Sidelines Activist: Charles S. Johnson and the Struggle for Civil Rights

CHARLES S. JOHNSON (*Courtesy of the Fisk University Library's Special Collections*)

SIDELINES ACTIVIST

CHARLES S. JOHNSON
AND THE STRUGGLE FOR
CIVIL RIGHTS

RICHARD ROBBINS

UNIVERSITY PRESS OF MISSISSIPPI 🌿 *Jackson*

99 98 97 96   4 3 2 1

The paper in this book meets the guidelines for permanence and durability of the Committee on Production Guidelines for Book Longevity of the Council on Library resources.

Library of Congress Cataloging-in-Publication Data

Robbins, Richard, 1922–
     Sidelines activist : Charles S. Johnson and the struggle for civil rights / Richard Robbins.
         p.   cm.
     Includes index.
     ISBN 0-87805-904-0 (cloth : alk. paper). — ISBN 0-87805-932-6 (paper)
     1. Johnson, Charles Spurgeon, 1893–1956. 2. Civil rights workers—United States—Biography. 3. Afro-American sociologists—Biography. 4. Fisk University—Presidents— Biography. 5. Sociologists—United States—Biography. 6. Civil rights movements—United States—History—20th century. 7. Afro-Americans—Civil rights. I. Title.
E185.97.J66R63   1996
301'.092—dc20   96-14472
     [B]   CIP

British Library Cataloging-in-Publication data available

For James Baldwin
        For Jimmy, friend

Where shall I be when the first trumpet sound?
Where shall I be when it sound so loud?
Sound so loud till it wakes up the dead!
Where shall I be when it sound?

God gave the people the rainbow sign
No more water, but fire next time,
Where shall I be?
Where shall I be?

                                —Traditional spiritual

CONTENTS

PREFACE

I first encountered the name of Charles S. Johnson in 1965 when I was visiting professor of sociology at Hampton Institute (now University) in Virginia. Hampton, a private institution among the more than one hundred historically black colleges, and rare among them for having a substantial endowment, was widely known as the place where Booker T. Washington was educated; he moved on to found Tuskegee Institute (now University) and to become, early in this century, "our national Negro leader." Years before I had read what are acknowledged to be Johnson's two best books, *Shadow of the Plantation* and *Growing Up in the Black Belt*, but I knew nothing of his life. During the year at Hampton I was honored to be asked to give the Charles Sumner memorial lecture and chose to speak on W. E. B. Du Bois. Nearly thirty years later I retain a vivid memory of that evening, for after the lecture several older men and women lingered at the lectern to reminisce about meeting Du Bois in various circumstances during his lifetime.

Preparing for this talk I decided to work into the presentation a brief comparison of Du Bois with two other eminent sociological contemporaries, E. Franklin Frazier and Charles S. Johnson. Just a few years later the American Sociological Association would institute its Du Bois-Johnson-Frazier award for distinguished work in the sociology of race relations, but in 1965 Johnson was not as well-known as the other two, partly because he was a more private person, partly because he was a less public advocate. I discovered, however, that the transit of his life, from boyhood in the segregated South, to higher education and research in race-volatile Chicago, to work as research director for the National Urban League and "entrepreneur" of the Harlem Renaissance in New York, to a return to the South to Fisk University and years of productive research on the sociology of race relations, to, finally, the presidency of Fisk, had much to tell us about American society and about the South, black and white, in the first half of the twentieth century.[1]

In the course of that lifetime Johnson came to know and influence a remarkable range of African American leaders, social scientists, writers, and artists. More, he forged a link between groups in the white community, capable of providing private philanthropic and public support, and groups in the black community dedicated, whether by research or advocacy, to the advancement of equality of opportunity. This critical bridging role, carried out under great difficulties and with no loss of dignity in a segregated society far more racist than today's, has been severely criticized as excessively accommodative and insufficiently militant, to cite Gunnar Myrdal's well-known distinction. I hope the pages that follow constitute a convincing rejection of that assertion. Here it suffices to say that if Johnson was not, nor ever intended to be, a militant radical, neither was he an acquiescent Booker T. Washington, much less, in one black critic's scathing words, "an establishment nigger." To hold him to some litmus test of militancy, constructed twenty years after his death and applied *after* the ensuing civil rights revolution and the collapse of racial segregation in the South, is to render an unfair ex post facto judgment.

Charles Johnson stayed his own course. He hated the racial discrimination he studied throughout his career and experienced personally innumerable times throughout his life. At the same time, however, he remained quintessentially American in believing that social change was inevitable, that the struggle for freedom and justice for black Americans could not be permanently denied. And he was quintessentially the social scientist in arguing that one path to social change, one among many to be sure, lay in demonstrating through disciplined research the full scope and dimensions of a pervasive racial system. That was his mandate for a "black social science." His committed activism in a moderate key—the work with the foundations, the advisory role as a race statesman, his contribution to formulating public policy, which he called his "sidelines activism," his quiet but effective role in the organization of protest movements—was grounded in his belief, rooted in his University of Chicago training, in the essentiality of research. And research, in providing a foundation for an informed activism, advances activism's cause. Charles Johnson, sociologist and advocate, integrated the two roles but understood each had its own ethos.

At the very end of his life Johnson admitted to some pessimism concerning race relations in the United States. Two years before his death in 1956, the Supreme Court, in its landmark *Brown* v. *Board of Education* decision, had declared racial segregation in public schools unconstitutional, a clear violation of equal protection under the law. Dismayed by the fierce resistance to implementation of desegregation in the South, he foresaw a deepening of racial conflict through the next decade. His characteristic realistic optimism seemed to flag. Yet he held fast to his lifelong conviction about social change and the democratic process. Ultimately racial justice and equality of opportunity would prevail. He argued this position persuasively in the final article he published in the *New York Times Magazine* in September 1956, titled "A Southern Negro's View of the South."

In this life of Johnson I follow his practice with regard to racial terminology. He employed "Negro" and "black"—"Negro" more frequently. The emphasis in this biography is on historical context, and both terms are appropriate to Johnson's era. Contemporary references are to "African American" and "black." The issue, of course, is not simply linguistic but ideological.

Over the years, working on Charles Johnson's biography, I have benefited immeasurably from the advice and support of colleagues and friends, some of whom knew Johnson personally. In my research I am indebted especially to Ann Allen Shockley, in 1974–75 the director, and to Sue Chandler, in 1974–75 on the staff, of Special Collections, Fisk University Library, which holds the Johnson Papers. I am grateful for a Guggenheim Fellowship in 1975 which enabled me to spend a year at Fisk researching the papers. Among those who have read my essays on Johnson or contributed to my understanding of his work, I should mention a goodly number; sadly, some are gone now. My thanks to James Blackwell, Leslie Collins, James Conyers, Lewis Coser, Rose Laub Coser, Theodore Currier, Thadious Davis, Robert Dentler, G. Franklin Edwards, John Hope Franklin, Nelson and Marian Fuson, Patrick Gilpin, Hugh Gloster, Joseph Himes, Ralph Hines, Everett and Helen Hughes, Blyden Jackson, Jaqueline Jackson, Guy Johnson, David Levering Lewis, Herman Long, Richard Long, Gordon Morgan, Nell Irwin Painter, John Shelton Reed, David Riesman, Charles U. Smith, Stanley Smith, John Stanfield, Charles Willie, and Bette Woody.

Patricia Johnson Clifford, Johnson's daughter, was most generous in granting me interviews in Nashville in 1975. I understood and accepted her decision not to give me access to more personal correspondence between Johnson and his wife, Marie. This decision, together with Johnson's well-known reticence to reveal his innermost thoughts and feelings, makes it difficult to construct a fully rounded portrait of Johnson.

Space precludes citing others on the Fisk faculty who provided a detailed picture of Johnson's tenure as director of social science and then as president of Fisk.

Finally, this book is dedicated to James Baldwin, to Jimmy, writer, witness, friend, gone now nine years and terribly missed. No two men could be so different as the eloquent, powerful writer and the austere, reserved sociologist, and yet, in his very first book of essays James Baldwin wrote this: "I don't think that the Negro problem in America can be even discussed coherently without bearing in mind its context; its context being the history, traditions, customs, and moral assumptions and preoccupations of the country; in short the general social fabric. Appearances to the contrary, no one escapes its effects and everyone in America bears some responsibility for it."[2]

"The general social fabric." Charles S. Johnson, sociologist, would say *Amen* to that.

Sidelines Activist: Charles S. Johnson and the Struggle for Civil Rights

I

CHARLES S. JOHNSON: AN ENGAGED LIFE

Wen Charles Spurgeon Johnson collapsed and died at the Louisville railroad station, October 27, 1956, he was, as usual, en route. He had descended to the platform for a moment before reboarding for New York, where, as president of Fisk University, he would deliver a report to the trustees. Nashville—New York—Chicago—all his professional life these cities, triangulated, were markers in the stages of a productive, many-sided career. It all started, however, in a small city in southwestern Virginia, Bristol, where he was born in 1893. Because racial segregation was then at its height, the family sent him to Richmond for high school, and there he completed his B.A. in 1916 at Virginia Union University, a private Baptist college for Negroes. In Richmond, venturing into the heart of the black community to do part-time social work, he encountered the appalling double system of racial discrimination and economic deprivation that would be his concern as a sociologist for the rest of his life. But how could he work social conscience into a disciplined, useful profession?

He moved, therefore, to Chicago for graduate study in sociology, with a concentration in race relations. Chicago was a good place to start— epicenter of urban-industrial America, "hog butcher to the world," vigorous and dynamic, a magnet of opportunity for European immigrant and southern black tenant farmer alike. And yet, in a setting different from Richmond's, Chicago was the scene of a system of exploitation by class and race only a little less severe than in the South. Negroes coming north in the Great Migration by the thousands had still to live, in W. E. B. Du Bois's metaphor, behind the glass wall, at once racial and economic. They could see into the better society; they could not share equally in its rewards.

Charles Johnson, returning in 1919 to the two Chicagos of the magnet and the wall after a year of military service in combat in France, found

3

himself squarely in the middle of the country's worst race riot. In personal danger, he had a narrow escape, but characteristically, when hired by the investigating commission to submit a report on the riot, he wrote in the spare, controlled language of the social sciences. The commission study, published in 1922, for which Johnson wrote the majority of the chapters, became a classic, comparable to though somewhat different in tone from Du Bois's *The Philadelphia Negro*. In *The Negro in Chicago* (1922) Johnson does not explicitly voice his commitment to the cause of equal opportunity or his compassion for those suffering racial injustice. His views, however, are manifest in the material itself, which includes data on employment, housing, and the criminal justice system.

The University of Chicago set the pattern for his sociology early on, conceptually and in applied research. Johnson's lifelong mentor would be Robert E. Park, a remarkable man. A sociological theorist and practiced journalist, Park was equally at home with abstract German social thought and with the urgent social problems in the urban neighborhoods just beyond the university. He had investigated and brought to worldwide attention the terrible atrocities perpetrated by the Belgians in their Congo colony and had served as secretary and ghostwriter to Booker T. Washington at Tuskegee. As president of the Chicago Urban League he got the young Johnson appointed its research director. Park's deep influence on Johnson and other students was not really in the area of broad concepts and theories. His emphasis on cycles and processes in intergroup relations—from conflict, to competition, to accommodation, to assimilation—his Spencerian evolutionary constructs, and his classificatory approach to collective behavior proved useful but not central to Johnson in his research. No doubt Johnson used Park's landmark sociological studies on the dynamics of social change, on the importance of conflict and (national) minority group cohesion in the first stages of the cycle, and on the worthlessness of theories of Negro biological and mental inferiority. But Johnson's lifelong commitment to scientific research as a necessary prelude to liberal reform and change in public policy was very non-Parkean. Park was contemptuous of liberal reformers as "damned do-gooders." What Johnson and other students—among them Everett and Helen Hughes, Louis Wirth, Robert Redfield, and E. Franklin Frazier—drew from Park was his great capacity to synthesize the European-based "working concepts" of sociology and the social facts of life in real communities, producing a unique genre that came to bear the stamp "Chicago school." (As

4

Everett Hughes expressed it, the system of this theorist/tough-minded former newspaperman was that there was no system.) Johnson's two best books, *Shadow of the Plantation* (1934), for which Park wrote the introduction, and *Growing Up in the Black Belt* (1941), were written in the Parkean spirit, not the letter. Park's impact, his insights and illuminations, can be found in the work of many sociologists in the succeeding generation of the Chicago school, in such fields as immigration, crowd behavior, community structure, folk culture, human ecology, and ethnic relations.[1]

In Louisville that October day, en route to the trustees' meeting, it is more likely that New York, rather than Chicago, was in Johnson's thoughts. For all the impact of *The Negro in Chicago,* he and his new wife, Marie, knew they wanted a wider horizon, a national setting. In 1921 they moved to New York, invited by the National Urban League. As research director for the league and editor of its journal, *Opportunity,* Johnson carried out or supervised more surveys of race relations, linking racial barriers to the changing economic infrastructure that was the focus of the league's program. But over and above this research, he would be known for the rest of his life for his pivotal role in the movement that came to be called the Harlem Renaissance. Not only did he open the pages of *Opportunity* to "the New Negro," the young creative artists and writers come to Harlem in the 1920s from across the country because that was the capital of black America where their voices could be heard. Just as important was to persuade publishers and editors downtown that those voices must reach a general audience. The Harlem writers would thus be heard, on their merits, beyond Harlem. For the literary imagination is both particular and universal—Langston Hughes's best poetry at once race-specific and timeless. Johnson's great success in this is seen in the titles bestowed on him, "entrepreneur" and "midwife" (with Alain Locke) of the Harlem Renaissance. Hughes, Zora Neale Hurston, Countee Cullen, Sterling Brown, and many other writers knew well his contribution. Some remained friends long after the Renaissance burned out, done in by the onset of the Great Depression, continuing racial restrictions, and its own inability to forge a voice true to a deep African American tradition. But the novels and poems endure.

At all events, passing through Louisville that day, it is probable that Johnson was much more preoccupied with Fisk and Nashville than with either Chicago or Harlem. By 1956 he had completed more than twenty-seven years at Fisk, seventeen as professor of sociology and head of the department of social science, the last ten as president. He had left New York, the league, and Harlem because he had always wanted to return to the South to conduct in-depth research on race relations and the socioeconomic regional structure in which race was embedded. And he had continued to believe he could be an advocate for social change on the race question as well. From 1929 on, Johnson produced an unprecedented number of solid studies of race relations and Negro life in the South. As director of the social sciences and the research center, his was the guiding hand behind the studies, the conferences, the community programs, the training of a new generation of black social scientists. The center's work rivaled that of the only other comparable regional institution in the South, that of the University of North Carolina at Chapel Hill under Howard Odum (1884–1954). In sending out so many young black sociologists to carry on the research, Johnson passed the baton on to them as Park had to him. (When the mentor retired from Chicago, Johnson brought him to Fisk; he died there, at age eighty, in 1944.)

In a sense, the race relations research center represented a gift to W. E. B. Du Bois as well as Park. Moving to Atlanta University at the turn of the century to teach sociology and history, Du Bois dreamed of founding and developing just such a comprehensive research center for the study of Negro life in the South. And, in fact, important research projects did materialize—the Atlanta University monographs. But Du Bois's center was not provided adequate support; it did not flourish, and thus Johnson "was able to do what Du Bois says so bitterly in *Dusk of Dawn* he had never been given the opportunity to do."[2] The two men knew each other well, though they were never close. It has been claimed that they disliked each other, that Johnson always remained envious of Du Bois's greater stature as a national leader and as, certainly, a far more creative and original sociological scholar as well. There was some tension between them, going back to Harlem Renaissance days when Johnson, editing *Opportunity,* and Du Bois, editing the *Crisis* for the National Association for the Advancement of Colored People (NAACP), both proposed literary contests for young black writers at the same time. Moreover, Du Bois regarded Johnson's agenda, research as ground for social action, as much too limited and conservative. "He is," Du Bois would say, "if not reactionary, certainly very cautious." Yet he himself embraced a similar philosophy, sociological research combined with moderate advocacy, during his first Atlanta sojourn, which ended

6

in 1910. Only later did he decide to concentrate on militant civil rights action at some expense to scholarship in social science. Much later, in the autobiography *Dusk of Dawn*, looking back to leaving Atlanta, he speaks candidly of becoming, with just a pinch of regret, "a propagandist" for racial equality and a movement leader.

After 1948, when Du Bois had been eased out of the NAACP for the second time and had embraced a much more radical political position, the paths of the two men diverged further. But Johnson never let personal considerations stand in the way of his respect for Du Bois's forceful leadership in the civil rights movement. In 1944, when Du Bois left Atlanta, Johnson persuaded Fisk's president to offer him a position in social science with very generous salary and perquisites. Du Bois declined graciously and returned to the NAACP in New York. And in 1951, at the outset of the McCarthyite persecution of the left, when Du Bois was indicted on a convenient technicality, failing to register as an "agent" of a foreign power, Johnson was the only president of a historically black college to support him publicly. Du Bois was easily acquitted in 1951; he expressed his gratitude to Johnson and his bitterness toward other prominent black leaders.[3] Du Bois's view in later years that racism was solely the product of capitalism, his changing positions on economic separatism for Negroes, and his refusal to acknowledge Joseph Stalin's severe repression of racial and ethnic minorities in the Soviet Union led to his estrangement from centrist civil rights leaders in the NAACP and Urban League. But his radical political dissent, his fellow-traveling with the Soviet Union, was not a crime but his constitutional right. The preposterous indictment and trial was simply one more expression of McCarthyism in the 1950s. In fact, he did not join the Communist party until 1961, shortly before leaving for permanent exile in Ghana.

Johnson's legacy, then, over against Du Bois's, would be the establishment of a major social science research center with a national reputation, which year after year produced studies of the race relations system and the economic and social structure of the South. And that accomplishment, in turn, flowed from his success in another capacity, the bridging role, carried over from his "entrepreneurship" of the Harlem Renaissance. With unbounded energy and determination he moved continuously between two worlds—between the black and white communities; between the philanthropic foundations of the white establishment that had the power and money to support black social science and black social services and the community of black social scientists and creative artists; between the burgeoning civil rights movement centered in Washington in which Negro leaders collaborated with a small band of white liberals in government positions and the higher administration leaders who, in the end, would be the movers and shakers in the attempt to pass an antilynching bill or legislation to aid the beleaguered tenant farmers, black and white, in the South. None of the usual metaphors— entrepreneur of the Renaissance, broker for sociological research on race relations, "sidelines activist" (his own term) in the shaping of public policy on the race question—does full justice to the bridging role. All his life he worked long and hard as a consummate negotiator to propose, carry forward, and conclude the initiatives he wished to pursue.

This work required frequent travel by rail on the circuit from Nashville to Chicago and New York. In Chicago there was the Rosenwald Fund, crucial to the bridging role. Julius Rosenwald, president of Sears, Roebuck, had a conservative but relatively enlightened view of how to reduce glaring racial injustice in America, and he backed it with his millions. Substantial sums for that time were granted for rural Negro schools in the South and for social science research in the region. The Rosenwald Fellowships, in the selection process for which Johnson played an important part, were of vital importance for an aspiring young Negro writer or artist. Rosenwald was especially fortunate in his executive director and foundation president, Edwin R. Embree (1883–1950). Embree necessarily worked within the general parameters established by Rosenwald. Over the years, however, he moved steadily toward a more liberal position favoring racial integration as the only way to achieve equality of opportunity in the long run, whatever the short-run necessity of allocating funding in the South within the strict confines of segregation. A man of deep conviction and integrity, he became Johnson's closest friend and confidant. Rosenwald had wisely decided to liquidate the fund in twenty years; either it would accomplish something in that time or it would not. Between 1928 and 1948 Embree oversaw the distribution of money to a wide spectrum of Negro institutions, with the research projects usually channeled through Johnson. John Stanfield has written that "Embree did more for black social scientists and the social science of race relations than did any other foundation administrator of this period."[4] When he died in 1950, Johnson paid moving tribute to him for a lifetime dedicated to justice and equality.

The other railroad line led from Nashville to New York to the strategic philanthropic centers of the American Missionary Association (AMA), the social service arm of the Congregational Christian church, and the General Education Board (later absorbed into the Rockefeller Foundation); in the 1950s the John Hay Whitney Foundation took its place with the others. In 1943, the bridging role was made more efficient when the research efforts of the Rosenwald Fund and the AMA were coordinated and Johnson was appointed research director for both. Given all this activity, it is not surprising that during his lifetime, and even more so after his death, he was subjected to considerable criticism for being a kind of "czar" of race relations research, an "establishment nigger" who always "had his hands in the pockets of all the foundations." The same criticism was leveled at his receipt of funding from the Carnegie Corporation, the Ford Foundation, and government agencies. But how could he have done otherwise? The foundations had the money, and they allocated it. They had confidence in Johnson. He needed their resources to get the work done; he went to them. If the relationship was criticized as "too conservative," "too safe" with respect to such issues as a head-on commitment against segregation, that had to be. And nowhere is there any record of Johnson being compelled to submit his work to censorship imposed by the foundations. In the milieu of his time, in an era of extreme racism, he managed to obtain the grants, get the studies done, and, conceivably, advance the understanding of racial oppression and what strategies could be deployed against it. That task fitted his own agenda, admittedly not as militant as Du Bois's or Frazier's: research in support of government strategies for bringing about incremental change toward eventual racial integration and complete equality of opportunity.

The same critics argued more broadly that in his constant activity and endless meetings, Johnson was excessively accommodationist and insufficiently militant, to employ Gunnar Myrdal's typology. One response is that Johnson's options were far more limited during that long period, from the 1930s to the 1960s, before the civil rights revolution began to shatter rigid racial segregation. After the 1960s, the foundations and public agencies actively sought out distinguished black social scientists, appointing them as directors of major research projects and even as heads of the foundations themselves as well as heads of cabinet-level federal agencies. That never could have happened in Johnson's day.

The long, involved bridging role exacted a personal psychological price for Johnson caused by the sheer mental strain of functioning within the upper reaches of the white establishment. Even his loyal wife, Marie, railed at the inordinate amount of time he felt he had to spend with John Hay ("Jock") Whitney to assure the flow of Whitney grants—though Whitney became a good friend as well. In Washington in the 1930s, when vital New Deal policies were being shaped, Johnson realized the limits, owing to race, that would constrain him as a direct player in the political process. In the run-up to the passage of the important Bankhead Farm Tenancy Act of 1937, Rexford Tugwell, directing the Farm Resettlement Program, requested one of "our trio" (Johnson, Embree, and the white southern liberal and activist Will Alexander) to serve as his deputy. It could not be Johnson. "Embree could not leave the Fund," he wrote, "and I was a Negro; that left Dr. Alexander; he went as Tugwell's assistant." Later, when Tugwell resigned, Alexander took over as head of the program.[5]

In both the research and the bridging role, the collaboration of black and white professionals in the South played out ironically in personal relationships in a setting of strict racial caste etiquette. Lodging, restaurants, and conference hotel arrangements could not be taken for granted in an interracial context. Johnson was elected the first black president of the Southern Sociological Association in 1945–46, and yet he could not be sure of getting a sleeping car reservation out of Nashville or a hotel room in Memphis. Out in the field, he and his research associates, had to be concerned not only with samples and surveys but with public accommodations. On occasion they confronted personal danger as well and possible violence. St. Clair Drake thought one source of the intense migraine headaches Johnson suffered arose from his having to make abrupt status transitions from being Dr. Charles Johnson, sociologist, to Charles Johnson, Negro, in situations integral to southern life through the 1950s.[6]

Whatever the tensions associated with these two roles, research-advocate sociologist and social science broker, Johnson, looking back in 1956 could take satisfaction in the last ten years of his presidency at Fisk, 1946–56. He had accomplished the usual goals—strengthening the curriculum, the endowment, and the physical plant and sending more and better students on to graduate school. In addition, with such innovations as the annual Institutes of Race Relations that brought leading national figures and decision makers, black and white, together with everyday community activists on an interracial basis on the Fisk campus, he had focused national attention on Fisk and the still unresolved racial problems of the South. The first black president of historically black

Fisk University worked ceaselessly to enhance Fisk's standing in the academic world at home and abroad.

So, in Louisville, en route to the trustees' meeting, he could think of the long road from his moment of sociological insight in Richmond in 1915 to the state of his presidency in 1956. Without being smug or complacent, he knew his had been a useful, committed, and successful life. In these days, however, he was not as given to introspection and reminiscence as in the past. In contrast with the heady Harlem Renaissance times, some friends contended he had become, as president, more reserved and deliberate, more guarded, though flashes of anger would still occur in the face of a difficult racial situation. (He left behind a vast collection of papers in the Fisk library archives, but they contain scarcely a word on his innermost thoughts and feelings; there are only countless papers on beliefs and positions on issues of race. This lack poses a challenge to any biographer seeking the "real Johnson.") In his formal dress and demeanor he seemed to some a staid Victorian of the twentieth century. That may be. But one central passion had been constant throughout his adult life—his belief in the inevitability of social change, of democratic social change, in the struggle to achieve racial justice. Naturally, he had to position that belief against the everyday reality of racism he saw all around him in the South. (He might have mused, on the railroad journey to New York that he had in hand the small triumph of no longer having to call the Nashville station master to complain that he had not been sent his reservation.) But the contradiction between ideal and reality did not change the fact that a lifetime of steady work had been in the service of such a belief. Holding to it enabled him to put on vest, tie, and suit and venture out each day to one more conference, to write one more article, to sign one more statement calling for an end to the poll tax. His favorite aphorism, drawn from his days in Africa in 1930, was "If you know well the beginning, the end will not trouble you much."

The optimism, tempered by realism, the faith in cumulative social change, however, sometimes seemed harder to summon in the mid-1950s. To begin with, Johnson knew he was wearing down physically; his health was declining. Just a few days before leaving for New York, he acknowledged as much in writing to his longtime friend Fred Brownlee, now retired as executive director of the American Missionary Association. And this was occurring at "one of the most difficult work periods of my entire career."[7] He had promised his wife he would try to slow down.

Then, too, by 1956 the initial exhilaration of the challenge of the Fisk presidency was wearing down as well. Without question, he had played the central role in enhancing Fisk's national reputation. But he was well aware that within the university his tenure as president was not regarded as an unmixed success. There was a sense on campus that he kept decision making too much to himself, sharing college problems with only a small circle of friends. No doubt the aloofness reflected a personal style. Away from the warmth and intimacy of family—he and Mrs. Johnson had raised four children now grown and away—he knew he came across as too distant, especially with junior faculty. At the same time, his sociological writing had diminished. As president he wrote mostly broad, exhortative essays on higher education or the general state of race relations in the world. Perhaps these writings were an expression of this work on an international scale—on the first American delegation to the United Nations Educational, Scientific and Cultural Organization (UNESCO) or on President Harry Truman's commission to recommend changes in the educational system of postwar Japan.

Even his crowning achievement, the research center on race relations, appeared to be losing momentum despite the fact that after the Supreme Court decision in 1954, finding racial segregation in public schools unconstitutional, the critical challenge of monitoring and charting the progress of desegregation loomed ahead. Johnson's guidance of the center, indirectly from the president's office, was subject to criticism. In an earlier era the young research scholars he had trained sometimes referred to him, with a mixture of affection and exasperation, as "Massa Charlie" of "The Plantation." Many of them had moved on to make their own careers in the South. Years later one of them would charge that Johnson had unfairly appropriated credit for research actually done by junior colleagues. But except for one instance, there is no evidence to support this contention.[8] He could be faulted not for his supervisory role in research but for his lack of resolve in not protecting academic freedom and the right to political dissent when, responding to the bullying tactics of a House of Representatives committee bent on ferreting out "commies" and "subversives," he dismissed a faculty member for alleged communist leanings (the Lorch case).

In those last days before the New York trip, as he turned from private problems to public issues, from his stewardship at Fisk to the state of the desegregation process in the South, there seemed to be further cause for some erosion of his lifelong confidence in the power of social change to bring down racial barriers. He had shared, of course, in the immediate euphoria in the black community when *Brown v. Board of Education* was decided in 1954. The Court had acted with unanimity; it had overturned the "separate but equal" doctrine of *Plessy v. Ferguson* (1896), affirming for Negroes their fundamental constitutional rights under the equal protection clause of the U.S. Constitution. But Johnson knew his South. He was dispirited but not surprised by the massive resistance that followed in the South and the widespread violence it sanctioned. The Court itself, in its implementation document in 1955, had in some sense contributed to southern intransigence, producing a legal oxymoron—let us proceed, it said, with all deliberate speed. That really meant that once again the legal aphorism would apply: justice delayed is justice denied.[9]

It was under the burdens of personal fatigue, persistent problems at Fisk, and dismay over the resurgence of racism in the wake of *Brown* that Johnson sat down to write a summary of race and the South. "A Southern Negro's View of the South" was published in September 1956 in the *New York Times Magazine,* exactly a month before the fateful last trip from Nashville to New York. He wanted, as so often, to reach a wide audience in the national political community. He wished, as usual, to argue that the sociological research he and his peers had conducted underlined the need for an accelerated national strategy to bring about the social change required to overcome racial injustice. The goal remained, as always, he said, nothing less than "full American citizenship" for all Negroes. An end must be put to the absurd, unscientific myth of Negro racial inferiority. Action to achieve a vague "good human relations" was totally inadequate; only fully enforceable new laws by "a stronger and higher authority," the federal government, would be effective. If massive resistance and southern white violence signaled an antithetical trend and contributed to a growing pessimism in the autumn of his life, he remained convinced nonetheless that a fuller measure of national civil rights ultimately would prevail. Neither regionally nor nationally could we default on that promise. In short, he wrote, he did not despair of "the system" however savagely it had oppressed the Negro throughout U.S. history.[10]

In this last article, Johnson expressed general agreement with the premise set out by Gunnar Myrdal and his associates in their comprehensive survey of the "Negro problem," *An American Dilemma,* published a decade before. (Under the elaborate scholarly division of labor worked out in this massive Carnegie-sponsored study, Johnson had contributed a volume, *Patterns of Negro Segregation,* 1944.) They argued that the quintessential democratic task in the years to come was to diminish the gap between the American Creed (exemplified in the Declaration of Independence, with its concern for the dignity and rights of each individual, irrespective of race) and the American Reality (the persistence of pervasive racial discrimination, in contradiction of that creed). Myrdal himself was largely responsible for developing this conceptual framework; most of the commissioned reports, like Johnson's, were largely descriptive and analytic, sometimes coupled with brief sections on recommendations. In social psychological terms Myrdal was mistaken. Americans and others are able to live comfortably for long periods of time with such contradictions. When they do move eventually toward resolving the dilemma it is likely they are compelled to do so because of militant counterassertion by the oppressed minority rather than by their own majority-group convictions. In Frederick Douglass's eloquent phrasing, "Power concedes nothing without a demand. It never has and it never will." The civil rights movement demonstrated the validity of this statement in the 1960s. And Ralph Ellison raised the essential question, "Can a people (its faith in an idealized American creed notwithstanding) live and develop for over three hundred years simply by *reacting*?" In 1945, when the Myrdal debate began, Johnson retained a degree of skepticism. He understood the sociology of resistance to change as well as the idea of change itself. *An American Dilemma* was written at the end of World War II, yet the "double victory" (over Nazism abroad and racism at home) was not achieved, even in the armed forces themselves which remained tightly segregated, as Johnson and others observed.[11]

Johnson must have had other reservations. In particular, Myrdal's treatment of the "pathological" elements in the social structure of the Negro community seemed to him to underestimate the countervailing strength and resiliency of Negro institutions, though he himself had dealt with family disorganization in *Shadow of the Plantation.* From a more personal standpoint, it should be remembered that Myrdal chose Frazier over Johnson as the best black social scientist to review critically the manuscript drafts. Myrdal thought Frazier could offer a more independent, less establishment view of the study. Johnson did, however, serve on the initial advisory committee, and he contributed the important sociological idea that became Myrdal's "vicious circle" thesis.

All the same, in this final testament, Johnson generally shared Myrdal's perspective. He remained persuaded to the very end that American society could be moved to reduce racial discrimination, that ultimately the barriers of both race and class could be breached and equality of opportunity for Negroes advanced. He believed with Myrdal in programs of social engineering, which could produce practical solutions to racial problems within the existing political system.

Setting out for New York that October day, then, he could reflect on all the books and research projects, on the work at Fisk, and the presidency. For all the public recognition and honors, the private or inner Johnson had not become accessible. He had his small circle of colleagues and friends—Embree, the writer Arna Bontemps and the painter Aaron Douglas of Renaissance days, both of whom he had brought to Fisk. There were his colleagues Giles Hubert and John W. Work, his younger protégés in sociology, Lewis W. Jones, Bonita and Preston Valien.[12] Scores of others presumed to know him but did not really. Unlike Du Bois, James Weldon Johnson, Langston Hughes, and other prominent figures of his era, Johnson wrote neither autobiography nor autobiographical fiction. There were short, impressionistic sketches on growing up in Bristol, on the Harlem Renaissance and its writers such as the poet Countee Cullen (his assistant editor at *Opportunity*), on the long association with Park and Embree. But even in these portraits he wrote as an exemplary social scientist, engaged and passionate about issues but circumspect about the personal characteristics of persons with whom he worked closely. It seemed that all he had written and done would have to stand for the self as the distinguished sociologist.

Thus his "spiritual autobiography," as the title indicates, is mostly a statement of his credo, with a few personal experiences threaded into a discussion of the moral principles by which he had tried to live:

> It has been impossible for me to escape concern over how people live and are permitted to live and earn their living in a free society. This conviction helps to explain my concern with wage earners, from sharecroppers to city factory hands, and my rational impatience with those entrenched prejudices which would divide human society into rigid castes, and seek support for the restrictions imposed, in the divine intent of the Creator himself. It explains why, in the logic of my life, I can take an unequivocal point of view regarding inequalities, believing that while there are inequalities in personal gifts there is no justification for the inequality in social and economic environment.[13]

His conviction about overcoming "the inequality in social and economic environment" was always quietly affirmed, not preached in moralistic terms. In the personal uses he made of power, in his "using" of the talents of younger colleagues, black and white, and in some of his prickly personal relationships, no doubt he did not always live up to the moral precepts espoused in the spiritual autobiography. Who does, every day, consistently? But on the whole, reflecting on his career before departing for New York, he could say in all honesty that they were his compass and guide, they made his work amount to more than sociological fact-finding and analysis. The resentment of some others over his manipulative tendencies and his attitude toward rivals seeking to occupy the "super Negro" domain over which he presided, his sometimes ruthless playing out of the role "operator," does not demolish his essential moral integrity. He would claim no more in the spiritual autobiography.

On the train between Nashville and Louisville, Charles Johnson might have summed up his life in that even, understated form that was right for him. He wanted, from the Richmond days, to be a good sociologist with a focus on race relations research, especially in the South. And he was. As did Du Bois, he believed it vital to establish and secure support for a dynamic research center where the South, its economic and social structure and above all its system of racial oppression holding the Negro hostage, could be studied intensively. And he did at Fisk. The center produced a new and talented generation of Negro social scientists. He hoped the many studies would do more than fill library shelves; he thought that social science could be joined to advocacy—in various degrees of militancy—in the sense that a solid foundation of research would serve the advocates (he among them) in demonstrating the depth and scope of racial inequality preventing millions of African Americans from achieving "full American citizenship." In the preparation of Thurgood Marshall's brief for the Supreme Court in *Brown,* and in many other cases, he saw that happening.

In the two years following *Brown,* Johnson watched and participated in what many whites called the southern ordeal in defense of segregation, what many blacks knew as the prelude to the struggle for liberation. He continued to the end to hope for racial change. If hope was sometimes laced with disappointment, he remained firmly convinced all the same that the burden of race was being lifted year by year. History, Thomas Carlyle says, is the essence of innumerable biographies. One of these,

Charles Johnson's, would have as its central theme his faith in our eventual capacity to effect social change, to form a society of equal opportunity and equal protection under the law. "He was," as John Egerton has observed, "a really important figure . . . present at the creation of every initiative to bring about social change in the South."[14]

That theme might be phrased in more earthy terms. Charles Johnson loved the blues. In a paraphrase from the "St. Louis Blues" we can say that in the matter of race this country has come a long, long way from the condition of slavery. But it still has a long, long way to go.

From Bristol, Virginia, to Chicago, to New York, to Nashville, Charles Johnson had come a long, long way himself.

II

NORTH FROM VIRGINIA, ON FROM CHICAGO

C entral and southern Appalachia, the spine of the Southeast, runs from West Virginia to Alabama. Much of that lengthy transit consists of rugged highlands, mountains and ridges cut by valleys broad at lower elevations, then deepening and becoming narrower as they penetrate into high country. The grandeur of its scenery, from the Blue Ridge Mountains to the Smokies, with the Great Valley in between, the commanding views encountered in western Virginia and North Carolina and in eastern Tennessee make the region a great attraction for tourists. Yet economically and socially central and southern Appalachia resonates in a different way for many Americans; they picture a rural and isolated region, burdened by poverty, still holding to a folklike tradition in the most remote hollows. And the area contains relatively smaller populations of African Americans than the seaboard and Deep South. (Myths and stereotypes about "hill people" abound on the television screen, but that is a cartoon Appalachia that does an injustice to the complexity of this sociocultural region and to the dignity of Appalachians.) To be sure, Appalachia also means coal mines, steel mills, railroad networks, and a cluster of urban-industrial metropolitan areas with a significant number of historic black communities. Despite these variations and the new superhighways and supermarkets, the general character of Appalachia holds on, altered but not submerged by change.[1]

Bristol, Virginia, where Charles S. Johnson was born and spent his childhood, was and remains a small city, set at the edge of the Great Valley in a triangular wedge of land in the very southwest corner of Virginia, in conjuncture with northeast Tennessee and northwest North Carolina. It is basically southern Appalachian but somewhat less poverty-ridden, more economically developed, and, whites at least will tell you, a trace more progressive or "border South" in race relations. Actually, there are two Bristols, separate municipalities on the Tennessee-Virginia line, sharing a common Main Street down the middle. In the eighteenth century, yeoman settlers moving into the expanding frontier from Virginia and North Carolina required protection. So these farmers, mainly Scotch-Irish, constructed their blockhouses as they built their cabins and tilled the fields. Fort Shelby, erected in 1771, became the focal point for the area. The Cherokee and Chickamauga Indians were ruthlessly pressed back from the settlements, even though the British Proclamation of 1763 was supposed to assure Indians rights in the western part of the mountains. Though slavery existed in the region, the majority of settlers had no economic need to bring with them from the tidewater the onerous slave labor of the cotton plantation system. This is probably the origin of the assertion, in part myth but with some truth, that racism was less oppressive in southern Appalachia.

Soon the early industrial revolution reached the agrarian area. The first ironworks, established in 1785, subsequently failed. The towns received their present names in 1852, when an Englishman, Joseph Anderson, laid out a tract for manufacturing and named it for the British industrial city. The key to development, as everywhere else, was the railroad; the Virginia and Tennessee reached Bristol in 1856, followed by the Norfolk and Western. Into and past the Civil War the towns grew as distribution centers for iron, coal, and lumber. Small factories—tanneries, pulp mills, tobacco processing plants—were established on both sides of the line. Population rose from only a thousand before the war to some three thousand (combined towns) by 1880, to ten thousand by 1900, of whom one thousand were Negroes. Within the framework of traditional white paternalism, the blacks of Bristol, though completely subordinated, were left free to build their own community institutions. The Lee Street Baptist Church, founded in 1865 in a tiny wooden shed, was transformed by its eighth pastor, the Reverend Charles H. Johnson (Charles's father) into a large, imposing brick church whose spire towered over Bristol. Completed in 1902 the church was an astonishing achievement for Rev. Johnson, whose stewardship lasted forty-two years, from 1890 to his death.

By 1890, when Rev. Johnson and his wife, Winifred (Branch), came down from Lynchburg, Virginia, to take up his pastorate, Bristol had become a flourishing, though never affluent, small city, hub of Washington County and transportation center for export of industrial materials to the southwest highlands of Virginia and beyond. When not subject to economic panics, as happened in 1896 and periodically thereafter, the towns provided a measure of stability to the white and, to a lesser degree, the black population, all within the tight boundaries of white supremacy. The local histories from the 1890s to the 1940s either minimized or denied that a racial problem existed. Local directories first listed white institutions, then "colored." Indeed, it was not until the 1960s that local histories carried the discussion beyond "we have always had good race relations here." As Charles J. Harkrader parades the usual clichés: "I confess a deep sympathy for the colored race and its struggle for recognition and reward. . . . We have always boasted the high character of our colored people. . . . Our colored people have been patient but hopefully passive." He then notes candidly that Bristol did not desegregate public places or hire the first black policeman and postman until the 1960s. As of 1964, of thousands of Negroes employed over the years as locomotive firemen, not one had been promoted to engineer.[2] Engineers were organized in a separate union that did not admit Negroes.

By all accounts Rev. Johnson was a remarkable man. Son of a slave, he had been taken in by the master and educated in the Baptist faith and in Greek and Latin alongside the master's own son. The white boy went off to Richmond College, the black boy to Richmond Institute (subsequently Virginia Union University), where he received his B.D. in 1883. A traveling preacher, he met his wife in Lynchburg. A house servant in the homes of aristocratic old Virginia families, she is described by her son as having "the poor best that the public schools of Lynchburg offered, to which was added an uncommon amount of intelligence and social grace." Small, wiry, and highly energetic, a "decorously dignified man of the cloth," Rev. Johnson felt secure in his education and was determined to pass on that heritage to his children. In Bristol he not only ministered to spiritual needs but helped to organize virtually all the economic and social projects of the community. Within the prevailing racial system the Johnsons had a mutually respectful relationship with the white families of standing. Toward the rough-hewn populist racism of the town, however, which the leading families deplored but did nothing to curb, Rev. Johnson had no patience or tolerance. In the one lynching that Bristol tried for years to live down, he stood in the middle of the street in front of the mob "shouting solemn warnings against their reckless and ungodly lawlessness" as the lynchers, bemused, streamed around him.[3]

Such was life in Bristol, white and black, in the 1890s. White "benign neglect" and indifference ironically contributed to strengthening black social cohesion as the community built its own web of social institutions. The Johnsons had to live with segregation along with the others, but like Lucas Beauchamp in William Faulkner's *Intruder in the Dust,* they never for a moment accepted the imputation of racial inferiority. And they were confident even then that change would come.

Charles S. was born July 24, 1893, the first of five children. (Three sisters, Lillie, Sarah, and Julia, and a brother, Maurice, followed.) The middle name, Spurgeon, probably came from the well-known Baptist preacher Charles Haddon Spurgeon (1834–92). The Moore Street home, a center of community activity for the small, fragile, but secure black middle class of Bristol, was a comfortable and comforting milieu for a young boy who was a bit shy but avid to read and learn.[4] If family income was limited, books were bought nonetheless, and the father guided the reading. Insulated from the white community and race friction, Charles took what he could from the Negro elementary school, and this was supplemented by an informal education in the Negro barbershop. There he shined shoes, listened, and observed. Life was relatively untroubled.

Racial segregation seemed remote. As he and his mother took their places for colored on the trolley, the conductor was friendly and courteous. They had their regular Saturday afternoon ice cream soda at the drugstore, along with the whites. Then, abruptly, things changed. Politely, the drugstore owner turned them away; he could no longer serve them. Trolley car segregation would now be formally and rigidly enforced. The planned new school building for Negroes would be sited at the edge of town, next to a still-smoldering city dump. A small boy confronted a new reality.

What had happened at the dawn of the new century was that the state legislature of the commonwealth and those of the other southern capitals were ushering in a new era, an intensification of segregation and discrimination so severe that the eminent historian Rayford Logan would describe it in its later stages as the Nadir for Negroes in the American South.[5] And what Richmond and Atlanta proposed, Bristol and the small towns of Georgia and Virginia disposed. Southern Appalachia had never been as liberal as advertised, but it was somewhat benign in certain states of the former Confederacy in the late 1870s and 1880s.[6] The slave system was not extensive in northeast Tennessee and southwest Virginia before the Civil War because there was no great dependency on the cotton economy and hence on slaves. East Tennesseans voted against secession, and the state was the last to secede, the first to rejoin the Union. Some historical basis was thus present for moderate groups in the ruling class to challenge the Old Bourbons, defeated but unrepentant during Reconstruction.

In Johnson's Virginia, a relatively liberal period, at least by southern definition, developed. William Mahone, a former Confederate general, who headed the Readjuster party, became a U.S. senator and a power in Virginia's government with the help of Negro votes. (The party's name referred to a readjustment of the state debt, but to some Negroes it meant a "readjustment" of their status.) In the 1880s a kind of liberal white paternalistic progressivism prevailed in Richmond. The legislature, which included a dozen Negroes, repealed the poll tax and established a Normal and College Institute for Negroes in Petersburg (today Virginia State College). Its first president, the Virginia-born lawyer John Langston, would be the first and only Virginia Negro to be elected to Congress, though for less than one term, until our own time. But by the 1890s the Bourbons, with their unreconstructed doctrine of white supremacy, regained control of state government, restored the poll tax and, under the new constitution of 1902, eliminated Negroes from the political process. White voters now sent Mahoneism packing, perceiving it as dividing white against white.

So by the turn of the century, in the South, in southern Appalachia, in Richmond, and then in Bristol, the road opened wide to the nadir. De jure segregation was nailed to the de facto foundation; disfranchisement drastically reduced the Negro vote; the two-party system that had gained some political leverage for Negro leaders was ended. The transition had been accomplished in race relations "from benign paternalism to overt white hostility."[7] Contrary to another part of southern mythology, Negroes did not remain completely passive. They sought to protest and resist. But the power die had long been cast, symbolized at the beginning by the withdrawal of the federal military occupation in 1877. Mahoneism and its counterparts elsewhere in the South were short-lived, a temporary diversion on the way to the nadir.

To be sure, even into the 1890s, alternative voices could be heard in the South, voices of tried and true white southerners, with the proper credentials. For a brief, extraordinary time, Southern Populism, a movement aimed at agrarian reform and the curbing of corporate industrial power, sought an alliance of farmers, small businessmen, and workers, white and black. "Negroes," one Populist saying had it, "are in the ditch just like we are." Tom Watson of Georgia, Populism's most important leader, preached that racism served the ruling class as a diversionary strategy. He denounced "odious" lynch law and appealed directly for colored votes. As the movement faltered, however, he abandoned racial egalitarianism. With Senator Ben Tillman of South Carolina and others, he became the most demagogic champion of white supremacy. Inter-racial class alliances ceased to exist.

In Virginia, though the triumph of white supremacy was clear in the long run, the system could be relatively benevolent at times, as young Charles Johnson and his mother saw, before the great change. The white establishment could ignore the racial rules when it chose; General Robert E. Lee's daughter was arrested in Alexandria for refusing to move forward when the trolley crossed the Potomac from Washington to Virginia.[8] Writing critical of Bourbon rule could still be found. In Richmond, Lewis Harvie Blair, distinguished southern merchant and member of the aristocracy, published in 1889 his celebrated "heresy," *The Prosperity of the South Dependent Upon the Elevation of the Negro*. White supremacy, he warned, was a doctrine rooted in the past and inimical to economic growth—"we look to the setting and not the rising sun." But he, too, like Watson, eventually recanted. In the same year in New Orleans, George W. Cable issued the revised version of his *Negro Question*, which argued for full civil rights for every black American. This eminent essayist and novelist, a wounded Confederate veteran, never changed his liberal credo, continuing to work for racial reform in Northampton, Massachusetts, where he settled in his later years.

Still, it would be wrong to represent these alternative voices, the early Watson, Blair, and Cable, as anything but a distinct minority. Sooner or later, the southern Bourbons, the Redeemers as they liked to think of themselves, would prevail and white supremacy would be restored. The term "Bourbons" is certainly the more appropriate, for like the French aristocracy in the wake of the Revolution, the southern Bourbons learned nothing and forgot nothing from the Civil War experience.

On the Negro side, on the road to the nadir, there were also leaders who protested and dissented. Monroe Trotter, Ida Wells-Barnett, W. E. B. Du Bois, T. Thomas Fortune, James Weldon Johnson, A. Philip Randolph (1887–1979), and others, differing in personality and sometimes at odds with one another, were united in their outspoken condemnation of racial injustice. Du Bois, in particular, would become ultimately the most important black leader of the twentieth century and the spiritual father of the contemporary civil rights movement. Born in 1868 in Great Barrington, Massachusetts, he went south in 1885 to attend Fisk. The South was a revelation to him, both the profound quality of black culture and the tyranny of the barbaric color caste structure (his words) in which it was embedded. After Fisk he returned north, studied further in Germany, and received a doctorate in history from Harvard in 1895. Once again he returned to the South to teach sociology and history at Atlanta University and to write research monographs on American Negro life. But he could not rest as social scientist and moderate critic of racism; he went on to an uncompromising militancy, a fierce and fearless propagandist (again his word) against racial discrimination. During the rest of his long life—he died in 1963 at the age of ninety-five—he sometimes changed direction with respect to short-run strategy and tactics. At one point, despairing of integration, he reconsidered his position on segregation, arguing for separate development of the black community. Later in life he embraced his own distinctive form of Marxism, valuable in the analysis of color in class terms but vitiated by his obdurate refusal to recognize the corrosive racism in the Soviet Union. Outrageously hounded by the American government in the McCarthy-era 1950s, an embittered Du Bois left the United States permanently to live and die in Ghana.

In 1903, in the midst of the triumph of white supremacy, Du Bois published *The Souls of Black Folk,* searing, powerful essays on southern black culture and on the consequences of racial injustice. In the famous chapter "Of Mr. Booker T. Washington," he laid out the conditions for waging the battle for freedom and equality of opportunity. He and other similar leaders (the Talented Tenth), the militant "radicals," would organize and consolidate an unswerving movement against racial oppression. Their energy would be concentrated primarily on this task, but they would also have to stand against the accommodationism of the "conservatives" led by Booker T. Washington with his acquiescence in segregation, his overemphasis on a self-limiting industrial education program, and his dependence on white philanthropy for support of his plans for black education and business. This framing of their differences may oversimplify. Washington privately railed against racism and segregation and secretly filed lawsuits against it. Du Bois was compelled to compromise at various times—for example, in agreeing to segregated training for black soldiers in World War I. But in broad terms the two men stood for strikingly different strategies for changing the racial system.

If Du Bois would be vindicated by history in the long run, it was Washington who in the early twentieth century was the recognized "national Negro leader" and whose "Tuskegee Machine" had the capacity to negotiate with, and win concessions from, the white power structure. Born a slave in 1856 on a farm near Roanoke, Virginia, some 150 miles due east from Johnson's Bristol, he made his way "up from slavery" to West Virginia and then to Hampton Institute which was then a vocational secondary school. After teaching there for some years after his graduation, he decided to apply the Hampton approach on his own. He founded Tuskegee Normal Industrial Institute in Alabama in 1881, and by the turn of the century it had become not only the most well-endowed and best-known black institution in the country but a solid base for his national political ambitions. Whatever influence and circumscribed power he was able to wield derived from the financial support of northern business philanthropy and the southern political establishment. Because both considered him "safe," he could achieve practical results in behalf of Negro Americans. The "radical" Du Bois, for all his militancy and eloquence, could not hope to match the "conservative" and pragmatic Washington in this respect.

Perhaps the most significant expression of the Negro side during the nadir was his dramatic speech, the Atlanta Compromise Address, presented to the Cotton States Exposition in 1895 and built around compelling metaphors. To southern whites the message was clear: we accept racial segregation as a permanent institution ("In all things that are purely social we can be as separate as the five fingers, yet one as the hand in all things essential to mutual progress"). To his Negro constituency he said, we must work hard, succeed in the trades and the businesses in our own community, earn the respect and support of the whites and thus persuade them eventually to do away with unjust racial restrictions (" 'Cast down your bucket where you are' . . . cast it down in agriculture, mechanics, in commerce, in domestic service, and in the professions"). Today, Washington's critics far outnumber those defenders who argue that for that time his political realism, his emphasis on Negro self-improvement and mobility through vocational education, and his appeal to white power to make changes in Negro lives represented all that *could* be done. Gunnar Myrdal summarized this ethos: "It is a political maxim that Negroes can never, in any period, hope to obtain more in the short-term bargain than the most benevolent white groups are prepared to give them. This much Washington attained." But Myrdal could not anticipate the 1960s, when African Americans acted and whites reacted, rather than the other way round.[9] After all, Washington was invited in 1901 to dine at the White House by President Theodore Roosevelt (who rejected most of his counsel) yet had to conform to lily white segregation in traveling to the capital. The fundamental criticism is that white power never delivered on the quid pro quo; Rockefeller and Carnegie money helped sustain the Tuskegee Machine but nothing changed with respect to the disfranchisement, segregation in a Washington, D.C., or total exclusion of Negroes from public and private white higher education in Virginia. It would be a half-century after Washington's death in 1915 before these changes were realized. Now, after all the revisionism, his greatness can finally be appreciated and his limitations better understood.[10]

Du Bois's pivotal role was as the most important race leader of the twentieth century. In contrast to Washington, however, he continued to be throughout his long life a sociologist and social historian whose work in social science was, in many ways, deeper, more penetrating than Charles Johnson's. *The Philadelphia Negro* (1899), written two decades before *The Negro in Chicago*, compares well with that volume. Both studies were innovative in making use of survey techniques and demographic data; both were grounded in the then optimistic social science conviction that research could lead to reform. Or as Du Bois expressed it in *The Philadelphia Negro*, "The final design of the work is to lay before the public such a body of information as may be a safe guide for all efforts toward the solution of the many Negro problems of a great American city." So, too, the Atlanta University monographs set precedent for the sociological research carried out much more comprehensively at Fisk by Johnson, in particular in *Shadow of the Plantation* and *Growing Up in the Black Belt*. Today, the two Johnson books bear rereading more than the Du Bois Atlanta monographs. We see in retrospect, however, that Johnson, for all his strengths as a social scientist, did not have Du Bois's unique gift, best revealed in *The Souls of Black Folk* and in countless essays and sketches for working sociological material into a powerful and moving document that could simultaneously illuminate the social world and strike a blow in behalf of black liberation and freedom. That was Du Bois's immense contribution—even when his research was criticized as faulty and his conclusions as more polemic than scientific.

When he left Atlanta in 1910, Du Bois was already drawing away from the value stand Johnson would take up a decade later. Du Bois saw that his sociological research in race relations to overcome ignorance was worthwhile but not enough. "One could not be a calm, cool, and detached scientist while Negroes were lynched, murdered and starved," he would say. Even so, as the propagandist and national leader replaced the social scientist, he could and would at any given time take up research, both for itself and also to advance "the cause." *Black Reconstruction in America, 1860–1880*, for example, with its controversial interpretation of that critical period, remains a significant achievement.

At the same time, Johnson's sociological work, though not of the scope and depth of Du Bois's, must be recognized as significant despite Du Bois's (and E. Franklin Frazier's) efforts to box in his sociology ideologically as too conservative and limited, too dependent on the white power structure, and thus not contributing to the overwhelming challenge to overturn that pervasive system, the evil of racial discrimination. Johnson was never silent about that evil. But he thought he himself could best contribute to its demise by pursuing in his own distinctive way the dual linked roles of sociological research and forceful advocacy. There are many routes to Rome.[11]

Charles S. Johnson was only eight when Washington's autobiography, *Up from Slavery*, appeared, only ten when *Souls of Black Folk* was published. Even later, as a young adult, working for the Urban League in Chicago, and at the start of the 1920s, for the National Urban League office in New York, Johnson, like Du Bois in the earliest years in Atlanta, was largely devoted to sociological research and moderate activism designed to influence public policy. But once he chose to found and edit the league's journal, *Opportunity*, in 1923, he had to take up a more forceful position with regard to the deterioration of the racial situation and the problems posed by the debate between the "radical" Du Bois and the "conservative" Washington. Where did Johnson stand on this issue of militancy? Du Bois, then editing the NAACP journal, the *Crisis*, and A. Philip Randolph, the dynamic labor leader and head of the Brotherhood of Sleeping Car Porters, who was then editing the *Messenger*, did not have any doubts on this score. They were first and last fighters for civil rights, prophets crying out against the inequities of racism. Randolph, in particular, a socialist and passionate advocate of nonviolent direct action, boldly took on the task of countering the legacy of Washington's more timid accommodationism. Johnson had to forge a somewhat different path. Though critical of some of Washington's program, he recognized that Washington had correctly understood that the struggle could not go forward without heavy support from powerful whites in the business community.[12] White support was needed as well for the league's social work programs in whose interest Johnson prepared and carried out his dispassionate research, the surveys of race relations in the industrial cities. Yet the research showed him that major changes in economic and political institutions would not come as readily as Washington supposed. The obstacles were great, and perhaps it was this realization that led him to increased preoccupation with the creative arts, an area in which talent might effect a breakthrough and invite a sustained white commitment.[13] Finally, at the other end of the political spectrum, the anti-Washington end, though he was as forceful as Du Bois and Randolph in his condemnation of lynching and all forms of blatant racial discrimination, he was not as interested as they were in mobilizing black people to form a militant sociopolitical movement, armed with the power of the march and the vote.

So he was not Washington, by any means. Neither was he Du Bois, the outspoken militant. A "conciliatory realist," he was also a liberal advocate for change, one whose realism necessitated interracial cooperation with white social scientists and philanthropic patrons but whose strategy of conciliation never required abandoning the core principle of total opposition to all forms of racial injustice.[14]

The child of eight or nine could know little of this problem of leadership and strategy in the early years of the twentieth century. But this detour has been needed from the straightforward narrative of Johnson's life to provide a national historical context for what happened to Mrs. Johnson and her son on the small scale of Bristol in the drugstore and trolley car. Indeed, in southern Appalachia these questions of black leadership and mobilization for change in racial patterns may have had a more muted character than elsewhere owing to the smaller proportion of Negro population and, with it, the smaller size of the middle-class pool for black leadership. In Richmond, for example, blacks were 40 percent of the population, in Sullivan County (Bristol, Tennessee) roughly 8 percent, in Washington County (Bristol, Virginia) about 10 percent. In some counties of Virginia's southwest corner the percentage was less than that at the turn of the century. At the same time, the larger numbers of poor whites in the towns and the rural mountain areas saw no reason to reach out to black workers and farmers.

In this setting, high school education for Negroes was bound to be even more limited than usual. The Reverend Johnson sent his son to Wayland Academy, a private preparatory school in Richmond affiliated with the Baptist college Virginia Union. He then went on to the college, completing his A.B. in 1916 in three years. College challenged him, and so did the urban community beyond the campus, which he encountered when working many after-school and summer jobs to earn his way. With help from his favorite teacher, Joshua Simpson, professor of Greek, he conquered a persistent stutter and a slowness in reading and was graduated with honors. A kidney injury ended his football career, but he managed the football and baseball teams, edited the school paper, and was elected president of the student council. He worked between school sessions as a waiter, mess boy, and watchman on the run of the New York—Providence boat (a perfect opportunity for reading). In his last year, working for the Richmond welfare association's Christmas basket distribution, the young provincial black bourgeois from Bristol was overwhelmed by the poverty and social problems he observed in the ghetto. One experience especially made an indelible impression. Asking why it had to be may have turned him toward the new field of sociology. Visiting homes he found a young woman, in tatters, in labor. The doctor he located would not come; finally, he got hold of a midwife to do the delivery. Later, when he tracked down the parents, they informed him they had disowned their daughter. As he told Arna Bontemps years later, this experience led to a lasting conviction: "No man can be justly judged until you have looked at the world through *his* eyes."[15] Richmond thus set the serious student on his career path. He was a serious student but not a narrow grind. At Virginia Union he enjoyed a full social life, once confiding to his friend Edwin Embree that he learned well how to bend the eight o'clock curfew that this Baptist college imposed then.

So he went on to Chicago in the fall of 1917 for graduate school, two dollars in cash in hand. He knew he represented a small middle-class segment of a large stream of black migrants from the tenant farms and small towns of the still heavily rural South to the growing urban-industrial complexes of the North. During the 1920s, from New York, Johnson would write frequently on the economic and social transition of these first-generation city dwellers (as well as the traditional Negro populations already there). Later, Arna Bontemps, Richard Wright,

Horace Cayton (1903–70), St. Clair Drake, and many others would describe what came to be called the Great Migration. There has always been a debate in social science as to the weight of the "push" of economic deprivation and racial discrimination in the South versus the "pull" of northern economic opportunity, extensive discrimination there notwithstanding. Johnson himself, starting empirically from the baseline of southern population loss, black and white, developed a "rough correlation" of the multiple factors involved. From studies he concluded that the primary driving force was economic, admitting that some of his expectations did not work out. For example, an increase in lynchings in particular counties could not always be associated with a rising curve of exodus. On the whole, Johnson argued for a largely economic interpretation for both blacks and whites. But in his studies, based in part on four thousand letters written by Negroes emigrating from the South, he emphasized as well how integral was the nexus between severe racial discrimination and the feudal economy of the plantation system. In the South, racism supplied the essential foundation for plantation owners' feudal control of black tenant farmers and for white businessmen to exploit severely the black urban labor force. At the Chicago end, a basic maxim was once again proved. Where there is a very real labor shortage and a very real need for cheap labor, employers' and government's demand for workers will override deep social and even racial prejudices—at least in the short term. Eventually, when demand slackens and domestic unemployment rises, the latent prejudices will surface as extensive discrimination against foreigners, blacks, Jews, et al.

In Chicago, industrial heart of America, the economic pull was strong already in the first decade of the twentieth century. Especially after 1917, during the wartime economy, the demand for labor was intensified by active recruitment. The industrial plants sent agents deep into the South; the "IC," the Illinois Central Railroad, carried black workers north at reduced rates. Robert Abbott, the celebrated publisher of the national Negro newspaper the *Chicago Defender*, gave maximum publicity to the drive, invoking the biblical slogan "Bound for the Promised Land." Chicago's Negro population, which Johnson would study so carefully, rose dramatically from 40,000 in 1910, to 109,000 in 1920, to 234,000 in 1930. The Great Depression drastically reduced the flow until the wartime economy and labor shortage in 1940–41 once again produced another great wave, this time directed toward the west coast as well.[16]

Once arrived in Chicago, Johnson got lodging in a family hotel on Dorchester Avenue and started work as a stevedore and night watchman. Enrolling as a graduate student at the University of Chicago, he came under the direction of Albion Small and Robert E. Park. Park would be his mentor, his sponsor, his friend, and a signal influence on his life and work. Park had an impressive background, an admixture of academic sociology and direct observation that could serve Johnson's style of research. Park's journalistic eye, his investigative skill honed in the inquiry into Belgian atrocities in their Congo colony, his theoretical-historical studies in Germany (Du Bois had followed the same route), his years as public relations secretary and ghostwriter for Booker T. Washington, and, above all, his keen interest in guiding and advising his students made him the ideal mentor for Johnson and for E. Franklin Frazier, another rising Negro sociologist.

In his classic *The Negro Family in the United States*, published in 1932, Frazier thanked Johnson for "valuable suggestions," but toward Park he was much more effusive—Park's "profound insight into the cultural aspects of the Negro life has been of indispensable aid." Frazier, who came to Chicago almost a decade after Johnson, after teaching high school at Tuskegee and at St. Paul's in Virginia and a year's graduate work in sociology with Franklin Hankins at Clark University, recognized the value of Park's general conception of social structure and the importance of the personal document in making community studies. So did Johnson. But Park's general sociological theory, expressed in essays and fugitive papers, was not at the heart of Johnson's and Frazier's interest. Race relations sociology was, and they made selective use of Park's. In particular, the well-known cyclical theory—the transition in intergroup relations from competition, to conflict, to accommodation, to eventual assimilation—seemed to some degree to be a sociological underpinning to Johnson's outlook on change. Assimilation could imply full racial integration.[17]

But Johnson was too young, too impressed with Park's stature and authority, and too grateful for his advice and counsel to see that Park's view on race rested on a premise, developed by William Graham Sumner as well, that it was futile to try to change deep-rooted racial and other social customs (mores) through central planning and national public policy (stateways). Yet as a social scientist and advocate, Johnson worked all his life from an antithetical premise. Further, Park retained scattered fragments of pseudo-biological theories, though he was forthright in

rejecting the doctrine of white supremacy with its imputation of biological Negro inferiority. Park would use phrases such as "the Negro's
metier is expression rather than action" or "he has a genial, sunny disposition" or "he is primarily an artist." And he had a limited view of black
consciousness and sense of community; they represented essentially a
transition on the road to assimilation.

In any event, it was not primarily Parkean theory, either general
or in race relations that forged the lifetime bond between Park and
Johnson. What brought them together at the start in Chicago was Park's
immediate recognition of his student's brilliance in ordering facts and in
conducting scrupulous scholarly research. Johnson, for his part, saw that
his mentor had access to the whites' resources; without these there could
be no sponsored research and, not incidentally, positions for research
directors. This in no way diminishes the depth of their long and genuine
friendship from Chicago days to the last nine years together at Fisk until
1944. It was simply the way things were—and in some respects still are—
in the professor-graduate student relationship.

In this context, Park, as president of the Chicago Urban League, was
able to place his research assistant with the league. Johnson established a
research department, got a Carnegie grant to study the Great Migration,
and undertook a survey of the Negro in Milwaukee. But it was Chicago,
even before the riot of 1919, that challenged him. With his Richmond
experience still in mind and with his "professional father" Park providing
sociological guidance, he saw at once how deep were the problems
and how long they would endure in this "black metropolis." And
he understood why the white power establishment in Chicago and
the handful of "Uncle Tom" Old Settlers who were their satellites
persisted in misreading the urban problem, perceiving the symptom,
civic disorder, as the cause. The East St. Louis race riot of 1917 and
the Houston riot the same year, when Negro soldiers were hanged and
imprisoned for life after a kangaroo trial, reinforced this misperception.
Johnson realized early on that his valuable contribution would be in
scientific study of the Negro's condition and not in his ability to effect
immediate change in this erroneous conception of the racial structure.

The conditions then—and now—in Chicago scarcely need recount-
ing. Negroes were essentially sealed into the ghetto (Bronzeville) for
life. Workers were locked into jobs at the lowest end of the employment
ladder. The middle and tiny upper class had achieved limited economic
mobility, but in all things social, to use Booker T. Washington's phrasing,

they remained excluded behind the color line. Housing, education, and access to social services were tightly bound by racial discrimination. In Chicago, as in other northern cities, a full range of institutions within the black community met the needs of the population. But Bronzeville could not generate sufficient political power to broaden the road to equality of opportunity beyond the South Side. Writing a new preface and concluding chapter to *Black Metropolis* more than forty years after Johnson's arrival in Chicago, Drake and Cayton recounted some progress, especially in the economic sphere, yet they still were not optimistic for the long term.[18]

Barely launched in social science research, Johnson enlisted in the army early in 1918 and was sent to France where he served as a regimental sergeant major in the 803d Pioneer Infantry of the American Expeditionary Forces. He was at the front in the Meuse-Argonne sector under direct fire. Why he wrote only a few cryptic lines about his wartime experience is not known. Possibly he did not care to dwell on the appalling contradiction of black soldiers fighting and dying at the front while enduring extreme segregation and discrimination at home and in France. Nearly four hundred thousand Negroes served in the armed forces in World War I, some 10 percent of them overseas. Yet they were barred from the marines and the new air corps and could serve only as messmen in the navy, while the majority in the army were confined to labor battalions and supply services.

War only reinforced what had gone before. In 1906, for example, in Brownsville, Texas, after three companies of the Negro Twenty-fifth Regiment were involved in a race riot, President Roosevelt dismissed the entire unit without honor and disqualified the soldiers from ever serving again. The outrageous Houston trial in 1917 exemplified the same institutionalized military racism. Once war began, the War Department announced it would train Negro officers only in a segregated camp in Iowa. Having battled so strenuously for black inclusion in the common war effort, the NAACP leadership, primarily the white, influential chairman of the board, Joel Spingarn, and the editor of the NAACP journal, the *Crisis*, Du Bois, had no recourse but to accept the humiliating compromise, calling it a "victory."

In France, the two Negro divisions, the Ninety-second and Ninety-third, fought as well and as bravely as the whites, the Ninety-second receiving the French Croix de Guerre. Nonetheless, the troops were subjected to constant racial harassment, and the high command did nothing to counteract the baseless assertion that black troops ran away from battle and stole French women from their men. The official Bulletin #35 summed up the situation succinctly: "White men made the 92nd and they can break it just as easy." As he was returning home after the armistice, Johnson witnessed assaults on black soldiers by whites at the ports of embarkation in France and at the port of debarkation in Norfolk. The message was not lost on any dark-skinned soldier: the "freedom" experienced in France would not carry over to civilian life.[19]

As if to underline that bitter irony, one week after Johnson's arrival in Chicago the worst race riot of all broke out. The young sociologist with a Ph.B. from the University of Chicago (1917), a much stronger version of his Virginia Union B.A., now found himself under direct civilian fire for a week in the hot July of 1919. To Embree, some years afterward, he described being shot at while dragging others to safety. All accounts agree that white mobs, roaming through the city's colored districts, bore the overwhelming responsibility, though there was, of course, black counterviolence, a fighting back. Thirty-eight died, twenty-three blacks, fifteen whites. In the wake of the riot came the demand for a commission investigation.

The formation of the commission, the appointment of Johnson as associate executive director (Graham Taylor, a white, was named executive director), and the value and limits of the six-hundred-page report remain of great interest today if we bear in mind the time frame of 1919 and how far we have come and not come from an era of such deeply entrenched racism. To take one instance, although the research strategy was his and he wrote at least seven chapters of *The Negro in Chicago*, his pivotal role is acknowledged in one line, listing his title. It was not simply that he had been recommended by Park. Just as he had originally caught the eye of Park in class with his incisively written reports, so he got the attention of the commission by submitting the best research plan for its work. The commission, consisting of six white and six black community leaders, with financial assistance at the start coming from the wealthy philanthropist and head of Sears, Roebuck, Julius Rosenwald (also a member), then set about its inquiry.

Thus was initiated, subject to later modification, Johnson's basic approach to race relations research.[20] It made him a major player for the next three decades, and the many subsequent studies are the source for the views of both his defenders and his critics. In essence, the charge was to frame the problem, define the historical background, do the research in living communities in the Parkean spirit, and arrive at conclusions that could be translated into recommendations for change. But though these recommendations represent truth speaking to power within the system, they do not question the system itself. It is simplistic to think that the limits, the proposals only for gradual incremental change, stemmed from the fact that the money and resources to do the studies came from the philanthropic power elite that set the parameters for the racial system. Johnson did actually have a measure of the social scientist's autonomy in doing the research he wanted to do. Rather, what was clear from the 1930s to the 1950s was that as a Negro, he was co-opted to lend his considerable influence to the movers and shakers in the making of public policy without being able to be a central participant in the ultimate decision-making process. Today, if he were alive and in middle age, he would still be supervising research and serving on countless boards and commissions. But he well might also be in Congress or the cabinet or president of a prestigious university or of the Ford Foundation or ambassador to India or Nigeria.

On the one hand, then, the Johnson approach would come to mean important and sometimes groundbreaking work in the sociology (and economics) of race relations. On the other hand, neither in conceptual theory nor agenda for social change did it cut deeply enough into the firmament of American society. In contrast, for all the criticism of the accuracy of their analysis of race in America, an Oliver Cox or (the later) Du Bois at least grounded the question of color in a Marxist framework of capitalist oppression and class conflict. Johnson shared with these and other, more militant social scientists and advocates anger and outrage at the South's system of segregation. To the end he remained a firm inte-grationist.[21] At the same time, his conception of what could be achieved required him, in the words of his student and friend Lewis Jones, to practice "the method of indirection"—forming coalitions with white liberals to press for immediate, realizable steps toward racial justice in the hope, in the long run, that the intolerable system of racial segregation would collapse. In these terms his sociological studies and his thesis of cumulative social change surely stand and endure, however conservative they seem to the present generation of black social scientists who have the advantage of the wisdom of hindsight and the better fortune to live in the rather more open, less racist, society Johnson envisioned.

To read the commission report, subtitled *A Study of Race Relations and a Race Riot*, with Johnson's mandate in mind and from the perspective of our own time, is to understand both its importance and its drawbacks. Basically, it provided a sociological context, thanks mainly to Johnson, that anchored the immediate traumatic event to economic and social conditions of long standing; thus the chapters on the Great Migration, on Chicago's demography, on the Negro's situation in industrial employment (practically nothing is said of white-collar and professional employment for obvious reasons), on housing, education, and organized labor, and on crime and the "vicious environment." Replete with detailed charts and maps, the report showed clearly how the black community was marginalized and segregated. The photo illustrations were candid, giving equal place to "Whites Stoning Negro to Death" and "Type A (Substantial) Homes Owned by Negroes on S. Park Ave." At various points official rhetoric was given a reality check. For example, only 8 of the 110 national affiliates of the American Federation of Labor expressly excluded Negroes, but the report showed that nearly all "eligible" Negroes were in fact barred.

When it came to the deepest levels of interpretation, "causes" if one will, the commission report ended mostly with conventional recommendations. If the report was nationally acclaimed, it was for its thoroughness and for its cautious conclusions. The commission presented sensible instructions to police and local authorities to prevent further rioting, then went on to recommend better housing and schooling for Negroes, mutual tolerance among different ethnic groups, and other improvements without demonstrating how these goals could possibly be achieved in the face of implacable hostility from groups standing to gain economically from continuation of the status quo. Even the potentially important recommendation to establish a permanent race relations commission took twenty years to be realized. Johnson knew exactly what was missing and what was unsaid. But we are in Chicago in 1920, he is Negro, and he is only *associate* executive director. Given the time and the reality, he had produced a scholarly, comprehensive study that could—but probably would not—result in the incremental changes he hoped for.[22]

By the time *The Negro in Chicago* appeared, Johnson had left. He had become restless in Chicago; he was primed to take his mandate, race relations research in the service of social change, to a national setting. At the headquarters of the National Urban League in New York the board was well aware of his work in Chicago and Milwaukee. If the league, founded in 1911 to develop employment, housing, and social service opportunities for Negroes in cities, were to fulfill its function, it would need more sociological surveys. Indeed, the directors in Baltimore, Buffalo, and St. Louis were calling for studies on the Chicago model. In July 1921, Johnson and his wife left for New York. Johnson was invited to become director of the new Department of Research and Investigation, funded by an $8,000 grant from the Carnegie Corporation. His salary was $3,600—remarkable for that time. Two years into the surveys he would add to the research post the founding and editing of the league's magazine, *Opportunity*. And not long after that he would turn as well to sponsoring black creativity in the arts, encouraging the work of "the New Negro," and thus taking on the role of "midwife," "nursemaid," "entrepreneur," "architect," "broker"—the metaphors vary with the writers—of the Harlem Renaissance.

On November 6, 1920, he had married Marie Antoinette Burgette in her home community, Milwaukee. She was a few months older than Charles, a lively, handsome woman. Save for some strains in the very last years, theirs was generally a satisfying and fulfilling marriage. They had four children (one daughter died at birth). Charles Spurgeon II (born in 1921) became a physician, practicing in Dayton, Ohio. Robert Burgette (born in 1922) grew up to carry on his father's profession of sociologist of race relations. Talented and creative in research, he worked for several human relations agencies before becoming a professor of sociology at Central State College in Wilberforce, Ohio. (His doctoral thesis from Cornell University earned praise from his father which pleased him greatly.) Troubled in mind in his middle years, he died in 1965. The one daughter, Patricia Marie (born in 1924), went to Fisk and married a doctor; the family settled in suburban Philadelphia. Patricia Johnson Clifford, as a committed alumna and trustee, was active for many years in behalf of Fisk. The youngest son, Jeh Vincent (born in 1931), received a degree in architecture from Columbia University, and then moved to Poughkeepsie, New York, to practice. There were a number of grandchildren who were Johnson's delight. Traveling often, he could visit family more than is usual. His letters to his wife describing these visits en famille, romping with the grandchildren, show a side of him very different from the rather forbidding and formal Fisk social scientist and president.

Marie Johnson, in her own right, led an interesting life. She came from a mixed background; her father had what was then called creole ancestry, her mother claimed Irish as well as Negro descent. Bright and talented, she combined high school with private lessons in piano and violin. The protégé of wealthy patrons, she attended the Wisconsin Conservatory of Speech and Fine Arts. A prominent member of the city's library board helped her gain admission to the Milwaukee Library Training School, which had a general policy of excluding Negroes, and subsequently she became the first of her race to work in the public library system. After moving to Chicago to teach school at nearby Harvey, she met Johnson while he was with the commission, on leave from the Urban League. Her early experience with music and her teaching of dance and theater in Chicago gave her an abiding interest in the arts. So she welcomed the opportunity to move to New York where the circle of young Negro writers and artists would soon form the Harlem Renaissance. The Harlem years were happy and stimulating.

There was another side to Marie Johnson, however, already evident to some of Johnson's friends and colleagues in Chicago. With her background, her refined aesthetic sensibility, and her sense of her position in the black bourgeoisie, she could be pretentious and, at times, imperious. ("Assertive" is a kinder word employed by some of her critics.) A considerable number of those in the Johnson circle did not like her. These characteristics were not prominent during the time in Harlem but emerged over the years in Nashville, where she presided on campus as the wife of the head of social sciences and then the president of Fisk. She grew more demanding and difficult. After Johnson's presidential inauguration, some younger faculty referred to them as President Johnson and Queen Marie. Be that as it may, there can be no doubt that theirs was on the whole a long, mutually fulfilling relationship, a solidly anchored marriage. In traditional family terms she played well the role of strongly supportive helpmeet in Johnson's work. Only toward the end, in the 1950s, did she indulge, angrily, in wrongful accusations that he was unfaithful during his endless travel away from home. In the years before the impact of the feminist movement on traditional role behavior, one may speculate that she came belatedly in life to the realization that, after Chicago, she had not grasped the opportunity to fashion a career of her own from the capacities and talent evident in earlier days. Widowed in 1956, she devoted herself to various worthy local causes and to working with the library at Fisk on the Johnson Papers. Mrs. Johnson died nine years later and is buried alongside her husband.

At all events, what mattered to the young couple in 1921 was not what the far future would bring but the promise and the challenge in what lay just ahead. With great anticipation they set off for New York, for Harlem. At the same time, from different communities all across the country, would-be writers and artists who would constitute the Harlem Renaissance were arriving in what was already the black capital of America with similar expectations. A special substream within the Great Migration, New York version, often middle class and sometimes lighter-skinned, they knew that Harlem was the place where their work would be nurtured.

Langston Hughes, clearly the most gifted and productive poet among them, also arriving in 1921, by way of Missouri, Kansas, and Ohio, would write of the drawing power of "this great magnet." It was he who, over a lifetime, would catch best the spirit of both the exhilarating and the grim Harlem. "I can never put on paper the thrill of the underground ride to Harlem," he wrote. "I went up the steps and out into the bright September sunlight. Harlem! I stood there, dropped my bags, took a deep breath and felt happy again."[23] Harlem—this great magnet for Hughes and for the Johnsons.

III

RESEARCH, RENEWAL, RENAISSANCE

When the Johnsons arrived in New York in 1921, Charles had mainly the first of three goals in mind. The Urban League hired him primarily to provide research reinforcement for its program to open economic and social opportunities for Negroes in cities and to seek the reduction—no one could think "elimination"—of racial barriers in the way. This he would accomplish with professional skill. Still, he wanted to renew the role of advocate for social change, nurtured in Richmond, and more or less set aside for research in Chicago. The challenge here was immediate and urgent: to end the horror of lynching, and to overcome resistance to hiring qualified Negroes in every line of work, white collar as well as industrial. This he would seek to do in founding and editing the league's journal, *Opportunity*, in 1923. The agenda called for a determined but gradualist strategy, forged, as we have seen, not from inner conviction—always at heart Johnson remained angry and dismayed about the conditions white America imposed on black—but from a tough-minded, realistic assessment that racial gains would be slow and a long time coming. Finally, this very slowness and resistance to the struggle for equality of opportunity in the economic, political, and social spheres led him to the one area where a swifter and more dramatic breakthrough might occur: the arts. Toward achieving this third goal he would open the pages of *Opportunity* to poets and painters and seek publishers downtown for a new generation of novelists. Or, as he put it in his straightforward way in *Opportunity* in September 1924, the task was to try "to stimulate and encourage creative literary effort among Negroes . . . to stimulate and encourage interest in . . . a body of literature about Negro life."

But something else beckoned, Harlem itself. As Johnson set about the Urban League job, he and his wife learned about, and were absorbed into, this striking community in upper Manhattan. Harlem, its history and development, would be woven into their lives for eight years. And in the 1920s Harlem was well on its way to becoming *the* black community in America, paradoxically the humming center for many-sided cultural expression and a place burdened with enormous social and economic problems. In that second sense, it did not differ greatly from the Richmond of Johnson the potential social worker, or the Chicago of Johnson the research sociologist.[1]

The Harlem of this double character emerged at the dawn of the twentieth century; before 1900 it was almost completely white. The city's some sixty thousand Negroes were then concentrated in mid-Manhattan's West Side, primarily in the San Juan Hill and Tenderloin districts. They had been slowly moving uptown since the end of the Civil War. The West Side pattern can be readily guessed: more than 80 percent in menial jobs; a small "black elite" separated from a large working class as much by social status as wealth; families crowded into tenement housing at overcharged rentals. The families not only battled discrimination from without but extensive vice and crime within the West Side. Yet as everywhere in urban America, segregation begat solidarity. Against Irish gangs—nondiscriminatory, assaulting Italian, Jew, and Negro alike—in the face of rapacious landlords and indifferent politicians, the community had its vitally important buffer social groups, especially the churches. And in the clubs and saloons the people could hear the new ragtime music. Negro vaudeville and musical theater flourished in the area.

In the first decade of the century, the in-city exodus from the West Side, the advance wave of migrants from the South, combined to change Harlem's composition. (Of Manhattan's Negro population 60 percent had been born in the South.) Deep white prejudice on the West Side was accompanied in a minor key by Negro middle-class resentment of the southern newcomers. A vicious race riot against Negroes in the Tenderloin in 1900 presaged further conflict. Small white and Negro middle-class reform movements could make little headway against white racial bigotry.

The pull of Harlem for West Siders, however, was as much economic as racial, the consequence of intolerable rent prices on the West Side and the need (and greed) of white landlords in Harlem, who rode the wave of land and building speculation only to find themselves, when the inevitable collapse set in, with great numbers of properties unwanted by whites. The solution, with the aid of Negro brokers, was to rent or sell to Negroes. Inflated prices might even enable them to recoup losses. Any whites who wanted to stay would leave as the Negro tide rose. By 1930 the transformation was nearly complete. Harlem, roughly defined as running from 110th to 150th streets, south to north, and from Morningside Heights to the East River, west to east, had become overwhelmingly black. White retail businesses still lined the streets; the white families, the Jewish and Italian enclaves, were nearly gone. Lennox Avenue and Seventh Avenue were now the arteries of the Negro community. The great majority of blacks in Harlem were American but growing numbers came from the West Indies. The poet Claude McKay (1890–1948) and Arthur Schomburg, who set about building a remarkable library of African American literature, were in that number. These two groups had different class alignments and varying cultures; conflict between them lasted through the 1930s.

"The most profound change that Harlem experienced in the 1920's was its emergence as a slum," Gilbert Osofsky wrote in his *Harlem: The Making of a Ghetto*.[2] This was true in large part. Undeniably, the system guaranteed it: the "color tax" meant overpriced rents for poorer housing. Transferring from the South or from the West Side, the largest proportion of Harlemites worked in unskilled or semiskilled, low-paying jobs in factories and businesses. Median family income came to far less than for whites. In the larger apartments lodgers or kinfolk from down home were often crammed into available space for extra income; the famous "rent parties" were born of economic necessity. Landlords, frequently absentee, could keep investment returns up by keeping repair costs down. For the tenants these conditions were reflected in higher rates of infant mortality, and shorter life spans. When the Great Depression arrived in 1930, some Harlemites would say sardonically: What Depression? It had always been there.

And yet, though Harlem was indeed a ghetto, perhaps in some ways a slum, it was at the same time a vibrant social community. The statistics added up to a grim picture, but people do not live by unemployment alone. If life in Harlem was intolerably crowded housing, it was also the extraordinary network of churches—Adam Powell, Sr.'s, great Baptist temple and the tiny storefronts—the popular culture of jazz and blues, the bars and restaurants, the variety of benevolent associations, the entertainment at Smalls and the Savoy, the theater at the Lafayette, and the vaudeville at the Apollo, the civic organizations, and, not least, the political mass movement in the form of black nationalism, Marcus

Garvey's United Negro Improvement Association (UNIA). Precisely because this vital social community and its varied institutions did not appear in the pages of the white press downtown, save on rare occasions, the *Amsterdam News* not only reported on "the problem" and on black political protest but kept account of births, marriages, deaths, and social events, the stuff of life of any social community.

Moreover, for all the constrictions imposed by racism and economic hardship on the community in general, there was room in Harlem for differing class levels, for Strivers Row as well as crowded tenements, for Edgecombe Avenue's apartments, for the black bourgeoisie. Within Harlem there could still be a small version of the American dream of upward mobility and "making it." That is where the Harlem Renaissance enters in. Some in the Renaissance circle, though white collar, were poor themselves, struggling to get by along with other Harlemites. But even those who were more comfortable lived, after all, in the same community with ordinary people, amid working-class families. Jessie Fauset (1882–1961) spoke and taught French and wrote about people with refined sensibilities. She was not completely insulated, however, from the other Harlem because she happened to be literary editor of the *Crisis*. Charles Johnson and Marie, moving to Harlem, entered the elite circle, joining doctors, lawyers, businessmen, and, of course, intellectuals, the writers and artists whose pretensions would be wickedly satirized by Zora Neale Hurston as "the Niggerati" and by Wallace Thurman in his novel *The Blacker the Berry*. Claude McKay, who was one of them, could still say that "the efforts of the Harlem elite to create an oasis of respectability within the boundaries of Aframerica is strenuous and pathetic." Perhaps so, but these men and women, for all the striving after status, were fully aware that because of their color, gifted poet and pullman porter shared in common confronting the white world beyond Harlem. For both, to travel downtown was to be tested along the color line.

Such was the Harlem of Charles Johnson. Each working day he went downtown to East Twenty-third and Madison, the location of the Urban League office. From 1921 to 1928, when he left for Fisk, he was occupied primarily in conducting or supervising a large number of sociological surveys and interpretive studies of the Negro's urban condition across the country. Added to this role in research were the two others, moderate advocacy stemming from the league mandate and the bridging role in the Harlem Renaissance. These were productive years for him.

The Urban League had been founded in 1911. The year before, the NAACP had been established by a group of prominent white and black men and women who first came together in 1905, meeting in Canada, near Niagara Falls (hence the term Niagara Movement), in protest against a new wave of lynchings and racial assaults. They wanted more "aggressive action" in the struggle for freedom than was promised by Booker T. Washington's discreet accommodationism. As formally organized in 1910 the NAACP's leadership, except for Du Bois, was white. Du Bois was appointed director of publicity and research and editor of the new journal, the *Crisis*. But the whites were not just conventional, conservative philanthropists. Most important among them were the distinguished writer William English Walling, Mary White Ovington, a social worker and organizer who lived on a Negro street and was a committed integrationist, Oswald Garrison Villard, president of the *New York Post* and grandson of the great abolitionist, and Joel Spingarn, who became chairman of the board and whose name graced the NAACP's highest award, the Spingarn medal. Forthwith, the NAACP established its agenda: to end the lynching and mob rule, to restore the franchise, to make use of the law, the courts, and the power of publicity to the end of breaking the hold of discrimination. The legal cases it won, the broadsides it issued in the *Crisis*—Du Bois would remain as editor until 1934—earned it a permanent place in the history of race relations.[3] Deemed by some Americans as radical then, it is now seen in the civil rights spectrum as moderate-reformist but subject to drift and confusion as the daunting problems of the inner-city African American underclass are now basically economic and social, no longer responsive to the old legal-political strategy.

The National Urban League for which Johnson went to work had a somewhat different genesis. It was formed in 1911 from a group of social service agencies. In contrast to the NAACP's agenda, the league concentrated on opening opportunities for Negroes in industrial work, social services, and decent housing. The founder of the organization from which the league developed was a Negro, George Edmond Haynes, who was completing a doctorate in sociology at Columbia and had gone on to teach and to train social workers at Fisk. He became the first director. Eugene Kinckle Jones, also a Negro, was appointed field secretary; much later, in 1918, he was named executive director. But the league's direction ("Not Alms But Opportunity") came from the board, like that of the NAACP a small group of influential white businessmen, lawyers, academics, and social workers, notably L. Hollingsworth Wood, William and Ruth Baldwin, and Professor Edwin Seligman of Columbia. Jones, black, and Wood, white, were precisely symbols of what the League hoped to achieve. Jones was somewhat like Charles Johnson. His father, born to a slave girl owned by an aristocratic Virginia family, was raised and educated in Richmond and then went north and was graduated from Colgate University in 1876. Returning south he taught church history at Virginia Union for a half-century. His mother, born into a free black family, was musically talented like Marie Johnson and had studied at the New England Conservatory. Jones, like Johnson, took his B.A. at Virginia Union, and again like Johnson, saw and observed how racial discrimination shackled black people in Richmond. After a graduate degree in social science and high school teaching in Louisville, he joined the league in 1911 and was executive secretary, from 1918 to 1941.

Wood's social conscience and commitment had a spiritual base. A lifetime Quaker and a peace activist, he went to Haverford College and Columbia Law School and built a lucrative practice in New York. Work with the New York Colored Mission and its Penn School for Negroes in South Carolina then brought him to the league. Later he served on the Fisk Board of Trustees for many years and was instrumental in the selection of Johnson as president in 1946. He was a central figure in the formation of what would become the American Civil Liberties Union. All these activities were of a piece, flowing from being of the Society of Friends. He would lead the league as president until 1941. Haynes, the third major figure in the formation of the league's program, resigned in 1918 after a conflict with Jones.[4]

This was the setting, and Jones and Wood were typical of the men active in that setting as Johnson went about organizing the research department. The many significant studies were of two kinds, community surveys of Negro life in selected cities, comparable to Du Bois's study of Philadelphia, Johnson's of Chicago, and Haynes's of New York, and sociological essays about special aspects of race relations, including studies dealing with white misconceptions and stereotypes concerning Negro life. Cities surveyed included Baltimore, Pittsburgh, Albany, Denver, Buffalo, Hartford, and East St. Louis. Often the surveys were undertaken at the request of an affiliate or of groups wishing specific information. Or an agency or business would request an inquiry; Metropolitan Life, for example, asked for data on Negroes in industrial plants with pension plans. All the studies followed the social science ethos Johnson absorbed at Chicago. According to Nancy Weiss, "They were never prescriptive; rather they provided the raw materials with which local agencies could devise local programs to meet local needs."[5] The methodology was simple: to provide factual description and basic statistics. Johnson would spend up to a month in the city organizing the study, and then the local group would proceed, in coordination with a staff researcher. Interpretive analysis was limited, cautiously optimistic, and in line with the league's economic emphasis, as opposed to the NAACP's agenda of political protest. Racial segregation and discrimination as a powerful system underpinning many of the specific problems received less attention, although a particular study could and would stress the key sociological concept of interrelatedness. "There is no use trying to improve recreational, housing, and health conditions for the Negro," Ira De A. Reid wrote in his Denver survey, "without attempting to get the race into better paying jobs."[6]

Reid succeeded Johnson as research director in 1928. He is not well remembered today but is an important, fascinating figure, not only in league history but more broadly in the sociology of race relations. Very tall, witty, urbane, at once thoughtful and forcefully articulate, he was a man who knit together the roles of scholar, advocate, even professional athlete. Though born in Virginia in 1901, he, like Wood, grew up in the Philadelphia area, where Quaker influence was strong and where his father was a Baptist minister. He went to possibly the best Negro college in the South, the private Baptist-affiliated Morehouse in Atlanta, then moved on to graduate work in sociology and economics at Chicago and Pittsburgh universities (his M.A. thesis was on the Negro in the building trades). He left the research position at the league in 1934 to return south to work with Du Bois. After Du Bois was forced to retire from Atlanta University in 1944, Reid succeeded him as professor and chair of sociology. During the 1930s he served with a wide range of southern human relations agencies; later he worked for the Social Security Administration. Johnson's intellectual equal, he mirrored him as well in effectively bringing together sponsor and social scientist in research. One of his books, *The Negro Immigrant,* can still be read with profit.[7] After leaving Atlanta at war's end he settled at Haverford College where he was professor of sociology and chairman of the department from 1948 to 1968. He joined the Society of Friends there, continued his research (though less creatively), and was elected vice-president of the American and president of the Eastern Sociological Association. Still, the Haverford years were quietistic; his young students had no idea of his vigorous work in New York with Johnson and in Atlanta with Du Bois, who called him "the best trained young Negro in sociology" when he recruited him. Reid died in 1968, one of the last survivors of the Renaissance era.

Today, the league's research studies are criticized essentially for what they did *not* do; that is, probe deeply into the racial oppression that locked Negroes into the deplorable conditions the surveys delineated so clearly. Moreover, the emphasis on facts and more facts, as well as the note of uplift and progress, exemplified in reports of Negro mobility despite discrimination, did little to advance the march toward racial justice. What the studies did accomplish, given the time frame of the 1920s and the ultimate dependency on white philanthropy, which meant obvious constraints, was to build a solid body of data in support of the league's admittedly moderate agenda. Johnson and the league research department did not claim more. T. Arnold Hill, director of the league's Department of Industrial Relations for many years, summed up the approach. Social reform rests on "the factual interpretation of authenticated data rather than emotional and sentimental appeal. . . . We like to be known as an agency . . . that bases its program and action upon such authenticated findings."[8] *Opportunity,* operating at an annual deficit and with a circulation of only eleven thousand (a third of its readers were white) even at its peak in 1928, could count the research reports as a significant accomplishment.

And advocacy was not altogether absent. Johnson fulfilled the second goal in editorials and in the interpretive essays he, Reid, and others wrote for *Opportunity.* In the same time period comparable essays appeared in the *Crisis* and in the *Messenger,* the socialist, pacifist, and labor review edited by the indomitable A. Philip Randolph (with Chandler Owen). As might be expected, Johnson's fairly bland editorials scarcely matched those of Du Bois and Randolph in stridency and emotional force, but they, too, were directed against the barriers of racial discrimination.[9] More important were the interpretive essays, wherever printed, for they attacked sociologically, scientifically, the prevailing racial myths and prejudices that helped to sustain the actions of discrimination. By now most of the myths have been demolished, but not then, in particular the idea of biologically mandated Negro racial inferiority. A small sample shows these writers at work, deploying scientific argument in the cause of advocacy.

Franz Boas, renowned professor of anthropology at Columbia and teacher of the exuberant Renaissance writer Zora Neale Hurston, insisted that so-called primitive Africans had in fact developed complex civilizations, including the use of iron, copper, and bronze, long before the Europeans. Who, then, were the "backward" people?[10] His student and later colleague of equal renown, Melville J. Herskovits, wrote in "The Negro's Americanism" that any understanding of the concept of culture would show the absurdity of equating it with one race because races are mixed and, in any event, many races shared in the evolution of American culture. Kelly Miller, professor of sociology at Howard University, did not simply describe that "national Negro university" but argued that since racial segregation, so inimical to the life of the mind, could not be changed in the near future, it was up to Howard to foster "future leadership and guidance from within the race" while remaining open to qualified candidates of all races, as any first-class university must.

Charles S. Johnson, too, wrote poetically as well as sociologically about the Negro's "new frontage on American life." These northern cities, "stern, impersonal, enchanting," he writes, "white and black these cities lured, but the blacks they lured with demonic appeal." He cites the boiling anger in the northern black ghettos induced by racial oppression and quotes Claude McKay's fiery response: "If we must die, let it not be like hogs / Hunted and penned in an inglorious spot." Even so, he holds to his tempered optimism and concludes that "a common purpose is integrating these Negro energies born of new conflicts, and it is not at all improbable that the culture which has both nourished and abused these strivings will, in the end, be enriched by them."

The young E. Franklin Frazier, already by 1925 director of the School of Social Work at Atlanta University, friend and colleague of Johnson in the 1930s at Fisk, then rival and acerbic critic of Charles S. after establishing his own sociological center at Howard, focused his essay "Durham: Capital of the Black Middle Class" on the remarkable history of the North Carolina Mutual Insurance Company and comparable businesses. A new class was arising, refuting the stereotypes of lack of Negro enterprise. Negroes were "becoming an integral part of the business life of America." (Frazier's later sociological research and his conversion to socialism soon persuaded him this hope was an illusion. He came to take a more realistic, in some ways more jaundiced view of the black bourgeoisie.) And Elise Johnson McDougald outlined "the task of Negro womanhood," sharing Johnson's and Frazier's tempered optimism, urging women to "keep striving" against great odds.[11]

Johnson's own anthology, *Ebony and Topaz*, selections from *Opportunity* which he edited and published in 1927, consists mostly of stories and poems, for by then he was pressing the cultural cause of "our little renaissance" (Alain Locke's phrase) whose aim would be to "stimulate and encourage creative literary effort among Negroes . . . a body of literature about Negro life." Yet a fair measure of the 160 pages is devoted to social scientists deploying research not simply to inform but to persuade. Here, in coda to the roll call listed above, is Ellsworth Faris, a leading light of the Chicago school, on "the natural history of race prejudice." Enumerating the complex sociological dimensions, he concludes, "But to call race prejudice a natural phenomenon is not to assume it should be endured or accepted any more than murder or suicide." The essay by Edward B. Reuter, the distinguished sociologist at the University of Iowa, who would join Johnson at Fisk in his later years, charting "the changing status of the mulatto," is explanatory for the most part, but his basic aim is to disabuse whites not only of the stereotype of innate Negro inferiority but of the equally wrongheaded derivative stereotype of the superiority of the light-skinned mulatto over the darker-skinned. Someday, he wrote, we can hope to put an end to the assumption that "his [the Negro's] capacity varies inversely as his skin color." Guy B. Johnson, a young white sociologist at the University of North Carolina and a specialist in Negro folklore, treated the celebrated legend of John Henry, the steel drivin' man, hero of song and story, who competed against a giant steam drill and "died with the hammer in his hand." What is characteristic in this essay is that Guy Johnson moves on from tracking origins and variations to assert that whether John Henry is truth or myth or both, he "died defending the dignity of common labor and its superiority over that symbol of the white man's civilization—the machine." The message to whites is not overly didactic, but it is there. The social science essays in *Ebony and Topaz*, then, are primarily addressed to overcoming white stereotypes and prejudices.[12]

Finally, as his third goal, Johnson aimed to invigorate the arts as a central expression of Negro life. If this idea was germinating even when he first arrived in New York, he could not do much about it until the end of 1923 when *Opportunity* was launched. With the first issues of 1924 he was ready; the reader could find poems by Langston Hughes and Claude

McKay, as well as studies of Negro employment and interpretive essays on race prejudice.

In Harlem in the early 1920s that upsurge in literary and artistic work about Negro life that Alain Locke would call "our little renaissance" was happening.[13] Poetry by Countee Cullen and Langston Hughes; stories by Zora Neale Hurston, Wallace Thurman and Rudolph Fisher; novels by Jessie Fauset, Nella Larsen (1891–1964), and Walter White; poetic sketches by Jean Toomer (1894–1967) and Claude McKay; essays on black cultural themes by Alain Locke, Du Bois, James Weldon Johnson, and Charles Johnson; drawings by Aaron Douglas and Charles Cullen—these and many other contributions by and about Negroes not only were disseminated to readers in Harlem but began to penetrate that wall of indifference, if not hostility, behind which stood white America. In the process the "new Negro" asserted the right to write or sculpt freely in his or her own terms about the whole spectrum of African-American experience. Some writers wanted to break through constricting white stereotypes, some wanted to break away from an earlier confining tradition in the black community that produced a too genteel creative work, some wanted to demonstrate that folk art, like the spirituals, blues, and African sculpture, far from being "inferior forms," represented true art, as worthy as any other. And all wanted, in various ways, to capture the quality and complexity of black life in America. *The New Negro,* an anthology of their stories, poems and essays, with a stimulating introduction by Locke, was their manifesto.

The call to lift up voices in behalf of art came from Johnson in *Opportunity* in September 1924: "*Opportunity* hopes to stimulate and encourage creative literary effort among Negroes . . . encourage interest in a body of literature about Negro life." Six months before, however, Locke and Du Bois had already sounded the same note (*Crisis,* February 1924): "Even as we ask 'Where are the young Negro artists to weld and mold this mighty material about us?'—even as we ask, they came." And indeed both the *Crisis* and the *Messenger,* the voice of labor and socialism, had been taking literary work before *Opportunity* entered the lists, although stories and poems appeared less frequently than in Johnson's pages in the 1920s. The *Crisis's* support for African American cultural expression took second place to its primary emphasis, a political and legal strategy to combat racial discrimination and injustice. Reaching a peak circulation of nearly one hundred thousand nationally, it could hammer away at an end to lynching and mob rule, a recovery of the franchise, a forceful strategy to open access to jobs and housing. Moreover, neither Du Bois nor Randolph had Johnson's passion for celebrating the work of the writers and seeing them through to publication. (Nevertheless, the *Crisis* was the first to print Langston Hughes's "The Negro Speaks of Rivers," later dedicated to Du Bois.)

Du Bois, for all the power and eloquence of his polemical writing and sociological essays, had a lesser eye and ear regarding the arts. His own fiction, written in a Victorian style, did not have the same force as his nonfiction. As a critic, he was inclined to reject work if he did not like the author's lifestyle. (It must be said, however, that a new generation of critics, among them Arnold Rampersad, has argued persuasively in behalf of Du Bois as a gifted novelist and poet.) The *Messenger* had a much smaller circulation but a more dramatic self-definition: "The Only Negro Radical Magazine in America." It championed socialism, pacifism, and radical social reconstruction. Later, Randolph, leader of the Brotherhood of Sleeping Car Porters, turned it into the official organ of the union, less doctrinaire in its socialism but just as militant as before on racial issues. Randolph went on to become a towering figure in the civil rights movement. Tall, handsome, ramrod straight, he led the brotherhood effectively, but the union came into its own only with the passage of the Wagner Act in 1935, guaranteeing collective bargaining. Over bitter resistance from the railroad companies, a contract was finally won in 1937. Even in the hard days of the 1920s, throughout a failed strike and constant company harassment, Randolph stood fast. Always courtly and dignified, he had a riveting speaking voice, honed in oratory school. In 1941 he challenged the president himself, demanding nondiscriminatory hiring in defense industries or threatening to march on Washington in the thousands. Franklin D. Roosevelt capitulated and signed Executive Order 8802 establishing the federal Fair Employment Practices Commission.[14]

Racism, for the *Messenger*, was but one manifestation of an exploitative capitalism and its destructive war machine. A Negro soldier would be twice duped, by racism and jingoism. Randolph bitterly criticized Du Bois and Joel Spingarn of the NAACP for acquiescing in the War Department's decision to train Negro officers in segregated facilities. Randolph and Owen were the first to reprint Claude McKay's "If We Must Die"—which came out originally in the *Liberator*—as powerful a fusion of art and racial protest as could be imagined.[15]

All these editors were always conscious that, beyond Harlem, they were working against the national grain.[16] America of the 1920s was anti-black, anti-Semitic, anti-immigrant, anti-Catholic, and anti-political dissent (the Red Scare). In such a national setting, minority cultural expression could hardly thrive. Black artists and writers with something to say were either simply ignored or explicitly denied access to publishing houses, galleries, and theaters. Augusta Savage, for example, an extremely talented Negro sculptress, was denied her French government scholarship by the American supervisory committee at the school of the arts in Fontainebleau, France.

And yet, in New York, in the white community, there were some individuals of influence and power who rejected the national assessment of the Negro. On the contrary, these publishers, writers, academics, and editors were concerned to bridge the distance between Harlem and downtown. That white interest has sometimes been dismissed as patronizing or condescending when, as Langston Hughes observed "Harlem was in vogue." Hurston called these whites "Negrotarians." This view neglects the genuine interest on the part of some white influentials, to say nothing of the fact that publishers, quite aside from wanting to improve race relations, also wanted to find authors whose books would sell. In any case, for Johnson, the question of motives on the other side was not central; making the connections, winning results, were. The important whites had their own agenda, whatever their reasons. He had his.

A case in point is Carl Van Vechten, writer, critic, photographer, and tireless friend of the renaissance circle and the cause. He knew the publishers; he knew Harlem; he could bridge the two worlds. His own novel *Nigger Heaven* dismayed many in the circle, partly because of the title. In fact the title was meant ironically, a satirical comment on the segregation of Negroes in the most distant reaches of the theater balcony. The book itself contained subtle insights into life in Harlem. Van Vechten himself was not on occasion above the "slumming," celebrating the Negro as exotic, which some in the Harlem circle rightfully resented. His other novels besides *Nigger Heaven* were slight, not to be taken seriously. But as Jervis Anderson notes, this was the man "whose assistance to the growth of the Harlem Renaissance— one of the most important stages of the development of black writing— was probably greater than that of any other white American."[17] He knew everyone—almost. In between the partying, he was a serious student of African American literature and culture. A talented photographer, his portraits of Zora Neale Hurston, Nella Larsen, Countee Cullen, and others were widely praised. The interracial parties he gave, with his actress wife, Fania Marinoff, were for enjoyment and not to make a political statement. (Years later he was still trying to do Johnson's portrait: "I've got to get you in color!")

So a line of transit developed from the black circle to a small number of whites and back again. Charles Johnson was the chief facilitator, connecting authors to publishers and editors, and he was the force behind two dinners in 1924 and 1925 that strengthened his hand greatly as the entrepreneur of the Harlem Renaissance.

In March 1924 the Civic Club Dinner was a gathering of about a hundred guests ostensibly to honor Jessie Fauset's novel *There Is Confusion*. But the real purpose was to allow a mingling of young black artists and writers with editors, writers, and publishers from downtown. Locke presided; Du Bois and Johnson spoke briefly, as did James Weldon Johnson. What drew the strongest response, however, was the talk by the eminent critic and editor of the *Century*, Carl Van Doren, which moved the audience by calling for more work from "the younger generation of Negro writers." Countee Cullen and Gwendolyn Bennett read poems. So the evening ended. But it did not end, for it led to the publication the next year of a special edition of *Survey Graphic*, which became in book form *The New Negro*. The book inspired publishers such as Horace Liveright and Alfred A. Knopf to take more books by Negro writers. The time was growing ripe. Jean Toomer's *Cane* had appeared in 1923, Claude McKay's *Harlem Shadows* the year before that, Du Bois's *Darkwater* just a few months earlier—all by mainstream publishers. At the same time, downtown, the recent plays of Eugene O'Neill, among others, seemed to signal a more honest and realistic attempt at a portrayal of Negro life.

The New Negro contained work by established writers and by young published poets and novelists and by the less well-known as well. Johnson contributed to it his "Frontage" article. The editor of *Opportunity* had another project in mind, however. In 1924, the magazine announced the first literary prize contest; there would be small cash awards and the chance to break into print in *Opportunity*. (The *Crisis* proposal for a contest had come out earlier, on a more modest scale. Du Bois was said to be upset that Johnson had taken over his idea.) The awards ceremony and dinner was planned for May 1, 1925, at the Fifth Avenue Restaurant.

May 1 turned out to be a memorable evening, more than fulfilling Johnson's expectations. More than three hundred persons were in attendance. First prize in poetry was awarded to Langston Hughes, only twenty-three; James Weldon Johnson, no less, read Hughes's "Weary Blues." Frazier won first prize in the essay category, Sterling Brown second. A second prize for the short story went to Zora Neale Hurston— $50, for "Spunk." The work of those who would eventually become well-known and of those who would not at all appeared in the pages of *Opportunity* and in *Ebony and Topaz*. Hurston seemed to follow both paths, flourishing through the 1930s, then retreating to Florida, only to be "rescued" from obscurity thirty years later. Some contestants from the South and West followed up their entries by coming to Harlem, expanding the literary pool. After three years, however, interest began to wane, and the money from white and black philanthropy diminished. The contributions declined in quality; after 1927 the contests were suspended. But Johnson had got what he wanted—a jump in the cultural pulse of Harlem and new connections between black writers and mainstream publishers. *The New Negro* anthology was a success. So was *Ebony and Topaz*. A little more than a year later (1928), he would make plans to leave New York for Fisk and Nashville, to return to the South for the kind of sociological study he had been thinking about since Chicago days. Yet the Harlem Renaissance and the memory of the *Opportunity* contests would have a special place in his heart. That was a stimulating time.

The two "midwives" most responsible for the flourishing of the Harlem Renaissance were undoubtedly Charles S. Johnson and Alain Locke. Langston Hughes, who would know, remembered a third, Jessie Fauset, literary editor of the *Crisis* and Du Bois's assistant there. The star of the Civic Club dinner worked diligently in behalf of many writers. At the very end of the period (1931) she published another sensitive novel of black middle-class life, *The Chinaberry Tree*, which lacked the appeal of *Confusion*. Hughes asserted flatly, "Charles S. Johnson did more to encourage and develop Negro writers during the 1920's than anyone else in America." Arna Bontemps and Aaron Douglas were of the same opinion. Zora Neale Hurston expressed hers in her irrepressible way: "This was *his* work, and only his hushmouth nature has caused it to be attributed to many others." Johnson, not usually given to personal, mean-spirited remarks about others, did say that Locke was "cast in a role merely of press agent" for the Renaissance. Perhaps it is best to note simply that Locke took great pleasure in grading black writers and artists by his exacting standards. For years after the Renaissance was done he continued to assess the passing parade in literature from his tower—his regular column in *Opportunity*—while Johnson took great pleasure in organizing projects, in getting the work known, published, and disseminated to the widest possible audience, black and white.[18]

At all events, Locke was *a*, if not *the*, central figure of the Harlem Renaissance. Born in Philadelphia in 1886 to a solid black middle-class family, he went through the educational cycle at the highest level, from Central High School in Philadelphia, to Harvard, to a Rhodes scholarship at Oxford (the first Negro to have one), to further study at the University of Berlin in the Park and Du Bois pattern. Returning to the United States in 1912, he settled in at Howard as professor of philosophy. He would have been superbly qualified for any prestigious university. But he took discrimination in stride; his concern was the relationship of race to culture, literature, and the life of the mind. Small, slight, effete, a closet homosexual, eccentric in his personal life but highly disciplined in his work, he liked to enjoy the good life in Europe, the ambience of Paris. But Harlem was his beat. There, in the community, he could bring into synthesis the singular qualities of Negro literature and the enduring Western tradition. His was no simple Eurocentric elitism—the collaborative work with Albert C. Barnes on African art alone would refute that notion. Rather, he would use his European-based gifts and education to be mentor, guide, critic and friend to Negro writers and artists. And he would argue that their work (as he judged it) would prepare the way for an era of triumph for African American art. As he said, "I am more a philosophical midwife to a generation of younger Negro poets, writers, artists than a professional philosopher." His proof was *The New Negro*, "an augury of a new democracy in American culture," wherein African American artists, freer than before from proscription and prejudice, would contribute to an integrated, not a separatist, society.[19] Both he and Johnson were persuaded of this.

The interpretive essays in *The New Negro* anthology by the social scientists, including Johnson, have already been described. The established leaders, including Johnson, have their place as well. Du Bois is represented typically by his worldwide view of race and the oppression of imperialism: "And thus again in 1924 as in 1899 I seem to see the problem of the 20th century as the problem of the color line." James

Weldon Johnson presents a brief portrait of Harlem, but in a sense his mere presence in the anthology is enough. Poet, playwright, diplomat, field secretary of the NAACP, lawyer, folklorist, he was a unique player in the Renaissance. In 1930 Johnson persuaded him to come to Fisk—as he did with Bontemps and Douglas—to become professor of creative literature, where he served until his death in 1938. Walter F. White, who was at that time assistant executive secretary of the NAACP and later, for many years afterward the organization's director, writes of "the paradox of color" and describes once again the bizarre irony that he could do the crucially important work of investigating lynchings on site because he was so light-skinned as to "pass."

But the heart of *The New Negro*, and the same is true for Johnson's anthology, *Ebony and Topaz*, is the attention given to young poets and novelists, many of whom were "lost" for three decades after the Renaissance only to be "rediscovered" in the 1960s when a new generation concerned with black consciousness, black culture, and black studies generated a renewed interest in the Renaissance. There is certainly gratification in seeing this happen. (Some of us, growing up white and Jewish of democratic socialist families in New York in the late 1930s did indeed read these writers, on occasion traveling uptown to the old Schomburg library to read there. We were not, obviously, typical readers.)[20]

Zora Neale Hurston, of course, has come back to an astonishing degree, thanks in large part to being "rescued" by Alice Walker and other contemporary African American writers. Countee Cullen, Johnson's assistant editor at *Opportunity* for a time, continued to be read fairly widely, even though he came to be lightly regarded. Langston Hughes, the polymath, the most brilliant star in the Harlem constellation, continued to turn out work after work in every genre. But there were others. A minimal list would include Rudolph Fisher, Nella Larsen, and Wallace Thurman, in addition to Hughes and Hurston. Fisher (1897–1934) had grown up in Washington and Providence, then had gotten his medical degree at Howard and came to Harlem in the mid-1920s. The doctor-writer, in his short stories and in his novels, *The Walls of Jericho* (1928) and *The Conjure Man Dies* (1932), had the capacity to draw sharp-edged, psychological portraits of Harlem's bourgeoisie and working class, satirical and yet touched with humor. Wallace Thurman, born in Utah, had come to Harlem to become its sternest critic. Sardonic, cynical, scathing in his criticism of pretentious artists, whether black or white, he flailed away at the Harlem circle. His work was fitful, wracked as he was by physical ailments and alcoholism, but the caustic wit and the anger come through in passages of the novel *The Blacker the Berry* (1929). The classic failed novelist, drowned in drink, he died young. Nella Larsen wrote only two novels, *Quicksand* (1928) and *Passing* (1929) before disappearing into relative obscurity (after a brief interlude at Fisk, where she was the wife of Elmer Imes, professor of physics). Yet *Quicksand* is a considerable achievement; it holds the reader tightly with its subtle interweave of color and class around the persona of the heroine, mixed racially, struggling to find herself. Reading *Quicksand* one always wonders what Nella Larsen might have accomplished had her talent not been closed down by various circumstances.

The Harlem Renaissance did not last very long. During the Great Depression, some of the writers redefined their work so that it became more inclusive of the "other Harlem" of poverty and depressed housing. As Alain Locke wrote a decade later, the writers would now have to address a broader community, "the Harlem that the social worker knew all along but had not been able to dramatize. . . . There is no cure or saving magic in poetry and art for . . . precarious marginal employment, high mortality rates, civic neglect." John Hope Franklin and others have rightly observed that the creative art and the scholarly work did not stop; impressive contributions continued to mount through the Depression and World War II.[21] That is so. But the special élan, the swirl of high-intensity activity and argument around the poems and plays and novels diminished. And the writers went their separate ways.

Johnson ended his stewardship at *Opportunity* in 1928 and left for Fisk. His first priority had been social science research and a return to the South with its great challenge, economic as much as racial, for those who yearned to place their professional work in the service of social change. During the Renaissance he wrote no fiction, nor did he ever. The stimulus of the Civic Club and awards dinners, meetings with publishers, the late night talk with the writers, the "entrepreneur" role would be missed but would not have kept him permanently in New York.

Surprisingly, in the many boxes of material in the Johnson Papers, there is not only nothing about his feelings on leaving *Opportunity* and the Renaissance, but there is practically nothing on how exactly he managed the entrepreneur role, exactly how things worked with an Alfred A. Knopf or Arthur Schomburg. This contrasts with the very full file on his research role with the Urban League. In the years after the Harlem period, he would on occasion give a talk about those days or write a special memoir, as when the James Weldon Johnson Papers were presented to Yale University. James Weldon Johnson, Arthur Schomburg (briefly), Aaron Douglas, and Arna Bontemps were reunited with him on the Fisk campus. Hughes would visit, staying with the Johnsons. Zora Neale Hurston, possibly the most innovative and talented of them all, wrote on into the 1930s and 1940s before falling into obscurity in the 1950s. Her first novel, *Jonah's Gourd Vine*, came out in 1934, followed by a fine study in black American folklore, *Mules and Men* (1935), and the wonderful novel *Their Eyes Were Watching God* (1937). She wrote to Johnson from Florida, describing her curious brand of conservative politics, defending segregation, denouncing "tragedy of color" writers of "the sobbing school of Negrohood" who let race get them down.[22] All in all, however, in the Fisk years Johnson seems to have regarded the Harlem period as a closed chapter, an interesting and exciting one, to be sure, where by day poets could be introduced to publishers, where by night the Johnsons could be at home to friends or out on the town enjoying blues and jazz at a club.[23]

For Johnson, Du Bois, White, and James Weldon Johnson, the Harlem Renaissance was one stage in lifetimes of work in organization and advocacy. Walter White would go on to direct the NAACP for many years, a national figure like Du Bois but much more centrist, leaving far behind White the novelist of *Fire in the Flint*. Du Bois resigned as editor of the *Crisis* in 1934, leaving the NAACP to return to Atlanta and the role of militant propagandist for civil rights. Locke returned to Howard to teach philosophy. But for three decades he continued his role as guardian of the Renaissance, keeping readers informed in the pages of *Opportunity* of the annual state of the Negro arts. When he died in 1954 he was championing Ralph Ellison's *Invisible Man* and predicting that Afro-American literature and art were on the threshold of a fuller, many-sided contribution to American cultural pluralism.

The poets and novelists experienced a more difficult transition because they would not be turning or returning to academe or organizations. Hughes, as always the writer who would keep on writing whatever the changes in his political position and personal fortunes, went right on with poetry, fiction, autobiography, and adaptations of musical drama, weaving elements of folk, blues, and jazz into his work. Who does not remember the readings, the poet up front, reading, the trio back of him moving the music along? Or the Jess B. Semple (Simple) stories, written originally as columns for the *Chicago Defender*? They were not simple at all. In the bar in Harlem, Simple talks race, race, race, but the talk is embedded in an earthy sense of life and love. His bar companion (Hughes), playing a kind of pedantic lay sociologist, keeps gently correcting Simple with liberal platitudes. Don't stereotype— aren't there good and bad whites just like "us"? Simple's response could not be more to the point. Try *that* theory in Mississippi!

The other writers did not fare as well. Countee Cullen, *the* black poet of the 1920s, moved into the prosaic life of New York high school teacher and wrote no more poetry; he died in 1946. Jean Toomer, who in *Cane* created perhaps the most impressive single work of the Renaissance, not only fled Harlem and poetry but even his own racial identity. Claude McKay, the most powerful African American voice, is still read today; selections from *Home to Harlem* and *Harlem Shadows* are in anthologies. His stormy passage, from radical politics, to exile, to embracing finally the Catholic church, underlined the problem of coming to terms with racial identity in America. Among the women, Jessie Fauset continued to write on the same middle-class themes, then married and settled quietly in the suburbs. Nella Larsen dropped out; Wallace Thurman burned out.[24] From Fisk, Johnson kept up his praise for Eric Walrond, the West Indian writer, author of *Tropic Death* (1926). But he, too, faded away, to Europe. The Renaissance was essentially over; the writers left Harlem. (Discussing the Harlem Renaissance with me years later, James Baldwin noted that he was the only writer actually born there.)

What can we say finally about the Renaissance and Johnson's pivotal role in it more than a half-century later? On balance there is as much criticism as celebration. In the Depression and New Deal era that followed, with the call for social realism in fiction, it is easy to see why some of the Renaissance writers were faulted for keeping a distance from Harlem's working class and poor, for the lack of concern for social movements beyond the moderate Urban League and NAACP, for missing the great significance of Marcus Garvey's black nationalism, his UNIA movement, which for a time had a powerful hold on people in Harlem. Du Bois was utterly contemptuous of Garvey. Johnson, as was sometimes the case, had better insight than the editor of the *Crisis*. He, too, deplored the theatrical posturing, but he understood the appeal to black consciousness and solidarity and the mass response to that appeal.[25]

Hughes and Hurston excepted, it is now sometimes argued that the young writers failed to summon to their work the deepest, most authentic material from their home base, the black community. Nathan

Irvin Huggins, for example, insists that for all the proclamation of the "new Negro," the writers remained in large part collaborators with the white establishment and thus in some ways the product of the very white world from which they needed to be liberated:

> The great innocence of the Renaissance is most clearly seen in the irony that, where its proponents had wanted to develop a distinctive Negro voice, they had been of necessity most derivative. . . . A white commerce had determined what was to be considered success in business, industry and art. A white establishment had really defined art and culture. As long as the white norms remained unchallenged, no matter what the Negro's reaction to them, he always needed to return to the white judge to measure his achievement. . . . So it was an encumbered legacy that the Renaissance left to the following decades of Afro-American culture.

The result, Huggins concludes, was a "crippled art . . . not fresh, not real" in form and content.[26] This may be a largely valid verdict but it requires some qualification. Not all the writers were caught in this dilemma. There is, as usual, the Hughes factor. In a stunning essay, "The Negro Artist and the Racial Mountain," written for the *Nation* in 1926, Hughes argued that those who said let me be a poet, period, and not a Negro poet, were really saying let me be like white poets. The racial mountain, whiteness, blocks true expression. "Let Paul Robeson singing 'Water Boy' and Rudolph Fisher writing about the streets of Harlem, and Jean Toomer holding the heart of Georgia in his hands, and Aaron Douglas drawing strange black fantasies cause the smug Negro middle class to turn from their white, respectable, ordinary books and papers to catch a glimmer of their own beauty." Let "the colored near-intellectuals" actually listen to Bessie Smith's blues. As for the whites, "If white people are pleased, we are glad. If they are not, it doesn't matter." The same was true for colored people. Negro artists must pursue their own vision, beautiful and ugly, until "we stand on top of the mountain free within ourselves."[27]

A different criticism involving the white world is that the Renaissance writers were naive to assume that a show of black creativity would undermine the racism constricting that very creativity. This was a cultural counterpart to Boas's contention that science, armed with fact and generalization, ultimately would undermine the tenacious myths about the superiority and inferiority of races. Of Locke and company, Hughes said, "They thought the race problem had at last been solved through Art." The Renaissance probably did contribute to overcoming both malevolent and benevolent stereotypes of black people. But not much. In the 1920s great numbers of whites continued to retain what Walter Lippmann called the pictures in our heads. At a sophisticated level, white critics still wrote of an innate black "expressiveness," sensuality, and emotionality that contrasted strongly with the Babbitry and Puritanism of their own society. At the popular level, images of the Negro as Darky and Sambo, naturally endowed for shuffling and dancing, images of the South of "the good negrah" who knew his place and earned respect seemed unchanged. Beyond Renaissance, Harlem, New York, there was indeed another country.

All this criticism and revisionism notwithstanding, the Harlem Renaissance had an enduring impact. Before being submerged by conditions Alain Locke referred to as "precarious marginal employment" and "high mortality rates," the Renaissance meant simply that a fresh current of literature and art had been set flowing. Writers then and thereafter were enabled, in Du Bois's phrase, "to weld and mold this mighty material," in Johnson's phrase to establish "that mood of receptivity among the general public for the literature of Negro life." To that end, "our little renaissance" was a bridge to the future, not a dead stop at the end of the 1920s. Those who made it possible were the writers themselves, the editors of *Opportunity* and the *Crisis*, the business and professional supporters, white like Van Vechten, black like Schomburg, and the reading audience downtown and in Harlem. Revisionism simply amends the contribution.

The last word might be left to Arnold Rampersad, author of the definitive biography of Langston Hughes, in a new introduction to the reprinted *New Negro*. The anthology "reflects the mixed record of the Harlem Renaissance itself. In spite of the fact that the movement was short-lived, and many of its works and talents of less than stellar quality, the Renaissance succeeded in laying the foundations for all subsequent depictions in poetry, fiction, and drama of the modern African-American experience; and the same claim can be made even more strongly of its music, in the compositions and performances of artists such as Duke Ellington, Louis Armstrong and Bessie Smith. . . . Even today it [*The New Negro*] remains a reliable index to the black sensibility at the point where art and politics meet, as well as to events in Harlem and elsewhere among blacks in the 1920's."[28]

Charles S. Johnson had his own last word. Just a little more than a year before he died he addressed a social science conference at Howard

University in April 1955 on "The Negro Renaissance and Its Signifi-cance." Much was familiar—praise again for Jean Toomer, assessment of Garveyism ("a desperate and pathetic mass fantasy" yet of enormous appeal to a people so in need of hope), review of Locke's role and praise for him (Locke had died in 1954). Then came the lesson to be drawn: the raising of black consciousness, the surge of black pride in a distinctive literature, was vitally needed. Too many white people were telling too many black people they were not capable of such a thing. Now, so self-conscious a movement was *less* needed. Though their focus remained Negro life in all its variousness and complexity, the black poets and painters could now develop that theme within the mainstream, "within the context, not of a special culture group, but of the national society and world civilization."[29] Prescient though he often was on many issues, Johnson could not foresee the enormous racial upheavals of the 1960s and the subsequent emergence of a new liberation movement that included a "special culture group" pressing as hard for black studies and rediscovery of the black cultural heritage as for civil rights in the Congress. Still, Johnson had it right for the long term. Already, in Johnson's time, such writers as Richard Wright, James Baldwin, and Ralph Ellison were of this domain, aligned with their peers in the world of American literature and yet linked deeper in time to their predecessors in the Renaissance. Today, the line of transit still runs that way, from the novels of Toni Morrison and the poems of Maya Angelou to the poems of Langston Hughes and the tales of Zora Neale Hurston. Indeed, Arna Bontemps used to argue for a specific bracketing—Ralph Ellison with Jean Toomer, James Baldwin with Wallace Thurman, Paule Marshall with Zora Neale Hurston, and so on.

In any case, by 1927, when *Opportunity* suspended the literary con-tests, Charles Johnson was not giving much thought to the question of the enduring value of the Renaissance, let alone to why someday it might be judged to have failed in its mission. At the end of the year he entered into preliminary negotiations with Thomas Elsa Jones, Fisk's last white president and a most interesting man beyond that "race fact." By spring 1928, he was discussing with Jones the principal reason for coming to Fisk. Having consulted, as might be expected, with Park and Embree, he wrote Jones on February 8, 1928, "my research interest is definitely committed to the South." Moreover, it had become clear to him that both the research and advocacy roles at the Urban League would remain just about the same into the far future. As for the Renaissance, the "special culture" had been well launched; assuredly more authors would find more publishers in the future. So on March 13, 1928, he resigned.[30] Reid took over the research, Elmer Carter the editing of *Opportunity*. Carter was an energetic, politically astute man. It was not his fault that *Opportunity* eventually languished. More and more attention was being given to racial problems and progress in the general press, the Negro press, and widely distributed Federal government reports. During World War II *Opportunity* became a quarterly. With the winter issue of 1947, it ceased publication.

The eight years of the three goals were over. Charles Johnson had moved ahead, continuing the sociological research, renewing the middle-way advocacy in the spirit of the league, being present at the founding of the new cultural surge, the Harlem Renaissance. Now all that must have begun to recede in his thoughts, the South—the changing South(?)—coming to the forefront of his mind. As he and Marie packed, memories may have crowded in: his indomitable father, affronted by the lynch mob, standing up to it in the street in Bristol; what the Richmond ghetto had to tell him about the real world and the possibility of becoming a sociologist; how those thousands of black men and women had traveled south to north, from Mississippi to Chicago, the Promised Land of the Great Migration, where he had lived among them and had studied their adaptation to the urban-industrial setting.

It was time to be traveling once again, south, from Harlem, New York, to Fisk University, Nashville, Tennessee.

IV

GREAT DEPRESSION
AND NEW DEAL

By the summer of 1928 the Johnsons were installed in their home just off the Fisk campus. The family joined the Congregational Christian church, and Mrs. Johnson began her participation in many charities and social service groups, local and national, activities that continued for nearly a decade after her husband's death in 1956. Johnson was ready to develop his job, really three jobs in one, at Fisk: professor of sociology, director of the Department of Social Science, head of the Social Science Institute (later the Race Relations Department).

Johnson regarded the new challenge as much broader in scope than the formal academic appointment. His position and outlook might be compared to a cross section of tree rings—first the commitment to the university; then living in and studying the community, Nashville; then the comprehensive research, to analyze the socioeconomic and racial structure of the South, as well as participation in a wide range of southern regional interracial advocacy groups; finally, the aspiration (later on) to play some part—important but less public and more indirect than that of Du Bois, the propagandist—in the formation of national public policy in Washington, especially in such matters as antilynching and farm tenancy legislation. In his usual methodical way, Johnson, having agreed to come to Fisk, set about negotiating the terms. The president, Thomas Elsa Jones, first broached the idea in 1926. He wanted Johnson—and James Weldon Johnson in the humanities and Elmer Imes in the physical sciences—not only because they would obviously enhance Fisk's national reputation but because they could help shore up Fisk's generally sound but underfunded financial condition. When Fisk received a five-year Laura Spelman Rockefeller grant to restructure the social sciences, Jones had a trump card to play. Johnson then laid out what he thought should be the priorities—a department in the University of Chicago spirit emphasizing urbanism, race relations, and Negro social structure, locally, regionally, and nationally. Jones concurred, and Johnson accepted the post March 8, 1928.[1] But even as the fall term began he was still sending memorandums to Jones on the need for good balance of teaching, theory, and research practice and emphasizing that the southern regional "matrix" was the most important place to study race and Negro life. He could personally assure Jones that funding would be steady and secure from the usual sources: Rosenwald, AMA, General Education Board, Laura Spelman Rockefeller, et al. Controlling budget and program, Johnson promised a research center of national standing. And so it turned out. Even when he became president in 1946, Johnson kept a strong hand in this work. Only near the end of his life would both finances and the stature of the research operation begin to decline.

Before Johnson accepted Fisk's offer, E. Franklin Frazier, then director of the School of Social Work at Atlanta University, interviewed in 1927 for the position of head of sociology and the graduate program in social work. He was eminently qualified, with strong references from Du Bois and from Franklin Hankins, his teacher at Clark University. In this instance, President Jones displayed uncharacteristic weakness and timidity; bowing to pressure, he decided against Frazier, ostensibly because of Frazier's "difficult" personality, in fact because of his uncompromising opposition to racial segregation and the white paternalism dominating boards of trustees at institutions like Fisk and Atlanta. When eventually Frazier did come to Fisk (1929–34), where Johnson would be his director, his militant activism made the establishment uncomfortable. The subsequent estrangement between these two eminent sociologists did not stem from job competition, however. They developed different political outlooks and strategies for changing the racial system.

Johnson's twenty-seven years at Fisk were good not only because of the productive research in social science but because Fisk was Fisk, not just one more historically black college. Founded in 1866 jointly by the American Missionary Association and the state's Freedmen's Bureau, commanded by General Clinton Fisk, it was incorporated the next year as a normal school of "broad Christian foundation," but it was not until 1871 that four college students entered. For a decade afterward it was primarily a school of secondary level, although the founders' purpose was the eventual establishment of an excellent liberal arts college. From the 1880s to 1915 Fisk struggled to meet that mandate in the midst

65

of a hostile white community and with inadequate financial support. Originally interracial, Fisk had eventually to conform to Tennessee's segregation system, but it never gave in entirely. A substantial proportion of the faculty were white; so were a small number of students (today, about 1 percent). In the 1870s Fisk was able to avert financial distress only through revenue generated by the Fisk Jubilee Singers, whose tours of Europe and America brought in thousands of dollars—$150,000 in just seven years. These difficulties notwithstanding, at the dawn of the new century Fisk was becoming the outstanding symbol of liberal higher education as Tuskegee was for industrial vocational education for Negroes. The contrast may have been overplayed. As early as 1904 Booker T. Washington said that "we need not only the industrial school but the college." His wife and son had gone to Fisk, and he was a trustee from 1909 until his death in 1915. The Tuskegee Machine and Washington acquired significant financial support for Fisk from the usual cluster of Rockefeller, Rosenwald, Carnegie, and Morgan. For W. E. B. Du Bois, a scholarship student at Fisk from 1885 to 1888 (he finished at Harvard), Fisk was a revelation, "an extraordinary experience." He got a sound classical education, edited the *Fisk Herald*, and taught during the summers in Negro public schools. But most of all this black high-minded New Englander experienced the searing effect of the color bar and the remarkable resilience and strength of character of black culture confronting that bar.

Fisk flourished in the 1920s. Johnson, at the Urban League, kept in contact. But all was not well. Some black colleges in the South had white presidents who presided over their campuses as fiefdoms for paternalistic, tightly controlling administration. Among them, Fisk's Fayette A. McKenzie, a renowned fund raiser but a complete authoritarian and a man uninterested in his Negro constituency, represented all that was wrong with an archaic system. In 1924–25 strikes and protests took place at Fisk, Hampton, Howard, and Wilberforce. Their timing gives pause to those who assert that black student protest was nonexistent until the 1960s.[2] At Fisk, aided by the powerful voice of Du Bois and other alumni, the students were able to depose "the dictator" and restore the silenced student newspaper.

Under the new, relatively progressive president, Thomas Elsa Jones, Fisk resumed its growth and development, deterred but not halted by the Great Depression. By the end of the decade its endowment was several million dollars; Embree termed it the best Negro college with

66

"the pick of the country" for faculty and students. As Joe M. Richardson notes, "Under the leadership of Jones and noted scholar Charles S. Johnson . . . the university experienced unprecedented growth."[3] Its preeminence lasted through Johnson's presidency (1946–56) on into the mid-1970s, when administrative mismanagement and financial difficulties almost drove it to the wall.[4] Fisk has now largely recovered and once again is grouped with Hampton, Howard, and the Atlanta complex as the leading black colleges.

Through the 1930s Fisk had the traditional relationship to the white community of Nashville, a functional part of the whole and yet isolated from the mainstream system of institutions. Johnson, who would live there for nearly three decades, placed a high priority on maintaining a comprehensive socioeconomic and racial profile of greater Nashville (Davidson County). For him and every other black faculty member there was also a personal dimension. When they ventured off the campus they immediately confronted segregation. Despite his national stature, Johnson had difficulties, as in his conflict with the station manager who at first refused his request for a sleeper reservation out of Nashville.

In 1930 Nashville had a population of about 154,000, nearly 26 percent of it Negro. The population had doubled since 1900 as Nashville, like a large-scale version of the Bristol of Johnson's youth, developed a range of diversified commercial enterprises and industries, served as a vital transport hub, and established a cluster of colleges, secular and religious; music and religious publication industries came later. This profile remained roughly the same through the Depression and early postwar years, when a new growth spurt set in. Today, the city and county are combined into a single metropolitan administrative unit of nearly a million, and the city proper has a population of more than half a million, of which 23 percent is black.

During Johnson's tenure in the 1930s and 1940s, the racial pattern was familiar to him even before he directed many local surveys. Not only pervasive racial segregation but very striking white-black disparities occurred on the major socioeconomic indices and were intensified by the Depression. Ecologically, the census tracts showed the Negro population concentrated due west and then north of the downtown center and near the Cumberland River (including Fisk and the public Negro college, Tennessee A&I, now Tennessee State University), with smaller segments across the river, east near downtown, and to the southwest just off downtown. Residential segregation, following southern tradition, was a little looser, with some lower-middle-class and working-class white enclaves on the margin of black areas. Through the entire 1930s, the statistical abstracts show that the black-white ratios remained about the same—much lower black family income, underrepresentation in white-collar occupations and years of school completed, overrepresentation in unskilled labor and illiteracy. For example, the infant mortality rate for Negroes in Nashville was nearly double that for whites all through the 1930s. With respect to segregation, Negroes were restricted to one branch of the library, had separate wards in the general hospitals, separate parks, segregated seating in transportation and theaters, and were excluded from all retail jobs.[5]

Nashville, however, was only a small part of the focus of Fisk's new research center. Johnson's basic concern centered on the economic and racial problems of the nation and of the South in general and the exploitation of the rural black poverty population in particular. This constituted a complex challenge, for the "New South" remained both distinctive from, and yet integral to, the nation as a whole. In calling attention to the South as "the nation's number one economic problem," "one-third of a nation ill-housed, ill-clad, ill-nourished," the new president in 1933, Franklin Roosevelt, had no intention of directly addressing racial questions directly in the South. To raise the issue of racial segregation would provoke total resistance from unreconstructed southern legislators, who, controlling strategic committees by virtue of seniority, could jeopardize urgently needed economic measures. President Roosevelt explained the situation to black leaders through their intermediary Aubrey Williams (1890–1965), the white southern liberal and deputy to Harry Hopkins in the relief agencies. When pressed to move ahead to eliminate the poll tax in the face of a certain southern filibuster, he cited the old clichés ("politics is the art of compromise") and the standard bottom line ("don't undertake anything unless you have a 50–50 chance of succeeding").[6] Nonetheless, it soon became clear that Negroes would turn to Roosevelt and the Democratic party even though the southern Democratic bloc constituted the essential linchpin in the defense of segregation and the fierce racial discrimination that sustained it. In the 1936 elections the black precincts gave FDR over 70 percent of their vote and in 1940 only a little less. The reasons were clear.

First, because of their disadvantaged position in the economy, Negroes stood to gain immediately and directly from New Deal programs in behalf of the poor, the needy, and the unemployed. Second, they were aware, if vaguely, that at last they had some access to government. A small but determined group of white liberals in the administration—Will Alexander, Eleanor Roosevelt, Harold Ickes, Aubrey Williams, Harry Hopkins, Clark Foreman, and others—detesting racial injustice, nevertheless agreed to tabling the thorny issue of segregation to concentrate on concrete and, they thought, achievable, goals: elimination of the poll tax, an antilynching law, equitable assistance to black and white farm tenants in the South. They—above all, Mrs. Roosevelt—were moralists to the core with respect to racial justice and yet were practical and realistic. Their necessarily pragmatic approach was summed up by Alexander: "We had no racial doctrine, except that we were not to discriminate in the distribution of these benefits—the care of these people. . . . I frankly admit it. We accepted the pattern."[7] These New Dealers were aided and abetted by an informal "Black Cabinet" whose members included Mary McLeod Bethune (1875–1955), Walter White, Robert Weaver, William Hastie, and Frank Horne. Charles Johnson was in this select circle, though more in the background in his by now familiar "indirect" advocacy role. But he was very important to the group in giving advice and counsel, particularly when Alexander succeeded to the leadership of the Farm Security Administration (FSA, formerly the Resettlement Administration) in 1937.

Johnson's two best studies, *Shadow of the Plantation* (1934) and *Growing Up in the Black Belt* (1941) were done at the beginning and the end of the Great Depression. So it is necessary to emphasize how the tumultuous events of that period functioned as a national (and southern) screen against which Johnson and his associates set about the daunting task of transcribing and analyzing race relations and Negro life in the South. As in Nashville, so too in the small towns and rural areas of the region, economic crisis only made more rigid and constricting the color caste system within the socioeconomic southern "feudal" structure. There were three periods: the initial deep crisis, a middle era of slow recovery and New Deal reform, and finally a recession and a slowing of New Deal change as the country moved—perhaps stumbled—into a national defense economy.

Of the initial crisis, much has been written about the way the general economic paralysis rendered even more precarious the Negro's hold in the employment structure. Yet from the first emergency relief efforts, to the construction of the earliest public housing projects, to the enrollment of people of all races in the work projects such as the Works Progress Administration (WPA) and the Civilian Conservation Corps (CCC), Negroes could sense that *their* government, however careful it might be in confronting southern political sensibilities, sought to be inclusive, not racially exclusive in seeing that African Americans received a fairer share of New Deal economic and social assistance.

The economic crisis went deep nationally, deeper for the Negro population, and deeper yet for southern Negroes in the rural areas. Nationally, in 1932 production was reduced by half, unemployment reached the unimaginable figure of 13 million or 25 percent of the labor force, nonfarm income dropped to the level of 1890, and homes were being lost to foreclosure at the rate of a thousand a day. The South, with its overreliance on the monoculture of cotton—though the New South had indeed attained much greater economic diversity—and its greater poverty suffered even more as the price of cotton fell. Southern banks lost millions of dollars, and annual family income dropped even more drastically than in the nation as a whole. At the end of 1933 more than half a million families in the former Confederate states were on relief, one-sixth of all the families counted in the 1930 census. And the most affected of all were the Negro farm tenants and sharecroppers (the most impoverished of tenants) in the South, the very population whose situation Johnson's research group proposed to study as soon as possible. Negro farm tenants in the South during this period numbered some seven hundred thousand families compared to a million white families, far higher than the Negro proportion of the population. Worse, white croppers were a third of white tenancy, Negroes more than half. As Arthur Schlesinger, Jr., describes it, "It was a gray and hopeless life . . . steadily engulfing the South . . . an endless belt of dirt, drudgery and despair."[8] These millions of people, white and black, weary and worn out from work, had to look in the end to the federal government.

The New Deal's emergency relief measures in the first period were supplemented in the second by more durable efforts to strengthen the southern economy and assist small farmers and workers. Without a doubt the New Deal made a real difference in the lives of Negro Americans.[9] To be sure, even the relief programs, as basic as they were, reflected the traditional racial structure of the South; in many counties unemployment benefits, for example, went disproportionately to whites despite high Negro percentages in the population. But at least there was assistance. The coalition of southern white liberals and Black Cabinet members argued, with growing insistence, for more equitable Negro participation in Federal Emergency Relief Administration (FERA) and WPA jobs. Blacks had 20 percent of these jobs by 1936 and a share of PWA-built public housing.

In the second period, following the reelection of Roosevelt in 1936, these gains were consolidated. If proposals to outlaw lynching and to end the poll tax could not get past congressional opposition, still they were proposed. But for the Washington group, white liberals and Black Cabinet, and for Johnson in Nashville in communication with them, the fundamental test would be in agriculture, in southern agriculture, and most especially in southern farm tenancy and sharecropping. (During the Depression more than a third of all black workers in the country were farm laborers or tenants.) At the outset of the Second New Deal, President Roosevelt could ban discrimination on all WPA projects, as he did by executive order in 1935, assuring Negroes, who in some southern areas were in WPA jobs at almost twice their level in the population, a weekly income of $12, far above what they had been earning.

To mend the farm problem, with its complex interweave of economic, social, and racial factors in the South, however, required much more than an executive order. Never an economic determinist, Johnson nonetheless always emphasized how economic factors reinforced race prejudice, an idea he asserted explicitly as early as 1929.[10] Moreover, the early New Deal remedy, the Agricultural Adjustment Act (AAA) had produced unanticipated negative consequences for the black rural population. Price stabilization of cotton and other products did nothing for tenants. Acreage reduction drove more black owners from the land, and at the county level widespread corruption and discrimination diverted federal benefits meant for them. The secretary of agriculture, Henry Wallace, though deeply shocked by what he saw on a trip to the South, was determined to avoid the racial question. (It was said that when Mary McLeod Bethune, equally determined to show him these inequities, came to see him, he fled to the back recesses of his office.) It was no surprise that in response to this dreadful situation, whites and blacks together organized in Arkansas the Southern Tenant Farmers' Union (STFU), a brave and astonishing movement in the Deep South for that time. Guided by committed southern white liberals such as the businessman H. L. Mitchell and the young minister Howard Kester, the STFU held its own for a time against the implacable hostility of the white landlords and business establishment. The STFU survived every form of landowner violence, including murder, but in the end was betrayed by a combination of reckless communist infiltration and lack of support by the New Deal administration and national labor leaders. Indeed, when the Wagner Act passed in 1935, a magna carta for labor, mandating collective bargaining, farm workers were deliberately excluded from its jurisdiction.

Charles S. Johnson's contribution to all this activity would have a familiar character, moderate advocacy in cooperation with the Washington group in the agencies and sociological research so as to reveal the true dimensions of the farm tenancy and sharecrop problem and its tragic consequences for black and white. In the context of research, a commission of three, Johnson, Edwin R. Embree, and Will Alexander, produced in 1935 a summary of a two-year study "on cotton culture and farm tenancy in the region commonly known as the Old South." Titled *The Collapse of Cotton Tenancy,* this report of seventy pages was based on research by students, directed by Rupert B. Vance at the Institute for Research in Social Science at the University of North Carolina and by Johnson and his associates at the Department of Social Science at Fisk. The summary, in its brevity, was intended as well to reinforce advocacy. "General readers," said the prefatory note, "as citizens, should know the outlines of a significant and tragic situation which is of immediate concern to public policy."[11]

The burden of the study, based on the assumption that white tenants and sharecroppers were as much involved as black, was that the system had become outmoded, wasteful, extremely exploitative (especially the oppressive credit structure), and inherently destructive because of overdependency on one crop, cotton. Tenancy was bad economics and caused degrading human conditions. Neither federal relief nor federal AAA policies could resolve the problem. Indeed, the AAA made matters worse; the landlords got the benefits of crop reduction and other programs, while the tenants remained as before, locked into the paternalistic ownership structure, or were displaced from the land altogether. Johnson, Embree, and Alexander proposed as "the way out" that the federal government buy up a vast amount of land to sell to tenants, transforming them into homesteaders. Government service agencies would then provide capital investment, previously supplied on crippling terms by landlords and lending institutions. "The Re-Homesteading Project is intended to establish in farm ownership a huge number of families heretofore excluded from ownership and now being cut off even from tenancy or crop-sharing arrangements."[12]

Now "the way out" had to be translated into public policy. Knowing that nothing would happen if the racial question were raised, Johnson and his two white colleagues simply excluded it. The words "segregation" and "discrimination" do not appear; the phrase "for both colored and white" to cover implementation appears just once. In emphasizing white tenancy—an appendix notes, for example, that in Georgia there were sixty-five thousand Negro share tenants and croppers compared with eighty-two thousand whites—the commission hoped to defuse southern political opposition and gain the support of those southern Democrats who were economic populists and social racists. The next step consisted of conferences with Frank Tannenbaum, the historian and specialist in Latin American agrarian reform, another of the white liberals in the Washington group, then at the Brookings Institution. President Roosevelt had already established the President's Special Committee on Farm Tenancy (of which Johnson was a member) and in 1935 created the Resettlement Administration (RA) to combat rural poverty and save small farm family ownership. Tannenbaum then reshaped the draft. It was accepted by the Special Committee, and Senator John Bankhead, Democrat of Alabama, agreed to sponsor it as a bill. Further administration support was assured because Roosevelt had appointed the liberal reformer Rexford Tugwell as director of the RA; he, in turn, made Will Alexander his deputy. Tannenbaum, involved in steering the bill (working with M. L. Wilson of the Agriculture Department), in extensive correspondence with Johnson advised him that he, Tannenbaum, "kept the race issue toned down" but that it might be well for Johnson to seek support "quietly" among other national Negro leaders. Finally, in 1937, Congress passed the Bankhead-Jones Farm Tenancy Act. It replaced the RA with the Farm Security Administration; Alexander succeeded Tugwell as director. In modified form the Johnson-Embree-Alexander proposal had been incorporated into law.[13]

Although resettlement, the "rehomesteading" of the *Collapse* report, never achieved "huge numbers," it did become part of the overall FSA program, one of the most significant achievements of the New Deal, and Johnson could rightly think that what he called his "sidelines activism" had played an important part in the process. The ultimate solution, of course, lay far beyond the powers of an FSA. Eventually the question of rural poverty and tenancy in the South would be forever altered (though never solved) by technological change in farming, by diversification in place of King Cotton dominance, and by yielding of the small family farm to large-scale production. What the FSA did accomplish, however, expending nearly a billion dollars by the end of the 1930s, was to institute a landmark social reform system for the rural South and rural America, benefiting thousands of tenants, croppers, and migrant farm workers. Low-interest loans enabled farmers to rehabilitate their land or to buy new land. The first efforts were made to house migratory farm workers in decent labor camps, for example, as seen in *The Grapes of Wrath*. In the South and border states some sixty "homestead communities" were established. The FSA also supported cooperatives for medical care and small producers. If, as Alexander and Johnson recognized, FSA assistance would have to flow for the time being through the channels of segregation, nevertheless "at the risk of its political life, the FSA was scrupulously fair in its treatment of Negroes."[14]

Will Alexander resigned at the end of 1940, still battling the major farm organizations and the southern white power structure. He became a vice-president of the Rosenwald Fund until its termination in 1948, then retired to Chapel Hill, North Carolina, where he continued as an adviser and consultant to human relations organizations. Alexander was born in Missouri in 1884 but spent his early life in the South as a Methodist preacher; his pastoral experience led him into race relations. A man of conviction, the classic white liberal of the 1930s and 1940s, he shared with Johnson a pragmatic—even progressive—outlook on race. He loved the South, hated racial segregation and spoke out against it, yet argued that his group had to postpone a direct challenge to it. He wanted nothing more in his life, he said, than to "help change the racial climate of the South." At the FSA he had done his utmost to advance that strategy.[15]

By the late 1930s, with a deepening recession and the waning of the New Deal, Charles Johnson's "sidelines" role in the formation of national public policy in race relations would take a new turn. Into the 1940s, he would be preoccupied with the national defense and then the war economy, with the new wave of Negro migration to the northern and western cities, and with the prospect of a more insistent civil rights movement. If, as Franklin Roosevelt observed, Dr. Win the War would have to replace Dr. New Deal, then the basic challenge would be clear: somehow to prevent a repetition of the shameful racial history of World

War I in the military at home and abroad and in the domestic economy at home.

In any case, during the entire decade, Johnson's priority had been regional, not national. That meant social science research in race relations in the South, from the Fisk base. It meant as well a more active advocacy role in regional southern human rights organizations, a more direct involvement than sidelines participation in the New Deal. That dual approach—regional research and advocacy—got under way in 1929.

The first task in 1929 was to structure the Social Science Department and the race relations research enterprise. Johnson had in mind a curriculum and a research agenda similar to the program at the University of North Carolina under Howard Odum. The parallels were almost exact except for one critical aspect. Whereas Odum placed primary emphasis on the sociology of southern regionalism and its folk-urban transition, with race relations—important as they were—fitted into that framework, Johnson made central, for obvious reasons, the structure of race relations in the South, with socioeconomic change in the South fitted to that framework. At all events, by the mid-1930s there were only two social science research centers of national reputation in the South, Odum's at North Carolina and Johnson's at Fisk.

Howard W. Odum was one more of those southern white liberals who, though more cautious than a Will Alexander, also sought to "change the racial climate" in the region while accepting that segregation would have to continue, because it was so deeply embedded in the social structure. (He knew it was nonsense in personal terms and did not hesitate to ignore the rules when he brought Negro guests to the campus. But he could not bring himself to declare it morally unjust and in need of elimination until the mid-1940s. By then the most distinguished sociologist in the South was too late.) Born to a farm family of modest means in Georgia, he went north after graduation from Emory College in 1904 and having earned a master's degree in English and classics from the University of Mississippi in 1906. At Clark he took a doctoral degree, writing his thesis on the religious folk songs of southern Negroes (a longtime interest) and then another at Columbia in sociology in 1910. Influenced by Franklin Giddings and Franz Boas, he wrote his sociology thesis on the social and mental traits of the Negro. Although it was Boasian-accurate in rejecting the imputation of Negro inferiority, it was muddled in its confusion of learned and inherited characteristics. Only much later would Odum fully absorb the succinct, one-sentence principle Ruth Benedict put forth in the early 1930s: race and culture vary independently.

Back in the South and after seven years at the University of Georgia, Odum came to Chapel Hill in 1920, where he remained for the rest of his life. There he founded and directed a new school of social work, established the Institute of Research in Social Science (funded by the Rockefeller Foundation), founded and edited the important sociological journal *Social Forces,* chaired the sociology department, and wrote many books on sociology, regionalism, research methods, Negro spiritual and secular songs, Negro folklore, poetry, and fiction, and bred prizewinning Jersey cattle, which he claimed jokingly to be more of a contribution than the books. His southern regionalist framework, long dormant but now experiencing something of a revival, posed against the destructiveness of political sectional conflict the possibility that through social change the more "backward" South and its traditional folkways could make a "convergence" with the national urban-industrial system and its "technicways," while yet preserving the distinctive core of traditional southern culture.

All this, including Odum's integration of scholarship and gradualist activism, impressed Johnson. They worked together in the Commission on Interracial Cooperation in the 1930s and on its successor in the 1940s, the Southern Regional Council. Their only serious rift occurred in 1945, and it was entirely Odum's fault. In a misguided effort to promote long-overdue racial integration in the Southern Sociological Society, he proposed that Johnson's candidacy for the presidency would be assured if the other (white) nominee, the distinguished sociologist T. Lynn Smith, would withdraw. Both Johnson and Smith were, rightly, infuriated; they were prepared to win or lose graciously on merit, not on skin color. Odum apologized to them. Johnson won anyway, becoming the first black president of the society, for 1945–46.[16]

With the North Carolina model in mind, Johnson drew up his plan for Fisk. Doing so required a well-grounded faculty, balanced between older and younger scholars, diverse in ethnic-racial background. In the 1930s and into the 1940s Fisk achieved a faculty list impressive for any institution, black or white; not all but many of the scholars were brought in by Johnson. Park arrived in 1935, establishing a tradition of visiting sociologists, among them Edward Reuter, Andrew Lind, Kenneth Little and Cedric Dover from England, Ruth Landes, and Hortense Powdermaker (in anthropology). In the department the regular faculty included, at various times, Bertram Doyle, Elsie Brunschwig, Donald Pierson (engaged in pioneering work in race relations in Brazil), Bingham Dai, a doctor who was also a specialist in social psychiatry, Eli Marks, Paul Edwards, Giles Hubert, Jitsuichi Matsuoka, Mark Hanna Watkins (a specialist in Caribbean studies and in the mid-1930s the only Negro with a doctorate in anthropology in the entire country), and, briefly, E. Franklin Frazier. In keeping with the centrality of race relations, beyond the department, in history and the humanities, the list would have to be broadened to include such outstanding figures as James Weldon Johnson, Lorenzo Turner, Sterling Brown, and Horace Mann Bond, a distinguished educator and a sociologist as well.

Frazier stayed only four years at Fisk, leaving for Howard in 1934. In his early research Johnson was an enthusiastic sponsor, advocate, and friend. But starting at Fisk, there were serious strains, not a matter of personalities, of Frazier's pacifism over against Johnson serving in the war, or of Frazier's socialism over against Johnson's faith in capitalism tempered by liberal reform. Rather, it had to do with their clashing perspectives over the direction race relations were taking and would take in this country. As Anthony Platt has correctly summarized, "Johnson was . . . a liberal who moved in the circles of interracial diplomacy that Frazier despised. Johnson tended to emphasize how race relations were improving, while Frazier grew increasingly embittered about the intractability of racism."[17] (Platt neglects, however, a degree of envy on the part of Frazier that, scorn for white philanthropy notwithstanding, he would not be allowed to play a bridging role as Johnson did.) At Fisk their problem was largely a matter of differences of degree in campus roles. Frazier was vehement and courageous on campus and off, in militant public protest against the terrible atrocities and humiliations constantly being visited against Negroes in Nashville and beyond, as well as outspoken in defense of left-wing black leaders, socialist or Stalinist, on civil liberties grounds. Johnson, just as angry over lynching and the cruelties of segregation, channeled protest into his sociological work. Once Frazier left Fisk, however, he made the deepening estrangement personal as well as ideological, especially in his critique of Johnson's studies.

In the final analysis it might be said that with respect to basic strategies for change in race relations, Frazier was somewhat less radical than Du Bois, the militant propagandist, but was certainly far more independent and militant than the liberal Johnson, the "conciliatory realist." The final irony is that all three, despite their differences, are joined in harmony as "founding fathers" for black sociologists, their names engraved in the annual Du Bois-Johnson-Frazier award, given since 1971 by the American Sociological Association to a sociologist for distinguished scholarship.

From the 1930s onward the national standing of an outstanding faculty like that at Fisk was closely linked to the graduate program. The undergraduate curriculum in the social sciences was well-conceived, if conventional, fitted to the usual liberal arts distribution system. President Jones, in both his deep Quaker faith and his educational philosophy, wanted to make the undergraduate experience at Fisk a spirited community of young minds thoughtfully at work. His mandate to Johnson in the social sciences, however, was to put the Fisk stamp on the nation by creating an outstanding graduate school. Both men recognized that Fisk could help to prepare for the day when the mainstream universities, those citadels of racial exclusion, would recognize excellence instead of skin color, accepting African American M.A.s as doctoral candidates and hiring them as faculty. We need to remember contextually once again this was the 1930s, not the 1960s. With an occasional exception, the private University of Chicago and the public Ohio State, the academic community showed no disposition whatever to end the marginalization of highly qualified Negro scholars.

The charge Jones gave to Johnson was fulfilled. By the end of the 1930s nearly forty students were enrolled in the Social Science Department's rigorous M.A. program. Substantively, much of the work centered on the comparative and historical study of race relations, a distinctive emphasis not duplicated at that time anywhere else in the country.[18] Typical was the advanced seminar in race and culture, with Robert Park presiding. The program in African and Caribbean studies was instituted in 1943, with Rosenwald funding, and aimed particularly at analyzing the remarkable Afro-Franco-American syncretism in the black republic of Haiti. That program had only limited success. It was probably premature. The explosion of black studies and African studies in American higher education had to await the postwar collapse of colonialism in Africa and the West Indies and the new black cultural consciousness accompanying the civil rights movement. But, again, Fisk was first. Local projects, such as the Fisk University Social Center in Nashville, or regional initiatives such as the field internship program, developed jointly by Fisk and Tuskegee, with support from the FSA, helped to sustain the black community. Students went out from Fisk and Tuskegee to become FSA interns in rural places like Gee's Bend, Alabama, and Hancock, Georgia. The same principle of relating class-room to practice applied to the internships placed with the Tennessee Valley Authority. The dynamic FSA project came to an end in the third period of the New Deal, when Alexander resigned, as described above.

The well-known annual Institutes of Race Relations (IRR) repre-sented still another dimension, an opportunity to bring together social scientists, community leaders, and field workers in seminars, confronting immediate problems in race relations. Once again financed by the Rosen-wald Fund, they were first held, with Johnson directing, at Swarthmore College (under Friends auspices) each summer, starting in 1933. The IRR program transferred, with AMA funding, to Fisk in 1944. In both places Johnson was able to invite nearly every leading specialist, black and white, in race relations, together with an amazing number of strate-gic public figures in a position to advance the IRR agenda.

A central goal of the department in all this activity was, of course, to train a new generation of Negro social scientists. (Frazier was engaged in a more modest version at Howard.) In recruiting and sustaining a group of bright and enterprising graduate students and young instructors, Johnson could play the trump card: an abundance of fellowships and assistantships paid for from the usual sources—Spelman, Rockefeller, Rosenwald, General Education Board, American Missionary Associa-tion, to name the principal ones. The Black Cabinet and the southern white liberals in the Washington group also helped. In the early 1940s, for example, Mary McLeod Bethune, director of Negro affairs in the National Youth Administration (NYA), obtained fellowships and assis-tantships for Johnson through the NYA. The grants to Johnson and Fisk are indicative of Bethune's effectiveness in a context far more difficult for black activism than today. She and others in the Black Cabinet, with support from white liberals such as Alexander and Aubrey Williams, were able to wedge a civil rights commitment into a number of New Deal programs, and they eventually got government cafeterias desegregated. But apart from Mrs. Roosevelt and Harold Ickes they had virtually no support at the highest levels. And until very late the president remained largely neutral.

Johnson's unceasing effort produced a significant number of next-generation sociologists, many of whom went on to earn doctorates and then to achievement in the mainstream as well as the black college system, as desegregation in higher education got under way. A partial list would include Bonita and Preston Valien, Herman Long, Charles Lawrence, Stanley Smith, Charles U. Smith, G. Franklin Edwards, Lewis Jones, Josie Sellers, Harry Walker, Horace Cayton, Mozell Hill, Ophelia Settle, and Lewis Copeland.

Mary McLeod Bethune was born in South Carolina, one of seventeen children of a farm family. She was educated at Scotia Seminary (now Barber-Scotia College). She went north to Chicago and trained as a missionary, but, because she was colored, was rejected for assignment to Africa. Returning to Florida, she realized a lifelong dream when in 1904 she opened an industrial and home arts training school for black girls along Booker T. Washington lines. Remarkably resourceful in obtaining funding, she built the school from a one-room shack into what became Bethune-Cookman College; she remained as president until 1942. At age sixty, wanting to be heard nationally, she founded and was president for many years of the National Council of Negro Women. Mrs. Roosevelt, a good friend, persuaded the president to appoint her director of Negro affairs in the National Youth Administration. Energetic and persevering, she sought to get NYA resources allocated to state NYAs on a nondiscriminatory basis, a difficult task in the face of resistance from southern states. Several times a year she met with the president to urge him to be more forceful on racial questions. Johnson worked with Bethune in several organizations and admired her ability to get things accomplished.[19]

But above and beyond the institutionalization of graduate work in sociology and social science at Fisk and the training of a new generation of sociologists there, the principal contribution made by Johnson and his associates in the 1930s and 1940s was the numerous research surveys, large and small, of race relations and Negro life in the South. They may have lacked depth and theoretical significance, as Johnson's critics have charged, but in their eye for the moving case history of real people as much as in the precision with which they laid out statistical detail, they still command our attention and hold our interest. They are Johnson's legacy.

In 1930, however, that work had to be set aside. In the fall of 1929 President Herbert Hoover asked him to serve as the American representative on the International Commission of the League of Nations of Inquiry on the Existence of Slavery and Forced Labor in the Republic of Liberia. From March to September of 1930, he was in Africa with his British colleague, assessing this grim situation. Liberia, proudly, the only independent black republic in all of sub-Sahara Africa, the living rejoinder to those who said imperialism must remain in place because an "inferior race" could not govern itself, was charged with the very oppression black brothers and sisters in the American South laid upon their white oppressors. Charles Johnson could hardly do other than to accept the challenge and responsibility. Liberia had to be judged.

That year had also seen the publication of Johnson's *The Negro in American Civilization: A Study of Negro Life and Race Relations in the Light of Social Research,* the result of a conference on the "race problem" sponsored by a committee representing the major human relations and race relations organizations in the country. Johnson, as the appointed research secretary to the National Interracial Conference, held in December 1928 in Washington, was charged with synthesizing the data and preparing the book. The result was a thoroughly competent compendium on the status of the Negro as of the end of the 1920s. All relevant subjects were covered—work, family, housing, education, health, citizenship, crime and delinquency, recreation. But deliberately the volume is almost completely restricted to facts; it constitutes an encyclopedia of Negro data. Only at the very end, when Du Bois discusses the problem of recovering the franchise do the mountains of data take on life. He knew what to say, as usual: "Until the liberal white South has the guts to stand up for democracy regardless of race there will be no solution of the Negro problem and no solution of the problem of popular government in America."[20]

Du Bois's presentation and all the others were followed by brief "summaries of discussions," including recommendations, for example, for improving health facilities or schools for Negroes. Yet the two hundred or so participants, who included virtually every major black leader and white liberal in the country, could do no more than agree that race prejudice was unscientific as well as wrong and that, with interracial cooperation, improvement was inevitable in all the institutional areas covered. So the contrast between Johnson's first general book and the challenge in the Liberian situation could not be more clear when, by accident, book and challenge appeared in the same year. In the one, Johnson was asked to present the research of an objective social science in the hope that the sheer weight of the evidence would reinforce the moral imperative to move more forcefully against the patent racial injustice disfiguring America. Thus, from Fisk, he continued the role of sociologist-advocate developed in Chicago and New York. In the other, Johnson was charged not simply with investigating and reporting findings to the League of Nations Commission of Inquiry. If the charges were true, he would have to break from his self-imposed role as scrupulously objective sociologist, the formal and reserved apostle of the survey and the study. As a writer, as a human being, he would have to speak out in eloquence and fury against a modern African version of the slavery that had engulfed his own ancestors in Virginia. That is what he did in *Bitter Canaan: The Story of the Negro Republic,* a book he wrote like none before or after, very different from *The Negro in American Civilization.* Both the value and the shortcomings of the book on the American Negro can be explained, as usual, by the time and context; this was the early 1930s, during the Great Depression, when economic considerations subordinated the racial issue, when even militant black leaders had to practice restraint. Twentieth-century slavery could not be so explained.

Bitter Canaan was not published in Johnson's lifetime. He certainly tried, although he was desultory about the manuscript until the late 1930s. Thereafter, the Johnson Papers at Fisk and the papers of others elsewhere are studded with references to getting the book out. The simplest and largely correct explanation is that Johnson, one of the busiest sociologists in the country, black or white, never got around to revising the draft or doing necessary updating and that he never vigorously pursued the matter with publishers until it was too late. When, finally, in 1945 he submitted the manuscript to the University of Chicago Press, the editors rightly insisted on extensive revision. After all, World War II had come and gone. More to the point, decolonization was cracking open the system of Western imperialism in what was to become known as the Third World, leaving "independent" Liberia, in many ways still a fiefdom of the Firestone Rubber Company and its compliant ultra-conservative black elite in Monrovia, a bizarre, anachronistic island in an Africa where the winds of change were blowing. Johnson, busy as ever and, in 1947, about to be officially inaugurated as Fisk's president, was neither willing nor able to make the required changes. Chicago turned back the manuscript. Exactly forty years later, in 1987, *Bitter Canaan* appeared with a perceptive introduction by John Stanfield.[21] Stanfield decided he needed to provide a second, reinforcing explanation. There was no blatant "power elite" conspiracy, but the accommodationist influential leaders in the black bourgeoisie and the white foundations with which they were allied had no desire to trouble the comfortable relationship with the governing Liberian elite, direct descendants of the original American-sponsored colonists. Nor did the militant pan-African nationalists in the West have reason to broadcast the news that Firestone had willing black African collaborators, the Amero-Liberian elite, in the severe exploitation of the indigenous masses who, elsewhere in Africa, were poised to expel the white masters. This was true despite evidence to show that both the State Department and the foreign offices of the European colonial powers, in their own interests, had earlier condoned the system of forced labor.

What of the two-member commission report, written entirely by Johnson? (The other member, Cuthbert Christy, a crusty, arrogant British health administrator and Africanist, though indignant about forced labor, was totally inept in all aspects of the investigation yet tried to appropriate Johnson's material under the name "Christy Commission.") The two-hundred-page report, submitted to the State Department, the League of Nations, and the Liberian government, confirming the existence of this form of "slavery," did contribute to reform of the worst aspects of the forced labor system in Liberia and in the Spanish colony of Fernando Po. If nothing else, international publicity compelled the various governing bodies to take minimal remedial action. But the fundamental problem remained. Liberia continued, de facto, to be an American economic colonial dependency, controlled internally by the Amero-Liberian aristocracy with little or no concern for the tribal population in the interior. Although the inevitable overthrow of the Tubman government years later brought a modicum of socioeconomic change, it also brought the chaos and carnage of civil war (1990–95). On the hundredth anniversary of the colonization of Liberia, Johnson foresaw "a new relationship of this free nation in an Africa of colonies to the world outside its troubled borders." Alas, although "the Africa of colonies" is now an Africa of independent states, Liberia itself has survived without changing nearly enough.[22]

Apart from the controversy over publication and the modest reforms resulting from the League of Nations report, *Bitter Canaan* is well worth reprinting and reading. It is a moving memoir in comparative anthropology, written at the height of the colonial era when too few Western anthropologists were engaged in defending the integrity of indigenous African cultures, however different or deemed "inferior." And in the manuscript, in the diary he kept assiduously, and in the letters home to his wife, Johnson, the quintessential "cool" social scientist, was for once working his empirical data into an impressionistic, vivid series of portraits painted by a (black) writer, an acute observer from America tramping through one country in Africa. In the arresting interview with the British anthropologist Bronislaw Malinowski in London, in the tough-minded (but still sympathetic) vignettes of the Monrovia elite caught in the middle between the American colonial power and the native interior tribes, in the conversations with Chief Jeh and others in the bush, in his sense of the sights and sounds and colors of that corner of Africa, Johnson offers a glimpse of a social scientist who is not just a technical specialist but a humanist writer. He might have been of the group of novelists and poets, instead of "the entrepreneur," of the Harlem Renaissance.

Here is a typical passage where the occasion is a formal hearing on the forced labor issue but where Johnson is, as always, alive to the sights and sounds of everyday village life deep in the interior:

> Morning in a village was full of the intimate touches of life. The men sheathed themselves completely in their heavily patterned *lappas,* and unwashed and yawning, moved to the edge of town to pass their morning water. They conversed in drowsy cadences in the shelter of the banana leaves. The women went off to another corner of the village. A boy with a wooden tray picked up the night's droppings of the cows with his hands, patting it in the tray . . . this manure was an essential ingredient for their cement-finished walls and floors. Little children were led out of the huts by their mothers and postured face to the wall. The querulous cows began sniffing about, prying into every cranny. From the blackened thatch of the huts smoke began to rise. There was brief sweeping with a short bristling palm brush or with a spray of *piassava.* Girls with water jugs balanced on their heads appeared, depositing their burdens casually. The chill damp began to lift, the sun rushed out with an almost sudden spray, and another day was on. Throughout the day there were loud shrill voices of children, the cry of babies scarcely to be distinguished from the noise of hungry or harassed goats; the laughter of men and the droning conversation of women, through the thin walls of the huts; the sharp crackling of the crows high up in the cottonwood trees, the shrill chirp of the crickets, the pounding of rice straws, the sifting of the grain, and far in the forest, the mournful cry of birds.
>
> At the meeting with the chiefs, we sat with the paramount chief, his speaker and interpreter, in the midst of the wide circle of men squatting on low stools. These old men represented, they said, the fifth generation of the Barrabo people in this place. The interpreter shouted "Bateo!" (silence).

At one sitting with the chiefs, the women stood around the rim of the crowd of men; afterward, they said they wanted to be heard. Their speaker was a woman of about thirty-five. She said in a ringing, clear voice:

> We stand here and listen to the men to see if they tell all. If they leave out anything, we tell it. But one thing we want to say. They took us to the barracks against our will. Yes. They took us in groups of 200 and we were there for nine months. The soldiers used us as their wives, we who had husbands and children. They had guns and we could not protect ourselves, and our husbands could not protect us.
>
> We pray to have us stopped from going to the barracks.[23]

V

FISK: RESEARCH
AND ADVOCACY

For Johnson, returning from Africa meant returning, in 1931, to the southern research studies. Some appeared before and some after 1934. But in that year Johnson published *Shadow of the Plantation,* perhaps the best of his social science monographs. For all its problems, in methodology and interpretation it accomplishes what Johnson desired. He wanted to show how the structure and possible decline of the feudalistic plantation system defined the status of some six hundred Negro families who were bound into it. He wanted to use the case study of Macon County, Alabama, to demonstrate how the institutions of black folk culture functioned in this setting. And, implicitly, in the by now familiar role of social scientist-moderate activist he wanted to persuade those charged with making public policy that the economic exploitation and racial discrimination inherent in the plantation system required government to undertake a more immediate and determined role in social change. Doing so would require linkage to Washington, the New Deal, and the Resettlement Administration. In the brief commentaries, spoken in folk language by the workers, preachers, wives, and midwives, Johnson is also invoking something of his approach in *Bitter Canaan.* He would carry this style, people speaking in their own words, into his next best work, *Growing Up in the Black Belt,* written in the late 1930s, a study of several southern counties rather than just one.

Johnson succeeded in what he set out to do. Indeed, *Shadow of the Plantation* has become a sociological classic still being read; the University of Chicago Press issued a fourth printing in 1966.[1] It is ironic, then, that in our own time an underserved shadow hangs over *Shadow,* the fact that at the same time in Macon County the United States Public Health Service (USPHS) was conducting a "scientific experiment" that was to last forty years and, like Johnson's study, was underwritten in

86

its early years by the Rosenwald Fund. The demonstration project, as explained to Johnson, was to determine the rate of syphilis among Negroes in six southern areas, Macon County having been selected as one because of the health technology available at Tuskegee Institute. (In the book, Johnson duly reported the high rate and noted that in the drawing of blood by the doctors, "the greatest kindliness was shown the patients.") In fact, in an experiment that was worthless scientifically and horrifying ethically, some four hundred syphilitic black men were deliberately left untreated to determine whether a racial differential existed in untreated disease. The men thought they were being treated. Some died who could have lived, some continued to die in the 1950s, including children of some of the men, even when a much more effective medication, penicillin, replaced earlier therapy. Not until 1973, after a public outcry, did the Department of Health, Education and Welfare end the project, declaring it "ethically unjustified" and holding that penicillin should have been provided to the men when first available. The issue still reverberates. In 1995, at the congressional hearing on the nomination of Dr. Henry Foster as surgeon general, Dr. Foster vigorously denied any knowledge of the project when he worked at Tuskegee as a young doctor. He called it "the most cruel and inhumane experiment ever undertaken by any government."

This was no aberration, no misguided scientific venture gone awry. The Tuskegee Syphilis Study, wrote H. Jack Geiger, a medical doctor and civil rights activist, was not a bureaucratic-medical mistake but an expression of a "racism that permeated all of America's institutions at least until the mid-1960's . . . [reading the report of it produces] rage, shock, disbelief, and finally an overwhelming sorrow."[2] And within a context of general racism there was the racism of the medical profession in government. Dr. Taliaferro Clark, the director, and his associates believed every "natural" stereotype about Negroes (whom several doctors described as "darkies" and "Ethiopians"). Given their way of life, they would not be likely to seek treatment anyway. Therefore, if they were recruited with the promise of assured treatment, but with a noneffective drug, they would serve as test subjects.

There was a connection between the projected syphilis research and Johnson's Macon County study, stemming from the Rosenwald funding of both. Dr. Michael Davis, the fund's medical director, and the USPHS chose the rural areas of the South where the venereal disease rate for Negroes was high. Davis then invited Johnson, in 1931, to study "the social and economic conditions" in the county as well as the black population's access to medical services. But the man of social science did not know of the cruel methodology of the men of medical science. The descriptive and analytic sociological inquiry would be concentrated on the socioeconomic patterns and the folk culture of southern Negro rural life which conditioned the perception of Negroes about health care. That the plantation system itself, with its interlocked forms of economic exploitation and racial discrimination, might lie at the root of health care and everything else did not seem too urgent a matter to USPHS or the Rosenwald Fund. In any case, Rosenwald funded the syphilis project for only the first four years. And although Johnson contributed sociological context to the medical study, his central concern was much broader than health care.

The statistical data presented, together with the qualitative materials and the deeply felt and insightful comments by the folk themselves, demonstrated to Johnson that health care, folk culture, family life, and elements of "social disorganization" all inhered in a changing, declining, but still oppressive kind of modern economic feudalism. Hence the "shadow." Its historic importance is that it took on a racial myth, the conception of the easygoing plantation and the happy Negro, and replaced the myth with the objective truth: Macon County was a twentieth-century form of feudalism based on cotton cultivation. "All is not exploitation," Johnson observed, yet in a sense all was. One folk respondent may be illiterate but he knows what he knows: "What kills us here is that we jest can't make it cause they pay us nothing for what we give them, and they charge us double price when they sell it back to us."[3]

In his introduction, Robert Park relates Negro folk or peasant culture of the rural South to that of other "marginal peoples" around the world in transition, be it in Mexico or Mississippi—in Robert Redfield's typology, from folk to urban culture. Park calls attention especially to the recorded individual stories which the poet John Crowe Ransom likened to art as much as science and which connect to both the realistic fiction of Richard Wright about rural Mississippi and the interwoven tape-recorded interviews of the anthropologist Oscar Lewis about the rural-urban transition in Mexico. But Park, too, for all his conservatism and his insistence on the inevitability of assimilation at the end of the race relations cycle, is forced to acknowledge that powerful universal obstacle to change, the "incurable ethnocentrism" of so-called primitive blacks in Africa and so-called primitive whites in Alabama. He does not, however, pin the social psychology of race prejudice to the plantation socioeconomic structure housing it.

Johnson does, however cautiously. *Shadow of the Plantation* is explicitly a statistical study and an "intimate record" of six hundred Negro families in rural Alabama, in plantation country. Implicitly, the chapters on the heritage from slavery, the family, the work force in cotton, the school, the church, and the "play life" provide a foundation of data demonstrating the consequences of structured inequality through the entire life cycle, from infant mortality to survival in old age. In the concluding section, following a pro forma acknowledgment of some "positive" aspects of the plantation in the past (i.e., social stability), he finds the traditional plantation economy doomed by change, though the poverty it generated could well continue in a different form. These are the final words: "The greatest pressure is being felt at present by the tenants, dulled and locked in by a backwardness which is the fatal heritage of the system itself. But the fate of the tenant is but an aspect of the fate of the southern farmer generally, and the plight of all these awaits a comprehensive planning, which affects not merely the South but the nation."[4] Let the New Deal reach into Macon County!

There is yet another reason why *Shadow of the Plantation* remains relevant to debate today. Beyond the central theme, "the pressure of the system," whereby farm tenants and croppers were often exploited to the point of near despair, where, as Johnson says, "nothing remains but to succumb or to migrate," is the challenging question of culture and cultural reintegration. In *Shadow* in the chapters on family, church, and play life, nothing is said of the concept of culture or of the possibility that cultural patterns with respect to family and religious expression might have African roots. Further, these patterns might well have carried over to this country, enabling the Negro community to survive and to bear better the shattering experience of slavery and the plantation system. On the contrary, both Johnson and E. Franklin Frazier insisted that any carryover of Africanisms was peripheral to the centrality of Negro experience in this country. In his only and fleeting reference to Africa in *Shadow*, Johnson says, "The Negro of the plantation came into the picture with a completely broken cultural heritage." Frazier, too, though not denying the impact of African culture, for example, in Brazil, argued that he was interested in African acculturation only insofar as it bore on the economic and social institutions of the Negro in the New World. Yet in *Shadow*, in language expression alone, revealed in those poignant, richly textured folkloric personal commentaries of Negro tenants, it is clear that there is more than a derivative tongue being spoken, more than a refraction from "white" English. The black church, too, was much more than a version of American "white" Protestantism.

Thus this book, and even more Frazier's outstanding social history of the Negro in the United States, have served as points of departure for a subsequent generation of anthropologists and folklorists, white and black, to rework our cultural understanding of the black experience. Beyond the Frazier-Johnson position, these scholars were led in this direction by the pioneer work of Du Bois, Carter Woodson, and the anthropologist Melville Herskovits whose *Myth of the Negro Past* did so much to open up and enlarge the debate.

An additional aspect of the debate, principally involving Frazier but also bearing on Johnson's *Shadow,* concerned the structure of the African American family and an asserted "disorganization" of family life. Johnson treated the matter briefly and neutrally as a social scientist, observing that in Macon County there were several family types. There were relatively stable "normal and natural" families (so far as possible, given the racism impinging on family life), and there were families reflecting "definite disorganization," a product of both outside pressures and internal "disintegration of traditional controls." He let it go at that. Frazier, in contrast, studying the increasingly volatile urban Negro community structure and not rural peasantry, had to treat the theme of family disorganization much more comprehensively. Although he did analyze so-called pathological elements in Negro family life, he also stressed the resilient and integrative strengths that characterized the history of the black family. Critics missed Frazier's treatment of the organizational as well as the pathological in contending that he underestimated the numbers of stable Negro families in both the middle and working classes, in spite of the great external racist pressures on them. Much later in time the debate resumed. Daniel Patrick Moynihan and others pointed to illegitimacy rates and unstable fathers in parental roles—similar statistics are given by Johnson for Macon County—as indices of serious fissures within the inner city black family. The rejoinder, from both black and white critics, emphasized, as did Johnson and Frazier, the range of diversity in Negro families as well as the countervailing integrative aspects. Today, the "disorganization" debate continues, and now Frazier's analysis is better understood. A consensus may be emerging of not debating the problem polemically but treating it as a reflection of class (or "underclass") structure rather than race.[5]

From the early to the late 1930s Fisk's Department of Social Science carried out many other research projects. Among them were the surveys ("compendiums") of black rural communities and schools in Louisiana and Mississippi; local surveys in Nashville and Davidson County (for example, on low-income housing by Eli Marks, on juvenile delinquency by Bonita Valien, on demography of the Negro population by Herman Long); comprehensive reports on the national and regional level of the urban Negro labor force in general and in particular industries such as tobacco and textiles (sometimes directed by Johnson from Nashville but assigned to veteran research specialists such as Robert Weaver and Ira De A. Reid); historical research projects on slave documents and slave autobiographies in the Parkean human document tradition; multiple "Southern Rural Life Studies" supported once again by the Rosenwald Fund; collaborative research with the University of North Carolina Institute group on such matters as southern human geography, the implications of "southern peasantry," the extent of lynching, and studies of the historic isolated Negro folk communities. In this last category were the celebrated agricultural demonstration projects and University of North Carolina studies in folklore. In North Carolina, in another parallel to Johnson's center at Fisk, a new young generation of sociologists worked with Howard Odum, among them Arthur Raper, Guy Johnson, Guion Johnson, Rupert Vance, Katherine Jocher, and Edgar Thompson.

In these studies and the even larger number conducted in the 1940s, Johnson would obtain the necessary support, lay out the general research design, and frequently would direct the first phases of the fieldwork before turning the project over to research assistants. In the 1930s and 1940s fieldwork meant not only technical problems but complications arising from segregation, particularly if white and black social scientists happened to be together. One group of researchers ran into trouble encountering a party returning from a lynching but they were able to skirt around it. The noted anthropologist Hortense Powdermaker, working on the black youth study, wrote to Johnson from Mississippi. Once she said, "I'm from Fisk," her Negro respondents were receptive, taking her for a light-skinned Negro. The black research sociologists worked almost entirely in the black community, yet contact with whites, high and low, was sometimes necessary. It went more easily if the researchers conformed to the norms of racial caste etiquette expected by whites. One of them wrote to Johnson from Memphis that he was getting tired of the smiling, bowing, and "yes suh's" "no suh's" in dealing with whites. Johnson replied with dry humor, a human quality he generally kept concealed outside his circle of intimates. "What you describe suggests stooping to conquer. Don't bend too low. You may be suspected of caricaturing the hallowed etiquette of the region." As Johnson and Frazier discovered in Alabama, however, the racial etiquette did not always govern so pleasantly. Once they were returning, with other colleagues, to Fisk from Alabama, in two cars. They stopped for fuel. When Frazier paid his bill the attendant evidently did not consider him properly respectful: "Nigger, do you know where you are? You ain't up there in Tennessee . . . and I am going to show you how we hang niggers like you in Alabama!" The cars shot out of the station. Frazier's classic comment is still quoted: "I preferred not to become a martyr to social research!"[6]

Despite a heavy research agenda during the 1930s, Johnson managed to write three more general books on race relations: *Race Relations: Adjustment of Whites and Negroes in the United States,* written with Willis D. Weatherford (1934); *A Preface to Racial Understanding* (1936); and *The Negro College Graduate* (1938). All were workmanlike and informative but in no way striking or distinctive like the research studies of Negro life in the Deep South. The textbook, *Race Relations,* was a particular disappointment. Weatherford, a cautious southern moderate, who aspired to be a white liberal in the Embree or Alexander mold, shared with Johnson the view that they were making a significant contribution simply by collaborating: "No textbook in sociology has heretofore been undertaken by a white man and a Negro as joint authors." The contents and the division of labor, however, reflect the conventional status relationships of the times. Weatherford, a leader in the YMCA and head of its "graduate school," is listed first, perhaps because he was older, perhaps because he had a Ph.D.; Johnson, without one—he had a Ph.B. from Chicago—is listed as "Litt.D." Neither segregation nor discrimination is discussed in sufficient depth, though in the section on political status of the Negro, written by Weatherford, there is a forceful analysis of Jim Crowism, coupled with a plea to open voting to all regardless of race. Strangely, Weatherford, rather than Johnson, was assigned the chapters on Negro literature and Negro leadership. The forthright discussion of slavery, including the slave revolts—nearly half the book—must have provided students with a sounder historical perspective on the Old South, but the closing chapter on "solution or amelioration" of race relations, again written by Weatherford, is essentially a plea for mutual tolerance and an end to stereotypes. Reviewing the book, E. Franklin Frazier, now out of Nashville and completing his first year at Howard, described Johnson as "using much labored learning to express the most obvious trivialities" while "the white collaborator speaks sentimentally about the Negro and treads softly where fundamental issues are concerned." In truth, the book is not weighty enough to be the target for so withering a review. Frazier was really interested in getting back at Johnson.[7]

In the last analysis, what keeps the book alive is the final chapter, written by Johnson, "Can There Be a Separate Negro Culture?" All his life, in the ongoing debate, Johnson argued, as did Frazier, that the question of black cultural expression was secondary to the goal of equal opportunity and structural integration, similar to Park's assimilation but without loss of racial pride and identity. Thus neither of them was interested in the striking effort by the anthropologist Melville Herskovits to show the powerful carryover of African cultural patterns to American Negro life. But here Johnson, in a discussion of folk culture, blues, and the talent of the Harlem Renaissance, moves toward a position of cultural pluralism, reminding us that even Garvey's black nationalism with its Africanist cultural overtones, for all "that the whole fabric of the scheme was illusory and impossible," had a profound, astonishing appeal to the consciousness of the black masses.

The little book *A Preface to Racial Understanding*, written two years later and intended for a popular audience, is better. It is a lively popular history of the evolution of black life in America, written at a time when corrective perspective was vitally needed, when the conventional histories both minimized the degree of racial oppression and ignored or patronized black cultural expression. Although *A Preface* broke no new ground, it did fulfill that purpose and did so in a brisk, deft Johnsonian style, with chapters on the Negro worker, family, church, and school. Especially appealing are the brief portraits of Negro Americans, well-known like the singer Roland Hayes, lesser-known but remarkable for their achievements like the Yankee educator Charlotte Hawkins Brown, who went to North Carolina and founded Palmer Memorial Institute (and, as Johnson notes, could never get over being shunted to the freight elevator when meetings were held in hotels). The book ends with Johnson's favorite proverb, from the time in Africa, in Liberia, on working now to reduce racial injustice in the future: "If you know well the beginning, the end will not trouble you much."[8]

The Negro College Graduate also made a useful contribution. It is a detailed statistical assessment of black higher education in the setting of the dual, segregated system. The work is dedicated, appropriately, to the teachers he admired most, Robert Park at Chicago and Joshua Simpson at Virginia Union.[9] It showed how incredibly underrepresented African Americans were in the mainstream system. After graduation, Negro college graduates, the overwhelming majority of whom went to Negro colleges, were, again, severely underrepresented in the white-collar occupations and professions, and their incomes were significantly less than those of comparable white graduates. The statistics need no annotation. From 1826 to 1936 the total of known Negro graduates was forty thousand. At the turn of the century the number totaled only twenty-three hundred. (In 1992 1.3 million African Americans were in college.) There were as many Negro college graduates recorded in the eight years 1924–32 as in the entire century from 1826 to 1934. At the graduate level, since the first doctorate to a Negro in 1876 (Edward Bouchet, at Yale), there had been by 1933 a grand total of eighty-five. As for occupation and income, the Great Depression only compounded what had gone before. The study, based on statistical analysis, replete with an enormous profusion of charts and tables, covered some twenty-five thousand living graduates, and within that universe, about fifty-five hundred, constituting a special sample, balanced regionally and by urban-rural ratios, were interviewed or were mailed questionnaires. The graduates were way overbalanced in certain professions, especially teaching, medicine, and the ministry, and represented in tiny proportions in fields such as engineering and banking, for obvious reasons—a segregated educational system with employment opportunities in the professions and general color discrimination everywhere else. It was difficult to measure comparative income of Negro college graduates; for one, the incomes of women in the sample—nearly two thousand of the fifty-five hundred—depressed the overall figures. Further, Johnson, Eli Marks, and their associates concentrated almost entirely on interesting internal differentials within the black college population. Moreover, they compared black college incomes to overall incomes in the *general* population. Thus the differences were small, and at the middle levels, the Negro graduates were, as expected, even a little ahead. But a college-to-college-level comparative sample would have revealed a very wide racial income gap that has since begun to close.

The Negro College Graduate remains a mine of useful information of a time when going to college was out of reach for many qualified Negroes. Given the tacit agreement that Negro social scientists would not question the wisdom and justice of a dual system of higher education, even if for Negro citizens the vastly superior public "white" college was often just a few miles from their own poorly funded institutions, it is not surprising that Johnson was silent on that subject. The concluding chapter on an "educational philosophy" for Negro students focuses on ways they might be better prepared for a technological world and advises them to maintain a racial sense of pride, not an "inferiority complex."

This plenitude of research studies, books, and consultantships made Johnson a national figure and leader. "A," not "the"—that ended with Booker T. Washington. At the start of the 1930s Johnson received the Harmon Medal, a highly coveted award like the NAACP Spingarn Medal, for notable achievement by a Negro in his or her field of activity. In 1934, the Rosenwald Fund made him a trustee which occasioned a funny, gracious letter to Embree that provides a rare glimpse of that other person, the "human Johnson." Dwight Macdonald once defined the Ford Foundation as an island of money surrounded by applicants. On the same theme, after thanking Rosenwald, Johnson anticipates the letters: "I honestly have no fellowships in my desk. . . . I cannot come to Newport News and look at the Nursery School of the Junior Club. . . . I could not fund a school building before Christmas even if I had one. . . . I will not need a house in Chicago or a car in Nashville, or a traveling secretary . . . or a Scottish plaid blanket, or more insurance." He received honorary degrees from Harvard, Columbia, Virginia Union, Howard, and the University of Glasgow and the distinguished alumnus award from the University of Chicago. He continued to receive honors through the 1940s and into the 1950s. (After his death in 1956, the Social Science Building, named for Park, was renamed Park-Johnson.) Johnson plainly liked the recognition; he knew he had earned it.

In the late 1930s, in the last years of the New Deal, a conjuncture of circumstances resulted in the publication of a series of research studies, one of which, *Growing Up in the Black Belt* (1941), Johnson felt to be his other best book, after *Shadow*.[10] The setting for these works and the sponsorship of them still make for interesting reading.

During the years of the Great Depression and slow economic recovery, American youth were more disproportionate than before in the ranks of the unemployed. The economic crisis impinged even more on young black people already hemmed in by traditional racial barriers. Among educators and in the foundations there was concern about the psychological impact of all this on Negro youth in the South, on their sense of identity, their aspirations, and their motivation to achieve. (Later, when Johnson's study was under way, the distinguished psychiatrist Harry Stack Sullivan came on board as a special consultant and went to Mississippi for the first time to conduct interviews. He was enormously impressed by the dignity and resilience, in the face of crisis, of both the adults and youths in the Negro community of Greenville. But "I'm in despair about the youngsters here—chiefly about their abysmal lack of opportunity." Only half facetiously he suggested that "the problem of the Deep South could best be solved by a holocaust" against the whites.)[11] To some degree the New Deal work programs of the CCC and the NYA helped to cushion the impact, but they were not nearly enough.

In 1936, a new nongovernment agency, the American Youth Commission (AYC), financed by the Rockefeller General Education Board, was organized within the American Council of Education. Its aim was to explore the developmental problems of youth twelve years and older. (The original sixteen-member commission had Will Alexander as a member, but not a single Negro.) In 1937, the AYC decided on the study and defined the terms: "What are the effects, if any, Upon the Personality Development of Negro Youth of their Membership in a Minority Racial Group?" Homer Rainey, the AYC's director, had requested Johnson to play a central role in planning the study, yet in the end neither he nor Frazier, the logical persons to direct the project, was chosen. That position went to Robert Sutherland, a white sociologist from the University of Texas, as was Rainey. A little less than three years later the study was completed—seven printed and three mimeographed volumes. From this study came the AYC books. Ira De A. Reid's *In a Minor Key* constituted a preface and a statistical summary; Lloyd Warner (with Buford Junker and Walter Adams) contributed *Color and Human Nature,* drawing on an analysis of eight hundred young Negro men and women by Horace Cayton in Chicago; E. Franklin Frazier contributed *Negro Youth at the Crossways,* focused on a sample of youth of different classes in Washington and Louisville; and Allison Davis and John Dollard in *Children of Bondage* also concentrated on class-color differentials

96

in a sample of Negro youth in the urban Deep South. In this group *Growing Up in the Black Belt* remains the most valuable, in substance, methodology, and style, a classic, the one most likely to endure.

Johnson and his associates designed the research on a more ambitious and sophisticated scale than *Shadow of the Plantation*. Eight counties (including Macon again) were selected, six of them traditional cotton counties, the other two representing diversification in agriculture (two counties surrounded metropolises). The counties were further subdivided on the basis of socioeconomic change. Bolivar and Coahoma in Mississippi exemplified still-functioning plantation systems, while in Macon in Alabama and Greene in Georgia the system was declining. In Madison in Alabama small farmers and tenants, black and white, were committed to one-crop cotton farming in a nonplantation setting. Johnston, in North Carolina, represented mixed farming (cotton and tobacco). Shelby (Memphis) and Davidson (Nashville) in Tennessee provided the mixed rural-urban setting. In each county the sample of Negro youth was balanced for class and gender. Almost all of the some two thousand southern rural Negro young people were given a battery of psychological tests, although some of the test items now seem poorly constructed.

Much more fruitful were the intensive, open-ended interviews with some four hundred of the youths and additional interviews with their families. As is also true of *Shadow*, it is the vivid, often humorous and often wrenching personal stories by the respondents themselves that give the book its depth and indelible impact. The themes in the "personality profiles" and in other fragments threaded through *Growing Up* are familiar enough—the pressure felt from the combined force of color caste and poverty, the lack of opportunity that Harry Stack Sullivan saw in Greenville, the yearning to get away to the city and to the North, the faith in education in spite of poor schooling, the sadness about family disorganization and a parent gone away. But more important, these comments of the young infuse the book with the intensive quality of a novel within the extensive scope of the sociological concepts.

As a response to the question raised at the outset by the AYC, the study showed black adolescence in the (mostly) rural South to be at once a product of the omnipresent color system and of the regular socialization process in any complex society where the life cycle is conditioned by age, sex, class, and the urban-rural dimension. As Johnson noted, growing up black in the South, "one lives a normal routine with its problems and tensions," yet one cannot escape "the shadow of the white world" falling on farm or on city neighborhood.[12]

How, then, can the young black adolescent escape what Harry Stack Sullivan, in a special appendix, describes as a potential "warping of personality," given the destructiveness of "the prevailing white view of the Negro"?[13] The answer is implied in the psychological tone of the personality profiles and conversations with the respondents and made explicit by Johnson in the final chapter in his criticism of the concept of a caste system as employed by a number of his sociological contemporaries. With respect to the first consideration, there is no doubt of the intensity of psychological pressure exerted on Negro boys and girls of a half century ago at the height of the era of segregation. In one of the profiles Essie Mae sums up: "They [the whites] think they are better than the colored and try to keep colored people down." But Essie Mae is not standing completely alone, altogether vulnerable to racism scalding her personality. For there is the "normal routine" of her socialization—family, church, school (even if segregated), peer group, the web of sociation in the Negro community. Sociologically, Essie Mae's situation would be desperate only if the condition of racial "caste" in the India sense fully obtained, freezing her hope for herself, her children, her children's children. Here Johnson explicitly argues that "the southern race system does not . . . appear to meet fully the description of a caste system." The very need to reinforce caste norms by law rather than relying on the traditional cake of custom, to use Walter Bagehot's phrase, the very struggle by whites to shore it up and by blacks to resist it, means whites cannot take it for granted as immutable, nor will blacks accept it passively, with resignation. Change, then, not the static condition of caste, should be the key to the prospects for better race relations.

So a Johnsonian belief, held since his Chicago days, informs his view of growing up in the Black Belt, a belief in accelerated change, even in the grim late days of the Great Depression. Always a realist, Johnson in no sense underestimated the tenacity of southern racism. When the Supreme Court decision finally came down in 1954, he warned of the strength of massive resistance to desegregation. Nevertheless, it is instructive to read the last sentence of the Black Belt book: "In general the Negro continues to occupy a subordinate position, but the fact that he is struggling against this status rather than accepting it, and that the white group is constantly refining its own status in relation to the Negro, indicates that in the future, if one cannot safely predict progress in race relations, he can at least predict change."[14] In the 1960s many people found Johnson's faith in continued social change as thin a reed as his faith in the power of social science to help us to reject racial myths and thus speed the day of that change. They remained, however, the twin pillars of his outlook on race and on democracy.

Through the 1930s, occupied with advising Alexander and the Black Cabinet in Washington on New Deal farm and racial public policy, even more centrally occupied with social science research on race relations and the changing socioeconomic structure of the South, Johnson had still to make room for one more important component of his role as social scientist—advocate. That was his work with regional interracial reform groups in the South. The intention here was not simply to study the racial problem or to advise the makers of public policy on racial issues but to participate with other black leaders and with southern white liberals in groups that could, in Alexander's phrase, "change the racial climate of the South." This required Johnson, given all the research-advocacy demands on his time, to be selective in the choice of groups and in the degree of his involvement.

The simplest part of that task was to be wary of groups that were tainted by association with the Communist party, such as the Scottsboro coalition or the National Negro Congress, directed by John P. Davis. Johnson did not take his position against the far left from a mindless anti-left reflex. In the first place, he saw clearly that even in the roughest days of the Depression, Negro workers and poor farmers would, in the main, turn away from ideological programs based on black-white class solidarity in favor of immediate practical assistance from New Deal reformism. As Norman Thomas, leader of democratic socialism, was wont to say, the New Deal carried out most of *our program*—then they carried *us* out on a stretcher. As for the communists, for all the genuine commitment to interracial association—and it was impressive—the Stalinists who ran the party were always ready to jettison the concern for racial justice whenever party directives dictated change. (To say this in no way detracts from the party's heroic work in behalf of blacks victimized by the infamous criminal justice system in the South. Without the party, the Scottsboro young men would have been executed.) The classic example occurred in the mid-1930s, when Stalin, citing the "glorious achievement" of the Soviet Union in eliminating racism and anti-Semitism, ordered the party to abandon participation in a democratic "popular front" and support for integration as concerned the racial issue. Instead, the party would argue for the establishment of a black republic in the South, just like the "autonomous" ethnic republics in the Soviet Union. Ultimately, Richard Wright saw through this and other crackpot party proposals and resigned; Paul Robeson, Benjamin Davis, William Patterson, James Ford, and other black intellectuals did not, continuing to give the party a shred of credibility on race matters. Frazier, though aware that the communist-front human relations and interracial organizations were concerned with civil rights only for narrow tactical and manipulative purposes, nonetheless supported them naively and blindly, in particular because they folded the racial issue into economics and ruling class power. But he had no interest whatever in, and was never a member of, the Communist party. Such distinctions would be lost, however, on the congressional committees and government agencies that harassed him unconscionably in the 1950s.[15] Johnson was steadfast in his hostility to these party-dominated groups. Unfortunately, in the 1950s, when anticommunist hysteria swept the nation and the party's clear right to existence under the First Amendment was ruthlessly trampled under, Johnson gave less attention to the urgent general need to defend civil liberties and political dissent alongside his strong advocacy of civil rights. To his credit he would stand with Du Bois, but he would not help Paul Robeson and Frazier in their travail. In far broader terms than concerns the Communist party, this has sometimes been a troubling problem for so-called national race leaders, when two separate issues are conjoined, especially when pacifism confronts war. A number of important black leaders were hostile to Martin Luther King's linkage of the quest for racial justice with his passionate opposition to the war in Vietnam.

Within the conventional arena of protest and politics, however, there were still decisions to make. Johnson remained a member of the Urban League through the postwar period in the 1940s and was a firm supporter of the NAACP. But his role here, though not peripheral, was certainly not central. The same could be said for some of the more specialized southern regional interracial groups. His economic orientation made him a strong advocate for the Southern Tenant Farmers' Union. He knew its leaders H. L. Mitchell and Howard Kester, and was dismayed by the violence the group experienced. But his direct involvement was minimal. The same was true for the Southern Negro Youth Congress. (He also expressed a certain wariness owing to its alleged "radicalism.") But to work interracially with more conservative establishment groups, such as the Council on Southern Regional Development, occasioned as much frustration as sense of progress, for on the white side, figures of some power and influence, such as the New Orleans business leader Edgar Stern and the widely respected Virginia publisher Virginius Dabney, who defined themselves as race relations progressives, forbade discussion, let alone recommendations, on segregation as a condition of their participation. It would not be until 1942, in the celebrated Durham (North Carolina) Statement, that southern black leadership finally came to terms with this fundamental issue, but even then a critical "however" had to be placed in the text to placate the Dabneys and Sterns: "We are fundamentally opposed to the principle and practice of compulsory segregation in our American society, whether of races, or classes or creeds; however, we regard it as both sensible and timely to address ourselves now to the current problems of racial discrimination and neglect." It fell to Johnson to synthesize the views of sixty black leaders gathered in conference at North Carolina College for Negroes—among them Benjamin Mays, Horace Mann Bond, Rufus Clement, Gordon Hancock, and Charlotte Hawkins Brown—and to issue the public report on December 15. Johnson, "whose coolness and detachment sometimes troubled the others," knew all too well what could and what could not be done.[16]

There was one burning issue, however, on which a white constituency of indignation did exist and could be summoned into coalition. That was lynching. With respect to lynching Johnson could exercise all dimensions of his accustomed role: research on the scope of the problem; advocacy in an interracial antilynching group; cooperative work with the Washington group (the white liberals and the Black Cabinet) to press for an effective antilynching law. On the first count he was a key member of the Source Book Committee of the Southern Commission on the Study of Lynching, which was chaired by George Fort Milton and included, besides Johnson, Will Alexander, John Hope, Robert Moton, and Monroe Work. The critically important task was to document the shocking, terrible facts and to get them to a wide reading public as soon as possible. With Work and Arthur Raper, primarily, Johnson worked on the pamphlets that described the general situation as well as the horrifying individual cases. It was clear to Johnson and his colleagues that ultimately even the most bigoted white southerners would have to yield. They might defend racial segregation and even political disfranchisement of Negroes as part of the "southern way of life," but could they say brutal, lawless killing was "what the Negro wants"?

Johnson's group worked for the same goal as an association of women, Southern Women for the Prevention of Lynching, founded by Jessie Daniel Ames in 1930. By the end of the decade it had an astonishing forty thousand members, more than a match for those enrolled in the Women's National Association for the Preservation of the White Race. Astonishing because there, in the heart of white supremacy country at the height of the era of segregation, they not only knew how to organize but how to make use of the velvet-glove strategy—directly and through their lawyer, and doctor, and businessman spouses—to get somewhere. Jessie Daniel Ames (1883–1972) was born and brought up in Texas, where in the family kitchen she heard both tales of lynching and the story of the denial of the suffrage to women. After college at Southwestern University she became (for the South) a full-fledged progressive, a suffragette, and an advocate for the Negro's rights. In the 1920s she worked as field secretary and head of the women's division of the Commission on Interracial Cooperation (CIC) based in Atlanta and headed by Will Alexander. Branches of Southern Women were organized all over the South by Ames after 1930. Their effectiveness was based on the root fact that as traditional southern women, in hats and gloves, they could reach receptive judges, sheriffs, and newspaper editors to persuade them that simply, in all human decency, not in the name of race relations, these men must use their power to try to stop the crimes. No more than the Black Cabinet in Washington or Johnson's team in Nashville could the women hope to get an antilynching bill past congressional filibuster. Indeed, as late as 1940, Ames was still opposed to the attempt—the Senate would always kill it, she said, ending an exercise in futility. Yet locally they made their impact, and they must have helped at least slightly in one year, 1939–40, when for the first time since records were kept no lynchings were reported. World War II, of course, put both antilynching and anti-poll tax legislation on hold. Southern Women, along with the interracial CIC, was absorbed into the new Southern Regional Council in 1943. Ames returned to Texas, where she was active in social reform causes. She lived long enough to see not only the achievement of her group's goals but much more far-reaching civil rights laws.[17]

The forthright and courageous writer Lillian Smith, just as deeply southern as any of Ames's ladies, did not have much respect for this kind of interracial group because these women would never denounce the whole corrupt and immoral racial system as an abomination, top to bottom. Lillian Smith (1897–1966) was not scornful of the white southern liberal men and women as persons, but rather deplored their refusal to face the heart of the matter racially in the South: segregation. In 1944, the Southern Regional Council was formed from the older groups like CIC. The SRC was certainly more progressive and more truly interracial than the CIC. Guy B. Johnson, a sociologist at Odum's research center at the University of North Carolina, and who was white, was appointed executive director. Ira De A. Reid became associate director, Charles Johnson was elected to the executive committee, and distinguished black leaders including Charlotte Hawkins Brown and Benjamin Mays, president of Morehouse College, were named to the board of directors. But Lillian Smith refused to join. She and J. Saunders Redding, writer and professor of literature at Hampton Institute and a vigorous critic of white liberal timidity, wrote scorching articles against the SRC for its refusal to oppose segregation publicly and for its unwillingness to discuss the pathological nature of white race prejudice. Still, she understood why black leaders were sometimes compelled to adopt publicly a moderate posture when necessary. She and Johnson were friends, though not close, and they wrote candidly to each other about racial issues.

Lillian Smith was born in Florida to a prosperous family of strong religious conviction. When her father's business failed, the family moved to Clayton, Georgia. After musical studies in Baltimore and three years of teaching music in a Methodist mission school in China (1922–25), she returned to Clayton to manage her parents' nationally known camp for girls for many years until her earnings from writing finally left her free to write full-time and devote herself to civil rights. In fiction and in essays she chose to tell the bone truth about white supremacy in the South. She found herself pilloried as a traitor to the region; twice her house was firebombed. Her best-known work, *Strange Fruit*, a novel about an interracial love affair, treated interracial sex with great sensitivity but confronted the South's deepest taboo. (The book was, of course, banned in Boston, but Eleanor Roosevelt got a White House order that vacated the postal ban.) In the 1960s, seriously ill but battling to the end, she resigned from the militant civil rights organization the Congress of Racial Equality (CORE) when it embraced a separatist credo of black power. In the history of southern white liberalism she is sui generis, a traditional southern lady with deep southern roots who yet dared to indict her region for its racism.[18]

The Jessie Daniel Ameses, the Will Alexanders, and the other southern white liberals are honored today for what they tried to do, against the grain, in the country of the 1930s and 1940s.[19] If Johnson was on occasion angry with them for not testing the fortress of white supremacy more steadily and more sturdily, he understood them. He respected them. He liked them.

Of all the groups and coalitions with which Johnson was associated in southern regional advocacy, three stand out: the Commission on Interracial Cooperation (1930s), the Southern Conference for Human Welfare, SCHW (1930s and 1940s), the Southern Regional Council (1940s and beyond). All three had mixed records of advances and retreats, but the last two would have accomplished nothing were it not for the presence, more precisely the intervention, of the federal government, a minimal presence in the New Deal era, to be sure, rising to a forceful intervention in the 1960s under pressure from the civil rights organizations. Johnson's relationship to all three varied in degree.

The Commission on Interracial Cooperation was founded in 1919, in the wake of rising prejudice and violence against blacks after World War I, and lasted for twenty-five years. Its longtime director, Will Alexander, set the course, to organize state and local interracial committees to combat racial violence, ameliorate race relations, and educate southerners misled by myths about race. That last charge meant research on such matters as lynching (by Arthur Raper, the 1930s research secretary) and encouraging southern colleges to establish courses in race relations. Thomas Woofter, the first research secretary, wrote the first textbook in this area, *Racial Adjustment*, adopted in some sixty southern institutions. In its educational function the CIC adopted the Boasian principle that scientific sociology about race would persuade people to change their attitudes and practices with respect to race. The textbook Johnson coauthored with Willis D. Weatherford, one of the founders of CIC, *Race Relations*, was written in this spirit.

The economic exigencies of the Great Depression drastically reduced the local reformist programs of the CIC but it maintained its educational and research function, sponsoring sociological studies such as Raper's analysis of southern peasantry and Horace Cayton's and George S. Mitchell's survey of discrimination against black workers in the unions, and focusing its advocacy function on working with the Washington groups to place more Negroes in New Deal administration. Johnson and Odum worked closely with the CIC; their centers in Nashville and Chapel Hill represented what the CIC aimed to accomplish. But by the end of the 1930s it was clear to both white liberals and black leaders in the CIC that in view of the magnitude of the racial and socioeconomic problems in the South, the CIC strategy, in particular the concept of progress within segregation, was outmoded and of decreasing relevance to the southern reality.[20] This led in 1943 to the merger into the SRC whose story properly belongs to the next chapter. It can be said, however, that the CIC's mandate to change the racial climate of the South, while maintaining its avoidance of controversy over the heart of the matter, the system of racial segregation, reveals a fatal contradiction, even granted the context of the 1930s when in the South it was possible to go so far and no further. No one knew this better than Johnson, but he kept his counsel; Alexander was his close friend and, after all, without the white liberals directing strategy the CIC never could have been formed. He contributed substantially to the CIC and SRC. Still, he wrote much later, in 1947, how does it so often happen "that the intellectual [white] liberals who know what should be done are torn between their private convictions and their public caution."[21] At least, in the Durham Statement in 1942, he and the other sixty Negro leaders might begin to free themselves of a similar wearying posture.

The Southern Conference for Human Welfare and its linked successor, the Southern Conference Educational Fund (SCEF), constituted a different development, and their advocacy had different consequences. Founded late in the New Deal period, in 1938, SCHW's aim from the start was to assert that economic equality of opportunity in the South would never arrive unless racial discrimination and segregation were confronted directly. In that sense and for that time it had to be more "militant" than "moderate" and its leaders had to brace from the beginning for virulent attacks on the membership as "radical," "communist," and "nigger-loving." It was essentially liberal left-wing until late in the day and its annual Thomas Jefferson Award to a southerner for advancing human rights went to such moderate liberals as Will Alexander, Mary McLeod Bethune, and Frank Graham (1886–1972), president of the University of North Carolina. What it did stand for completely and unequivocally went far beyond the CIC: total opposition to segregation, support for new federal laws to ban discrimination, and the solidarity of black and white workers in the trade union movement. Thus controversy was embraced, not avoided as in the CIC.

SCHW had an impact in the South from the late 1930s to the 1950s not so much because of its strength—the numbers remained relatively small, perhaps no more than ten thousand—but because it proposed in forthright form a different path for the South to take if it wished ultimately to throw off the twin burdens of economic underdevelopment and racial oppression. For all its misfortunes, bitter internal conflicts, and eventual failure, it laid out the direction for the evolution of a more effective Southern Regional Council and the far more effective civil rights movement. As Linda Reed has observed, SCHW-SCEF "played a major role in raising the national consciousness on the issue of civil rights and . . . for the creation of a new democratic South."[22] Charles Johnson was a member of the board until his Fisk presidency in 1947; he was less active but still involved after that. So he shared in the defining goal: integration.

Clark Foreman, the central figure in the establishment of the SCHW in 1938, served an apprenticeship in the Alexander-Johnson-Embree school of southern liberalism. A graduate of the University of Georgia, he went to work for Alexander as secretary of the Georgia chapter of the CIC. After a doctorate in political science from Columbia, he took positions with the Phelps-Stokes and Rosenwald funds. His passionate commitment to civil rights came partly from this work and, even earlier, from observing the humiliation to Negroes of segregation (at seventeen he saw a lynching which a friend said "burned a hole in his head.")[23] He became part of the Washington group during the first New Deal period when Harold Ickes, secretary of the interior, hired him as special adviser on the economic status of the Negro. It goes without saying that the adviser on Negro problems had to be a white man. But Ickes did permit Foreman to take on a Harvard-trained economist as his assistant, Robert Weaver, who years later became the first black cabinet member in government, in the Lyndon Johnson administration. The southern white liberals—Foreman, Frank Graham, Lucy Randolph Mason (a consumer and labor economist), Joseph Gelders (a physicist from Alabama), and others—then enlisted Mrs. Roosevelt, who arranged a meeting with the president. The group sought and got support from other relatively "progressive" associations such as the Southern Policy Committee. (Again the pattern prevailed: the Committee was totally white with the exception of one member—Charles S. Johnson.)

On November 20, 1938, some thirteen hundred delegates, white and black, representing a wide spectrum of political positions in the South, met in Birmingham, Alabama, and set the SCHW agenda. It was a historic, dramatic, symbolic event. As Johnson noted, "It was the first bold emergence of the liberal South responding to action by the devastating government's report on the region's economic and social plight."[24] The delegates were required to conform to segregated hotel and dining facilities, of course; the actual sessions were completely integrated. Mrs. Roosevelt not only attended but gave the principal speech and sat, integrated, with everyone else. The police department, on orders from the city commissioner, Eugene "Bull" Connor, to become infamous in the 1960s for setting police dogs on civil rights demonstrators, ordered the delegates to resegregate or face arrest. They had to do so. But Mrs. Roosevelt, knowing they would not arrest her, placed her chair in the center aisle and sat there during the entire conference. That set the tone for the SCHW; it did not meet segregated again.

Into the 1940s and beyond Johnson's role in groups such as the SCHW and the SRC was not only to participate in policy decisions but to try to show the southern white liberals who controlled and directed the programs, the anomaly in the underrepresentation of the black community in organizations devoted to improving the Negro's economic and social status. Black community participation is now seen as essential to achieving progress in race relations. It was not so seen then. Neither the FSA in Washington nor the SRC in Atlanta fully accepted that principle, although compared to the general prevailing southern attitudes and practices these agencies were far ahead of their time.

The members of the liberal coalition did last long enough to transmit their experience to the civil rights movement. Johnson, Alexander, Bethune, Embree, Eleanor Roosevelt, and Odum did not live long enough to witness the passage of the Civil Rights Act of 1964 and the Voting Rights Act of 1965. But they might have imagined the transformation of race relations strategy that eventually took place. Their contribution, despite its limitations, is linked to the continuing effort to overcome racial injustice.

At the very end of the decade of the 1930s the national condition underwent a significant change that altered Charles Johnson's multiple roles. As international affairs and the aggression of Nazi Germany in Europe came increasingly to preoccupy the president and the country, the New Deal's economic and social initiatives as well as the praise-worthy but narrowly defined effort in race relations were subordinated to other considerations.[25] The great debate over isolationism versus interventionism, the decision to make the United States "the arsenal of democracy" in support of democratic allies in western Europe, and the rapid transformation of the economy around the needs of national defense required the southern white liberals and the Black Cabinet in Washington to refit their concern for combating racial discrimination to the larger, reshaped national interest. So it is not surprising that the confrontational protest movement outside government, such as it was in the early 1940s, had now to assume the lead in reminding the Roosevelt administration inside of its obligation to improve equality of opportunity in defense industrial employment and in the military structure. The Negro press proclaimed, when war did come, the goal of "Double V for Victory"—over fascism abroad and racism at home.

The controversy over A. Philip Randolph and his proposed march on Washington, scheduled for the summer of 1941, is a classic example of this changed situation. In January, the president of the Brotherhood of Sleeping Car Porters proposed this dramatic form of grievance to express the anger Negroes felt at their rigid exclusion from all but menial jobs in the defense industry. By June, thousands were ready to march for racial justice and against hypocrisy in government. But as might be expected now, Mrs. Roosevelt, Aubrey Williams of the NYA, Walter White, and others in the Washington group argued strongly against the march. For Mrs. Roosevelt this was an uncharacteristic response; almost always on matters of race relations and human rights she prodded the president to lead the battle against bigotry.[26] (Johnson, too, might have opposed the march, but his papers contain no record of his personal opinion.) At the last moment, in a session with the president himself, Randolph called off the march. The quid pro quo was, of course, the celebrated Executive Order 8802—"there shall be no discrimination in the employment of workers in defense industries or Government because of race, creed, color, or national origin."[27] To assure compliance, Roosevelt established the Fair Employment Practices Committee (FEPC) to deal with complaints, though it had only limited enforcement power.[28] That widespread discrimination continued does not change the fact that Randolph's strategy worked and that the Washington group's inside approach had now to be necessarily muted. The lesson was not lost on the civil rights movement of the 1960s when

Randolph, Bayard Rustin, Martin Luther King, and others planned and carried through the March on Washington of August 1963.

The research function of the Department of Social Science at Fisk was even more important in the 1940s, for changes in public policy, even if limited, required a solid research base that would demonstrate in depth how entrenched was the system of racial discrimination. The number of studies, community racial self-surveys, and race relations conferences increased on a rising curve. Johnson and his associates knew that sooner or later in postwar America this body of work would play a part in policy recommendations. The report of President Truman's Committee on Civil Rights, *To Secure These Rights,* issued in 1947 and grounded in research, was for its time a path-breaking document, calling for "the elimination of segregation" among its recommendations.

In retrospect, Johnson's years at Fisk, from 1929 into the early 1940s before his ascension to the presidency in 1946, would seem to constitute his basic and enduring contribution to sociology, to social science research, to the never-ending commitment, in Alexander's phrase, "to change the racial climate of America." In the 1930s he wrote his best books, *Shadow of the Plantation* and *Growing Up in the Black Belt.* He solidified and developed more effectively the mediating role with white philanthropy and with government which made possible advances in the discipline of race relations and, perhaps just as important, helped to provide the support for a striking number of young black scholars and artists, the Rosenwald and later the Whitney Fellows. Though constrained by the racism of that period in the professions and in government, which placed restraints on an up-front public role for a Negro in policy decision making, he did his best to see to it that New Deal programs in such areas as farm tenancy and community social services were as free of racial bias as could be hoped for in the era of segregation.

The central question remains whether in all these roles he could have been more. That is, should he not have been more like Randolph, or Frazier, or Du Bois?[29] In the interest of seeking justice for his beleaguered people, should he not, like Du Bois, have been more the propagandist, the militant, less the master of indirection, less the practitioner of sidelines activism? The answer is that he could not have attempted to be more and still have remained true to himself, sociologist *and* advocate on terms he judged best for him. He played that role; he stayed that course. "Throughout the thirties and forties into the fifties, only a small number of black Southerners (and even fewer whites) were able to stay in the region and fight their way to national recognition in the long campaign for racial equality. Charles S. Johnson was one of them."[30]

Hemingway once said the end is to last and get your work done. Johnson lasted (though not long enough). And he got his work done.

VI

FISK:
WAR AND POSTWAR
IN THE SOUTH

In 1940, as the new decade opened, the state of the nation defined the status of African Americans. Looking back at the 1930s they knew that economically they had suffered more from the Great Depression than whites, yet precisely because of that disadvantaged position the New Deal's economic and social assistance helped materially to sustain them, even acknowledging that the programs for the most part followed, rather than challenged, the system of segregation and discrimination. The novelist Chester Himes has his character in *Lonely Crusade* say, "Roosevelt! All he ever done for the nigger was to put him on relief. . . . How he done it I do not know—starve you niggers and made you love 'im."[1] But millions of black working-class Americans thought differently; the New Deal helped them survive, and they left the Party of Emancipation in droves and voted Democrat for decades thereafter (they still do). Du Bois, as usual, got to the heart of the pragmatic matter, writing in *Crisis* in February 1934: "The New Deal is organized and conducted chiefly to relieve white distress and give work to white folks. What are we going to do about it? Denounce segregation or organize to relieve black distress and give work to black folks."

Looking ahead into the 1940s, however, they had grounds once again for apprehension. Within the larger curve of slow economic recovery, the recession of 1938 seemed to drag on. In January 1939, in his annual message, Roosevelt himself had signaled that in view of the grave international danger there would be no new domestic New Deal reforms. If that meant an oncoming defense boom with thousands more jobs, there was no assurance Negroes would obtain a fair share of them. And if a military draft were to be required and if war were to arrive, there was even less assurance that the segregation and discrimination of World War I would not be carried over into the new

III

armed forces structure. The economic transformation of the arsenal of democracy and the new global warfare were not slated to transform the color line.

The evolution of race relations in the 1940s largely substantiated these predictions. Not until nearly the end of the decade, marked by efforts to implement the recommendations of President Truman's Committee on Civil Rights report *To Secure These Rights,* the Supreme Court's overturning of racially restrictive covenants in housing, the first tentative efforts to undo military segregation, and a rising degree of counterassertion in the established black civil rights groups, would institutionalized racism begin to yield. The slowly rising curve of change can be seen, as in the 1930s, in three periods: the defense boom time of national mobilization, World War II, and postwar adjustment.

National mobilization of the economy was in direct response to Nazi Germany's overrunning of Europe, and Negroes, Jews, and other minorities had as much if not more reason than other Americans for supporting it in view of Hitler's racial doctrines—Jews were "untermenschen" and blacks "baboons." Du Bois often said that Nazi racial propaganda would go over better in Richmond or New Orleans than in Berlin. In 1936, for example, for the Olympics in Berlin, the German government persuaded the U.S. Olympic Committee and a cowardly State Department to get two Jewish runners barred from the four-hundred-meter relay; the participating Negro athletes were meanly treated in Berlin. But the nature of the enemy had little effect on opening up significantly, on a race-neutral basis, either the domestic labor force or the rapidly building military. The great demand for labor frequently meant white mobility into skill-level jobs, with Negroes filling in below. The profusion of nondiscriminatory proclamations issued by the various production agencies required only voluntary compliance. Nor did the newly created FEPC, the result of the president's executive order, have real enforcement power. (It had an annual budget of $80,000 at the start.) The Selective Service Act of 1940, the draft, forbade discrimination, but it was widespread at local draft board levels. The permanent army reflected rigid military racial policy carried over from peacetime. Of 230,000 enlisted men in 1940 only some 5,000 were Negro; Negro officers numbered under 100. (There was some improvement, of course, in all these areas, as the war went on.) In fall 1940 came the definitive War Department statement: segregation would prevail down the line. "The United States had committed itself to maintaining a white army and a black army . . . to carry on the fight against the powerful threat of fascism and racism in the world."[2]

During the four years of war some important changes were made. The Marine Corps finally opened its doors to Negroes; the navy finally permitted blacks to get beyond the messmen category; officer training camps were integrated; the air corps established a program (segregated) to train Negro pilots for the first time at Tuskegee Institute. The army even allowed sociologists to study soldiers' attitudes toward integrated units in Europe. Half a million Negroes overseas served as well as whites in combat and support. Yet especially in the training camps for enlisted men, many of them in the South, discrimination on the posts and in the surrounding towns was rampant. In civilian industrial employment, there were dramatic breakthroughs in selected industries, thanks in part to pressure from the FEPC, but this was still very far from equal opportunity in industry and in the unions. The race riots in major cities, in Detroit especially, were a symptom of deep racial unrest. Conditions changed but not the racial system itself.

All this did not surprise Charles S. Johnson, decorated combat veteran of the battle of Argonne-Meuse in World War I. He was a firm supporter of the war but under the banner of "in spite of"; that is, the cause was just despite the racism that contradicted its very purpose. He worked even harder on the research surveys, engaged in some advocacy in cooperation with the Washington group (though less than in the New Deal period), and continued his active participation in the regional groups, the SRC and the SCHW. He also watched with pride as his two older sons did well in air corps training. And he kept up a lively correspondence with assistants who had gone into military service or into federal service in Washington.

The postwar years, until the end of the 1940s, did not go well for race relations. As Johnson predicted during the war, there would certainly be the cumulative change after the war that was a central theme in his democratic creed. At the same time, as a realistic sociological student of the South, he knew there would be some backlash, in particular on the part of returning white southern veterans. The country in general remained relatively indifferent to racial issues, as the first postwar polls showed. What changed matters, however, were a cluster of new factors. Returning black southern veterans were just as determined to change the status quo as the whites were determined to hold to it. In the northern cities black voters were now an important part of the so-called liberal-labor coalition which included labor groups, Jews, and white ethnic populations, often Catholic in religion, who attributed part of their socioeconomic mobility to the helping hand of the New Deal in the Depression. The vehicle of their political expression was the northern wing of the Democratic party, which finally had the power to challenge the unreconstructed southern Democrats fiercely defending the race line. Only much later, in the 1960s, would the coalition commence to fray, setting in motion conflict between blue-collar white ethnics and blacks in the inner cities of the North. Then starting in the 1970s, the "southern strategy" commenced. Unwilling, for reasons based on both race and conservatism, to stay in the Democratic party, southern whites moved increasingly into the Republican camp.

The great symbolic event in this context occurred in 1948 at the Democratic party convention when Mayor Hubert Humphrey of Minneapolis gave a stirring, unprecedented plea for civil rights legislation which helped to induce an important segment of the southern conservative wing to defect from the Democrats and to organize the Dixiecrat party, pledged to permanent segregation.[3]

The changed political climate also emboldened the major Negro civil rights groups to take a more aggressive stand in waging legal actions against discrimination. And the federal courts were at last beginning to move from attempting to make "separate and equal" reality, with a bizarre statistical precision, to the recognition that segregation per se was the core of racial discrimination in the South, unconstitutional and unjust. What seemed inconceivable before the war now seemed possible after it. When Justice J. Waties Waring of the federal court in South Carolina ordered the Democratic primary opened to Negroes in 1947, southerners were astonished that it was done by a distinguished southerner, "one of us." But they knew more was to come.

Finally, there is the story of the remarkable transformation of President Harry S. Truman on questions of race and civil rights. (The president knew of Johnson's reputation. Immediately after the war he had Assistant Secretary of State William Benton appoint Johnson to the first UNESCO delegation and then to the commission to restructure the educational system of Japan.) An ordinary politician from a border southern state, Missouri, a product of the Pendergast machine, he worked his way slowly up the political ladder until he reached the Senate. His basic honesty compelled him to acknowledge the human aspect of civil rights, the right of a man or woman to a decent life irrespective of skin color. He voted for FEPC, abolition of the poll tax, and antilynching legislation. Not that he was a liberal ideologue. On the contrary, as president, he would on occasion propose a striking initiative in civil rights only to proceed very slowly toward implementation, not wanting to alienate altogether either the southern conservatives on the far right or the Henry Wallace Progressive party on the far left. This canny political figure saw both groups defect yet, amazingly, he won the 1948 election without them, taking a liberal-populist strategy directly to the people—and winning the black vote. It is true as well that he never quite got over his early socialization. The champion of the Fair Deal and human rights would not be above the everyday stereotypes of the comic Negro, as was true of his successor, Dwight Eisenhower. This was the "other Truman" of narrow-mindedness who could impose a mindless "loyalty oath" without a qualm.[4]

Nevertheless, his moral conviction and innate decency never really deserted him. In 1947 his Committee on Civil Rights, in its landmark report, *To Secure These Rights,* made sweeping recommendations which he then incorporated in his speech to Congress, February 2, 1948; until 1948 there had never been a special message on civil rights. (To be sure, this committee of fourteen included only two Negroes, Sadie Alexander and Channing Tobias.) The formal speech called for a permanent FEPC with actual enforcement power, a federal antilynching law, federal protection of voting rights, elimination of racial discrimination in interstate travel, an end to the poll tax (still existing in seven southern states), and compensation for Japanese-Americans unjustly put into detention camps during the war "solely because of their racial origin." Later that year came the executive order beginning the process of desegregating the armed forces. These were the formal proposals. Behind them was something simpler, Truman's outrage at the beatings and killings of Negro men and women in the South in 1946 and 1947. And his own capacity to grow, to move beyond his conventional background, reflected a still vague but authentic general stirring in the country to come to terms, finally, with race. It was what Johnson meant in writing that if there could not be progress there could at least be change. The committee report and the February speech, like the work of the southern white liberals and the Black Cabinet in the New Deal era, were markers, faint though they may have been, pointing to the new activism in civil rights in the 1950s that came to full expression in the next decade.

This, then, was the prewar, wartime, and postwar setting, one of change and resistance to change, against which Johnson worked out his agenda in research and advocacy. There was, however, a shift in emphasis. With respect to national public policy and regional activism his commitment was less intense, especially after 1946, when he became president of Fisk. But he could still show, as in the Durham conference in 1942 and the Atlanta and Richmond meetings that followed, his leadership skill in "conciliatory realism." This time the familiar role was in the service of finally inducing the southern white liberals (and some cautious black leaders as well) to join in a direct challenge to segregation. At the same time, in the new arrangement with the Rosenwald Fund in 1943, Johnson agreed to a division of labor with Will Alexander which might keep alive the connection with the Washington group and national policy in race relations. They would be co-directors of race relations in the Rosenwald, but Johnson would concentrate on research from the Nashville base, while Alexander would focus on the development of civil rights policy in Washington, activity fairly restrained by the wartime emergency but to be renewed energetically with the end of the war. At the same time, Johnson assumed the directorship of the American Missionary Association Race Relations Division.

From the Nashville base, throughout the 1940s, including the first two years of the Fisk presidency, Johnson and his associates turned out an extremely large amount of work in race relations—more than the Odum group at Chapel Hill—in the form of studies, programs, institutes, and conferences. To the discipline of sociology Johnson's research groups added very little, if anything, to theoretical concepts and methodological innovation. They drew upon the social psychology of race prejudice, the literature on the meaning and forms of racial discrimination, and the conceptual framework in the growing field of social change (with limited use of Park's cyclical typology). That, however, was not the point. What Johnson wished to do, as in the 1930s but more so, was to deepen the sociological understanding of racial conflict and tension, train the next generation of black sociologists to carry the work further, and, perhaps most important, bring to as wide a general public audience as possible an awareness of the enormous social damage resulting from the perpetuation of dangerous misconceptions and attitudes—M. F. Ashley Montagu had rightly titled his book *Race: Man's Most Dangerous Myth*. He wanted to set out a full and detailed scientific record of a system of economic, political, and social discrimination that deprived a tenth of the population of its rights and aspirations. In other words, if the studies and institutes did not serve in some way as prolegomena to social action and social change, however modest, then they were of limited utility. If the sociological research added to the theoretical literature or provoked a stimulating scientific argument from sociological peers, so much the better.[5]

It is a herculean task to sort out from the Johnson Papers in the Special Collections at Fisk University Library the results of some eighteen years of this work. Altogether Johnson's "Fisk Machine" produced an impressive record of achievement, unique in the nation and in the Negro college network.[6] The main lines of activity in the 1940s can be roughly catalogued.

Most important, most enduring, were the major studies of specific communities or of a central problem within the southern region. In these Johnson's role ranged from complete participation and supervision in the research and writing, to coordination of the research of others and complete writing of the report, to light participation through designing the research, securing the funding, and revising the final report. This was all done in the midst of countless other obligations, principally his functioning as director of the AMA's programs in race relations and the Rosenwald department of the same (with Alexander); administering the Social Science Department and Race Relations Department at Fisk; and seeking to have some impact on national public policy in racial matters mainly through participation in national associations with specific goals such as the NAACP in mounting its legal cases, or writing his syndicated column for both the newspapers in the Associated Negro Press, directed by Claude Barnett, and selected mainstream papers such as the *Minneapolis Morning Tribune*. Close involvement in the informal ad hoc coalition of black leaders in the South also had a high priority in the 1940s as this group prepared, at last, to "come out" on racial segregation in the Durham Statement and other declarations. Throughout, he carried on a huge volume of correspondence—with old Harlem Renaissance friends such as Langston Hughes, with sociological colleagues Frazier, Gordon Hancock, and Odum, and with a wide range of citizens, high and low, who wanted to know why he was being either too slow or too radical in respect to segregation. Edgar Stern cautions him to stay the more moderate course; a Negro communist journalist tells him he has sold out lock, stock, and barrel to capitalist imperialism. He can't please them all.

In view of this many-sided activity from the Nashville base it is not surprising that long before August Meier, his research assistant for one year and subsequently a distinguished historian of American race relations, raised the issue of whether he was appropriating the work of others as his own, some of Johnson's contemporaries raised the same question. The response is best made study by study, but in general it can be fairly said that he was consistently correct, and at times generous, in the matter of attribution. In a good many interviews with his younger colleagues and with former students, I recorded some candid criticisms of Johnson's tenure as head of departments and college president, but they did not fault him on the score of attribution. Bonita Valien, his trusted research associate, tried to set the record straight: "Because I was always the person who put the thing to bed I know what each person contributed. . . . People who went into the field did not write his books."[7] Ophelia Settle Egypt, another research fieldworker, insisted, "The final draft was uniquely his own." Herman Long and Grace Jones received full credit for the collaborative work, *The Negro War Worker in San Francisco* (1944), as did Long for their volume on restrictive covenants, *People vs. Property* (1947). One reason for some confusion on this issue was that often the drafts were extensively reworked by senior staff such as Eli Marks and Valien before reaching Johnson.

The war did not change the fact that in the 1940s, as before, black social scientists had to work under special difficulties, coping with problems of travel and accommodations in the segregated South. It was the uncertainty, not knowing whether one would or would not be served, that galled. Not only the fieldworkers but Johnson himself would encounter the unexpected. In 1946 when the Southern Sociological Society held its annual meeting at the Biltmore Hotel in Atlanta, President-elect Johnson was charged with informing Juliette Pfifer of Fayetteville State Teachers College in North Carolina that she would have to take a room at Atlanta University where Ira De A. Reid had arranged lodging for Negro sociologists. "Do you wish us to cancel your reservation at the Biltmore," he wrote to her, "or would you prefer to do so?" In this instance Johnson had no alternative. The year before he did. It happened more than once that the Nashville railroad station clerk first accepted Johnson's reservation, then, learning of his race, denied it. He pointed out that in fifteen years of train travel in Pullmans "as a professor and officer of the Rosenwald Fund and the American Missionary Association of the Congregational Church not a single instance of passenger objection has come to my attention." He asked whether it was official Pullman policy to deny reservations to Negro citizens or was it simply race prejudice. And then this pointed aside: "There is a little irony (which I have not yet exploited) in the fact that I had considerable difficulty with one of your clerks in securing reservations to attend the hearings in Washington of the Railroad Carrier Industry Committee of which I was an official member!" He received a stiff reply from the chief ticket agent that it was not the policy of the Louisville and Nashville Railroad to refuse Pullman accommodations to Negroes "when some are available."[8]

Of all the studies published in the 1940s *Growing Up in the Black Belt* is the most thoroughly documented in the files of the research center, though the fieldwork was actually done at the very end of the 1930s. But there were many, many more. The Johnson team conducted a comprehensive, long-range inquiry into the education of Negroes as part of the Louisiana School Survey. The Johnson-Long study of housing discrimination, *People vs. Property* (1947), focused on two case studies of real estate practices in Chicago and St. Louis, documenting the conditions that led a year later to the Supreme Court decision in *Shelley* v. *Kraemer* declaring restrictive covenants not enforceable in law; Johnson contributed to the brief. Preston Valien continued his studies of Negroes and the trade unions. An extremely valuable project, making use of Park's human document approach, was the recording of the autobiographies of aged living former slaves. The interviews, done by graduate students under the supervision of the anthropologist Paul Radin a decade earlier in 1929–30, were produced in typescript as the "Unwritten History of Slavery" in 1945. How fortunate, Charles Johnson wrote, "that these rare fragments of history, these glimpses into the mentality of a group so rigidly regimented by a unique economic structure . . . could be recorded before the last of these ex-slaves have passed irrevocably into history."[9] The Parkean human document technique was also employed in continuing studies of southern Negro youth, based on the American Youth Commission material compiled earlier.

There were also the innumerable community surveys and "self-surveys." Both were intended as "social engineering," that is, providing factual material and analysis on cities confronting racial tensions so that local community organizations could make use of the data to initiate social action to change local practices in race relations. Two case studies, in Minneapolis and Pittsburgh—Allegheny County, funded by the AMA Race Relations Division, Charles Johnson, director, resulted in policy recommendations. The studies of these and other cities were along the same lines as those conducted by Johnson years before at the Urban League. At the local level, in Nashville, Fisk established the University Social Center in the low-income area near the campus. It was both a community settlement house and a social laboratory—a place for practical application of social research.

The value of this research is self-evident. But Johnson and his associates did not discuss publicly a fundamental limitation on its effectiveness. When the data were compiled and closely analyzed—and they were often devastating in showing the consequences of racial discrimination for a particular community or region—the researchers then either had to pass on the material to policy makers ("we were fact finders only"), or if sections on "conclusions and recommendations" were included, they were proposals to majority group and minority group agencies to take action cooperatively to obtain voluntary compliance from the power institutions in the economy or education. Neither enforceable legislation nor nonviolent mass protest were discussed as possible solutions. Of course, this represented the lifelong Johnsonian ethos: social science research, providing a factual and analytic foundation to be used by policy makers. A solid scientific basis, as well as a moral basis, is thus laid for social action and social change—with the actual agents of change taking up a wide range of strategies ranging from goodwill voluntarism to complex legal and political challenges. If that social science ethos gained the Fisk center a national reputation and got its research closely studied, effectiveness and follow-through would often be problematic.

In some cases it did not matter. For example, in 1941 Johnson and his associates published *The Statistical Atlas of Southern Counties,* a compilation of hard data on 1,104 counties in thirteen southern states. (The associates were Lewis Jones, Eli Marks, Buford Junker, and Preston Valien.) Funded partly by the Rosenwald, the study established a socioeconomic and racial profile for each county based on such factors as population, race, educational levels, illiteracy, occupation, and agricultural-industrial balance. This profile enabled the researchers to construct a typology of variation of social systems in the South. A statistical light was thrown on both regional "backwardness" and clear racial disparities within the region. The facts spoke for themselves so that it required only a relatively brief analysis to show, by implication, the consequences of the

South's racial system. *The Statistical Atlas*, an invaluable storehouse of information, that "foundation of data" in Johnson's research strategy, was made available to planners and agencies of social change, if they would but make use of it.

In Volume 4 of the *Louisiana Education Survey* (1942) on Negro public schools in the state, prepared by Johnson and many assistants in the Department of Social Science, however, the facts are just as damning as in the *Atlas* but forthright commentary is required; the state is said to want better schools for both whites and blacks. At the same time, all discussion must assume the permanence of a framework of segregation. The researchers are thus compelled to conclude with a critical but oblique assessment of the future of Louisiana schooling for Negroes. There is frank admission that "the center of gravity of the Negro schools is outside the Negro community." In the recommendations section on higher education the research staff, finding no graduate school for Negroes and eyeing the fine "white" facility at Louisiana State University, concludes: "The state is faced with the alternative of setting up a graduate school for Negroes or providing scholarship funds for those demanding graduate study to go elsewhere. Both are evils but the latter appears to be the lesser of the two." Stressing the urgent need to lift the deplorable level of Negro vocational education, the research group is impelled to insert a bizarre sentence: "This (practical) education for the Negroes will pay dividends to the State. Shiftless Negroes, wasteful Negroes, dishonest Negroes, undernourished Negroes . . . are a costly liability. Honest, intelligent, hard-working, well-trained, healthy, happy, and thrifty Negroes will greatly increase the wealth of the State and the safety and happiness of the white race as well as the Negro race." In short, the statistics were devastating—for example, the median annual salary for Negro teachers in Louisiana was $377, 36 percent of the salary for whites—but the research group had no alternative but to arrive at an accommodationist set of conclusions.[10] To be sure, in the studies of northern cities like Pittsburgh and Minneapolis, the researchers were freer to be somewhat more candid and forthright.

There is abundant evidence that Johnson in these years was generous in advising others engaged in research unrelated to Fisk sponsorship. He was a good sociologist and a good writer, more than willing to give a close reading to manuscripts by the Odum group at Chapel Hill or by friends and colleagues. Nowhere is this more evident than in his relationship with Horace Cayton, working in Chicago as director of Parkway Community House. All through the preparation of *Black Metropolis* he was in extensive correspondence with Cayton, advising on sociological concepts, urging Cayton and Richard Wright (who wrote the introduction) to come to Fisk for the Institute on Race Relations or the music festivals. When the book appeared in 1945, with St. Clair Drake as coauthor, Johnson wrote to him enthusiastically, "good going . . . altogether unique and valuable contribution to the literature of sociology and of race."[11]

The focus on race relations in the Department of Social Science had an impact on the curriculum as well as on the research agenda. Useful as they were, the surveys of Pittsburgh, Minneapolis, Kalamazoo, Trenton, and other cities, the special studies of Negro packinghouse workers and longshoremen, and the widely distributed *Monthly Summary of Events and Trends in Race Relations* did not carry students into what would become known in the postwar era as the Third World. The comparative and historical study of peoples of color in Africa and the Caribbean was of growing interest as it became clear that momentous changes were coming that would drastically change the map of empire and white domination. So to the curriculum, Southern Rural Life, and the curriculum, Race and Culture, Johnson added, cooperatively with the two Africanist specialists, Mark Hanna Watkins and Lorenzo Turner, the Interdepartmental Curriculum in African Studies in 1944, with related courses on Mexico and the Caribbean built into the program. Special attention was given to Haiti, for obvious reasons. This was a very important innovation in 1944. The rush to African and Afro-American studies did not occur in mainstream academia until the early 1960s. With a few exceptions the same was true for the other historically black colleges. When I taught at Hampton Institute (now University) in the 1960s there were only two courses on Africa in the social science department, both taught by a white historian.

Still, the basic emphasis at Fisk was always on American society, and here Fisk had great success with an even more important innovation, the annual Institutes of Race Relations. Johnson had directed earlier versions of the institutes in the 1930s at Swarthmore, Cheney State, and New York University, and that model was carried over to Fisk, starting in 1944 and lasting until 1966. The purpose was to bring together each summer social scientists and leaders of community action groups to study racial problems with a view toward taking practical measures to reduce racial tensions and further equality of opportunity. To that end the major national human rights organizations and nationally recognized political figures, white and black, were invited. The first institute (July 3–21, 1944) set the pattern. There were 137 registrants, almost all southern, whites predominating over blacks about eight to five (this evened out as the years went on). The mixture of participants was itself an achievement; it included, of course, Alexander, Embree, and Fred Brownlee, secretary of the AMA, from the foundations; Charles Houston, the distinguished lawyer who, with Thurgood Marshall, later prepared the case for *Brown;* Robert Weaver, Ira De A. Reid, Guy Johnson, director of the Southern Regional Council, Charles Thompson, dean of Howard's Graduate School, and others from the Washington group. The noted anthropologist Ashley Montagu, Otto Klineberg of Columbia, who had done so much to refute the myth of a racial intelligence, Allison Davis, Helen McLean of the Institute of Psychoanalysis who had dared to treat the "silent subject" in the South, the sexual aspect hidden in white ambivalence toward Negroes, and the Fisk social science faculty—all represented the academic side.

Other noted participants over the years included Lester Granger, director of the Urban League; the historian Eric Williams (later prime minister of Trinidad-Tobago); the psychologists Gordon Allport and Kenneth Clark; courageous southern white liberals like Representative Brooks Hays and Frank Graham; well-known specialists in race relations like Ina C. Brown, Louis Wirth, and Rev. John LaFarge; the distinguished historians Henry Steele Commager and C. Vann Woodward; Willard Townsend and others from the labor movement. (Du Bois and Adam Clayton Powell, Jr., were *not* invited; Johnson thought it simply could not be risked, given the implacable hostility toward Fisk of the white power structure in Nashville.) Martin Luther King came to the final week of Johnson's last institute in 1956 and spoke stirringly about the Montgomery bus boycott, then entering its ninth month. Through the years the workshops on anti-Semitism and on American Indian culture and the Hispanic community were increased. As Patrick Gilpin has observed, the institutes may have been Charles Johnson's most important contribution in race relations, for they established in the heart of the South a continuing forum on the most complex and profound problem troubling the region, where the establishment saw to it that discussion of race was either taboo or suppressed.[12]

And in the later institutes, the participants, men and women of different races, meeting unsegregated on Fisk's campus, did not hesitate to define racial segregation as the South's millstone. Southerners mostly, they insisted desegregation must be the primary goal.

The evolution of the institutes commands our attention even now for another reason—they helped precipitate the first faint cracks in white public opinion on the race issue in the South. At the outset all was as before. The *Nashville Banner* and the *Tennessean* denounced the enterprise as a diabolical plot to undermine "Western civilization and white culture," organized by that "outside agitator" Embree and his Rosenwald Fund. This may have been offset by favorable tributes in the national press, the *New York Times*, for example, noting that the small number of white students attending Fisk, despite the law, had not caused the sky to fall. At the end of the second institute in 1945, the publisher James Stahlman, infuriated by the scandal of interracial residences on the Fisk campus, pressured President Thomas Elsa Jones and the Fisk board to terminate the institutes. For once, Charles Johnson blew up, threatening to resign and go elsewhere, with his associates, if this were allowed.[13] He was backed to the hilt, and at the next year's Institute the "provocative" Embree was especially chosen to give the opening address. And of course the white power elite of Nashville soon realized that the IRR was only talk speaking to power and never could be power challenging power. Moreover, the institutes showed, they came to say, that segregation or no the South was an open society (*pace* "northern radicals") receptive to free exchange in the marketplace of ideas. Until the crisis over implementation of *Brown* escalated in 1955, the institutes functioned in Nashville in a relatively benign climate of white public opinion.

In the 1940s, as in the 1930s, Johnson found time to write three general books on race relations (four, actually, if one counts the *Statistical Atlas* as a book rather than a compilation).[14] In 1943, *To Stem This Tide*, subtitled *A Survey of Racial Tension Areas in the United States*, appeared, written by Charles S. Johnson "and associates" (this time not named), funded by the Rosenwald Fund, and sponsored as well by the AMA's race relations department of the Board of Home Missions of the Congregational Christian church. In his Preface, Fred Brownlee, the AMA general secretary and a close friend of Johnson's, makes it clear, as Embree had in Chicago, that the goal must now be not simply improving race relations but "eliminating segregation as such."[15] Most of the book is just as the subtitle says, a survey of limited gains being made in employment, housing, the law, transportation, services to farmers and tenants, and political participation and, at the same time, obstacles still in the way of further gains. The even-tempered analysis comes within hailing distance of an indictment only in discussing the treatment of Negro soldiers and Negro morale during the war. But even so, after noting some gains such as the prospect for success at last of the anti-poll tax campaign, the effort to get the Red Cross and the army to stop the scientific absurdity of separating blood by race in the blood banks (successful later), and the elimination of racial exclusion in some branches of the armed forces, Johnson ends with his usual tempered, realistic confidence in social change. "In spite of the acute annoyances and racial discriminations of the present, the changing balance is favorable to the Negroes along with other handicapped minorities of the world."[16] And then, the nation must "free itself from those [racial] inequities which it shall have fought a war to eradicate from the world at large." To the text is appended the Durham Statement of Negro leaders (1942) and the Atlanta Statement of southern white liberals (1943). But Johnson makes no comment on the extraordinary debate over the texts which went on in 1942–44 wherein Negro leaders flatly denounced "the principle and practice of compulsory segregation" while the white group made no mention of segregation and used the passive voice to say that "there has been widespread and inexcusable discrimination in the South" which could be corrected by actually making "separate and equal" fully equal.

Charles Johnson's *Patterns of Negro Segregation* also appeared in 1943, a year before the encyclopedic Carnegie Corporation study, Gunnar Myrdal's *An American Dilemma,* of which it is a part. (Originally *Patterns* was one of twenty comprehensive memorandums requested of distinguished scholars on the Negro question by the strategic advisory committee under Myrdal—Shelby M. Harrison, William F. Ogburn, and Donald Young, chair, all, like Myrdal, white. The committee decided to publish some of the manuscripts separately from the overall report.) A highly interesting and extensive literature, practically a cottage industry, has now developed around the division of labor in the research and publication of *American Dilemma.*[17] It need not concern us here except to say that neither Johnson nor Frazier, or any Negro, was ever under consideration to direct the study; nothing had changed in that respect since the Chicago Commission days, although Johnson's 1930 volume, *The Negro in American Civilization,* was Myrdal-like in scope and could have been grounds for considering him. (The corporation's point of view was that choosing an outsider, in this case a Swedish social scientist, would better assure objectivity.) Beyond that obvious fact, the selection of Myrdal, it is clear that Johnson and Myrdal greatly respected each other as social scientists sharing a faith in the power of research and the possibility of change in a democratic society. When the book came out in 1944 and was hailed as "magisterial," even Johnson, who liked Myrdal personally, must have been skeptical of Myrdal's defense of the average white American's intention to become less prejudiced—Johnson did not see all that many of them in Nashville. But he said nothing like that in print. Nor did he criticize Louis Wirth when his old Chicago friend recommended to Myrdal that he choose a young white sociologist, Arnold Rose, and not the much more knowledgeable Horace Cayton, as his chief assistant.

Horace Cayton, sociologist, activist, writer, will always be known for *Black Metropolis,* but he had a long, interesting, and frequently deeply troubled career. He was born in Seattle into a black middle-class family whose journalist father, like Johnson's, had been in a slave family as a small child. He was a delinquent as a youth, leaving school to wander across the country in a four-year journey working at various menial jobs. Eventually he made his way to college, obtaining a B.A. from the University of Washington in 1931. Then as a graduate fellow at the University of Chicago he began an interesting research career though he never finished his doctorate. He worked for Harold Ickes as a special assistant in the New Deal era and had a long series of teaching-research jobs well into the 1960s, including two years at Fisk (1935–36). In the 1940s, he was director of Parkway House, a community center. He brought up to date the research on Chicago he had conducted with W. Lloyd Warner in the 1930s, and wrote an insightful column on race relations for the *Pittsburgh Courier.* He settled in California in the 1960s but lectured across the country. Cayton actively campaigned for the Myrdal job.[18]

What mattered in all this—beyond the parts played by Wirth, Cayton, and the others—was that in the end Johnson and his associates produced the most thorough and comprehensive classification of the commonalities and variations in the practices of racial segregation and discrimination in the South up to that time—at work, in schools, in residential housing, in law, in public accommodations, in the professions, everywhere. Further, drawing on the typological approach in sociology and social psychology developed by the Chicago school, they worked out an insightful typology of the Negro minority's response and counterassertion to this degrading system: acceptance, avoidance, hostility, and aggression. The methodology consisted of integrating a vast amount of material from the literature with interviews so that the Parkean human documents—the voices of those actually experiencing the discrimination—break through periodically to give additional meaning to the tables and descriptions. The basic research was done by associates and assistants, and in his preface Johnson gives full credit to his field staff for the interviews (Lewis Jones, Harry Walker, Joseph Taylor, Edmonia Grant, Anne DeBerry Johnson) and to his colleagues for analysis of the data (Estella Scott, Bingham Dai, Lewis Copeland, Preston Valien, G. Franklin Edwards). Especially revealing are the ways in which whites try to do the right thing in spite of the rigid system and blacks try to adapt without yielding their dignity and self-respect; both are caught in different ways within the iron cage of racial segregation:

> Manager of a hotel in Dayton: We recently let Marian Anderson stay here, but it was all arranged beforehand, so that when she came in she didn't register or come anywhere near the desk. She went right up the elevator to her room and no one knew she was around.

> A Chicago middle-aged, middle-class Negro, refused service in a restaurant: I was plenty hot but I didn't show it. When you show it you lose your point. That's what they are trying to do—make you hot so you'll cuss and start something; then they can have you arrested for disturbing the peace.

> A Negro social worker in Richmond: Every time I went into one of the stores the clerk called me "doctor," so I decided one day to ask about it. . . . The clerk told me that in their training schools they teach their clerks to call Negro men who are well-dressed "doctor." . . . He seemed to think Negro men would be glad to be called "doctor." They didn't know most of us feel like a fool having somebody call us "doctor" when we have not earned the title. They rarely ever give a title to a colored woman.

> The secretary of the Chamber of Commerce in Shreveport, Louisiana: You treat them here as servants. They realize they are subservient and not equal to white people. They say the happiest people in the world would be a cross between a Jew and a Negro; the Jew would always have a dollar and keep it and the Negro would always be happy if he had one.

> An elderly Negro school principal in South Carolina, addressed by whites as "professor" so as not to use the title "Mr.": I address older white men as "Mr." and white women as "Miss" or "Mrs." when I know them and "ma'am" otherwise. Young white men I give "Sir"; I reserve "Mr." for settled men.

At the end of *Patterns,* Johnson makes an important point, against the grain of the Sumnerian argument that social change is slow, that racial discrimination will decline when mores change, not when laws are imposed on society. "To preserve the democratic principle" the federal government has been compelled to impose rigid controls and regulations, to prevent child labor, to assure security in old age, to guarantee a decent minimum wage, and so on. World War II especially has required extensive government regulation. So "before the present war is ended" why should not government do the same thing in race relations "to ensure to all its racial minorities not only free but equal participation in the economic and political life of the country."[19]

As if to counteract the grim news from race country, revealed in *Patterns* in the racial restrictions still imposed on Negroes in World War II, in the backlash of violence and mayhem against Negroes in the South after the war, Johnson published his last significant book in 1947, *Into the Mainstream: A Survey of Best Practices in Race Relations in the South. Best Practices* was supported by the Race Relations Division of the American Missionary Association. Here Johnson's research associates are listed with him on the title page: Elizabeth L. Allen, Horace M. Bond, Margaret McCulloch, and Alma Forrest Polk. Acknowledging that postwar demobilization had been accompanied by considerable racial tension in the South, he hoped some balance could be achieved by emphasizing for a change the credit side of the ledger, the "best practices." The war accelerated the momentum. "It is by no means an ideal situation, but clearly it is not static." To anyone reading this book who experienced the tumultuous events of the 1960s involving civil rights, these pages of Johnson's must seem hopelessly naive and optimistic. But again, this was the 1940s. Johnson had some reason to think things might change. In the years after he died they did. But of course new and complex racial problems presented themselves after that. At the end of the century we still wrestle with them.

Best Practices consists of a series of linked illustrations of "re-awakened concern for the rights and interests of all American citizens through many organizations, local and national." In that sense it is a positive mirror image of the book on segregation. It is dated in one respect because the numerous interracial councils and commissions cited have long been superseded by government agencies, local and national, with power to enforce laws against discrimination, just as Johnson hoped for in the last chapter of *Patterns.* But in another respect it retains some value. For it shows us, at a critical moment in time, in the wake of World War II when many black Americans, veterans in particular, said "this time it is going to be different," they had some reason to believe so. Calamitous events in the South in the 1950s and 1960s severely shook the faith of a new generation of African Americans in the realization of equality of opportunity. But it was not lost. Johnson's book ends on a religious note. "Of all the signs of promise in today's world, none is more heartening than the growing rebellion of youth against the un-Christian [racial] practices of their elders."[20] Sixteen years later, Rev. Martin Luther King, the apostle of religious, nonviolent direct action against southern racism, could recite the litany of "worst practices" in the South—the bombings, the killing of children—and yet go on to say to the thousands assembled in front of the Lincoln Memorial, "I Have a Dream!" to triumph over "the un-Christian [racial] practices" of so many Americans.

In the course of *Best Practices* Johnson cited the organization of the Southern Regional Council in 1944 and the Durham-Atlanta-Richmond conferences in 1942–43 as "the biggest single development in the field of citizenship and race relations in the South within recent years." If that was to some degree hyperbole, it was also true that this activity represented very well what has been called here the regional research-advocacy dimension of his social role. Curiously, there is virtually nothing said in the book about the Southern Conference for Human Welfare (it is simply listed by name, twice). Nor is the electrifying 1938 SCHW interracial conference in Birmingham and the role of Mrs. Roosevelt even mentioned. By 1947 SCHW was already doomed, for it was the chief target of the fury of the white establishment in the South, the very symbol of the "radical" and "commie" influence of "northern outside agitators" (though its white liberal leadership was southern born and bred). Thereafter, Johnson and the southern white liberals in the "respectable" antisegregationist coalition would plan to distance themselves from SCHW. Most did, with a few heroic exceptions, including Clifford and Virginia Durr, Clark Foreman, and Aubrey Williams, all notable New Dealers in the Washington group, all from the South. In any case, in 1946 Johnson was named president of Fisk and needed to reduce participation in all regional advocacy groups, including his board membership in SCHW.

The point is more than academic, for in the very year of the publication of *Best Practices,* the House Un-American Activities Committee

(HUAC), the Keystone Kops of the American political inquisition and the forerunner of the far more dangerous witch-hunters of the 1950s (Senator Joseph McCarthy and the Subcommittee on Internal Security of the Senate, SISS), turned its attention to the South and the insidious doctrine of racial integration. Representative J. Parnell Thomas of the committee issued a report stating that SCHW had passed under the control of the Communist party. While it is true that the small communist faction—the best estimate was 0.4 percent of the membership—did its best to wreck SCHW for its own purposes, just as it had done in the 1930s in the Southern Tenant Farmers Union, this had nothing to do with SCHW's enormously important central goal, to challenge segregation directly and politically and to address the severe economic problems of the region through an alliance with the ever-growing trade union movement. The Thomas report and SCHW's endorsement of Henry Wallace of the Progressive party for president in 1948 sealed its fate. Sponsors and members deserted en masse. The successor SCEF was but a shell of SCHW. Thus ended ignominiously the only serious social-political movement in the South in that time attempting to change fundamentally the conditions of economic poverty and racial exploitation in the "backward" region.[21]

The establishment of the Southern Regional Council and the organization of the conferences at Durham, Atlanta, and Richmond represented a significant step toward resolving the age-old dilemma of the coalition of southern black leaders and southern white liberals: how to overturn the system of southern racial injustice, democratically of course, without alienating the white community. White support was vitally needed, at least for the time being. Both the black and the white groups had to be especially conscious of this problem in wartime because the claim of "hurting the war effort" or "undermining the country's morale" was bound to be used against them. Hence, at the very end of the Durham Statement, with its clarion call, "we are fundamentally opposed to the principle and practice of compulsory segregation," comes the sentence, "It is a wicked notion that the struggle of the Negro for citizenship is a struggle against the best interests of the Nation." It is no accident, as Marxists were wont to say, that the chairman of the editorial drafting committee was Charles S. Johnson, the "conciliatory realist." Other members of the committee included F. D. Patterson, president of Tuskegee, Benjamin Mays, president of Morehouse, Rufus Clement, president of Atlanta University, James Jackson of the Southern Negro

Youth Congress, and P. B. Young, conference chairman and editor of the forceful Negro newspaper *Journal and Guide* of Norfolk, Virginia.

The background of Durham, the debate at the conference, and the final document, have been amply described by Johnson, Mays, and Gordon Hancock, among others.[22] Hancock (1884–1970) was one of the most interesting participants. Born and brought up in a small town in South Carolina, like Johnson the grandchild of slaves and the son of a preacher, he confronted early on the oppressive southern racial system. A terrible lynching and riot took place in the nearby town of Phoenix in 1898 when he was fourteen; an unknown number of Negroes were killed. Education was severely restricted. Not a single real four-year high school for blacks existed in the state, and all the schools were rated third class, the lowest level. Hancock went to Benedict College, a Baptist school in Columbia, South Carolina, and was ordained for the ministry in 1911. But he felt hemmed in, unable to use his talent for theology and sociology. Two white professors at Benedict, Colgate men, persuaded him to go there for an additional B.A. and B.D. At thirty-seven, with an M.A. in sociology from Harvard, he returned south to Virginia Union (Johnson's school) in 1921. The white president had worked hard to recruit him and was able to offer him a salary of $1,200. Arriving at the president's house he and his wife, Marie, were met by the president's sister-in-law. Not knowing him she said they would have to use the back entrance. The president rushed to the door, ushered them in, and apologized profusely. In fact, Virginia Union had an outstanding reputation in the South for the cordial relationship between black and white faculty. Hancock spent the rest of his life as a professor of sociology at Virginia Union and was involved in some of the same advocacy groups as Johnson.

The record of the Durham conference is instructive in revealing how complex and difficult a task it was, in the setting of World War II, for black leaders and southern white liberals to work out a coalition strategy on race. Jessie Daniel Ames, still working as secretary for the nearly moribund Commission on Interracial Cooperation and realizing a new regional advocacy force would have to be brought into being (eventually, the Southern Regional Council), wrote to Hancock. She was interested in his ideas about Negro economic self-help, his pragmatic view of segregation (he was against it but believed black economic development had to come first), his unwillingness to accept W. E. B. Du Bois's more radical argument for separatism (i.e., let segregation stay, Du Bois proposed, but build a black "economic nation within a nation"). She wanted Hancock to convene a conference of black leaders to draft "A New Charter on Race Relations in the South." It would have to be neutral on segregation but would not equivocate on the need to reduce discrimination. The black and white New Dealers in Washington, such as Will Alexander and Clark Foreman, Mary McLeod Bethune, and Robert Weaver should not participate because they were from Washington and Washington did not understand the South. In February 1942, the two met in Richmond. She stayed in the white hotel; he arranged the meeting in the colored YMCA. Hancock organized the conference, and in October 1942, some sixty black leaders met in Durham, North Carolina, reached a consensus after much argument, and drafted the "Charter."

The Durham Statement was indeed, as Johnson argued, a significant document. The segregation issue aside, it called for abolition of every form of racial discrimination: poll tax, white primary, abuse by police, lynching, exclusion from juries, exclusion because of race from employment and union membership, gross inequities in education. It demanded equal participation in all branches of the military, an end to the scandalous inequalities in the distribution of agricultural aid, and more. If the states were unwilling to act, the federal government must. (The only temporizing was curiously on transportation; segregation was accepted only if facilities "were equal in kind and quality.") Before they reached the stage of consensus and signing (December 15, 1942), however, the participants had to undergo a storm of controversy involving the dilemma sketched above. The more militant (militant being a very relative term in the South) roundly criticized the chief planner, Hancock, as "timid." Du Bois, of course, declined the invitation. Northern Negro leaders, purposely excluded by Hancock and Ames, denounced the conference as an agency of appeasement. Ames and other southern white moderates, worried about the segregation issue, nonetheless in the end concurred with all the recommendations. "A difficult job well done," wrote Ames to Hancock. These conflicts, sometimes bitter, over what Hancock grandly termed "the most constructive departure in race relations since the emancipation of the Negro," made much more complicated the next important stage, the response by white southern liberals and, subsequently, the formation of the Southern Regional Council. Nonetheless, the Durham Statement was, for its time, a landmark. Hancock admitted the paragraph on segregation was "weak" but the best that could be done. Even Du Bois said he "would not be unwilling to sign—a pretty good document." Only the ultra-cautious "liberals" like Odum found the document too radical.

The test for Johnson's kind of moderate advocacy would come in the southern liberals' response to Durham. Ames worked hard, endured rebuffs from scores of members of the white establishment—the president of the Atlanta Chamber of Commerce said he would come in only if the conference would produce a ringing endorsement of segregation—and finally was able to hold a conference in Atlanta in April 1943, with 113 southern moderate and liberal white leaders from business, education, and the churches attending. The Atlanta Statement endorsed the Negro struggle for fairness and equity, supported the Durham program for change, except for segregation, and praised its "evolutionary . . . not revolutionary" methods. Not much more could be expected; even the governor of Virginia signed.

But the key would be the forthcoming conference in Richmond, in June 1943, of representatives of the two groups. The segregation dilemma would undoubtedly reappear. In the first place, the thirty-three blacks and twenty-seven whites could meet interracially only in a church; they did so, in the sanctuary of Grace Street Covenant Church, but the two delegations sat apart. The "collaborative" conference soon broke down, mostly because of the conservative white delegation's heated argument that the racial strategy had to be more prudent. Odum saved the day with a conciliatory speech, but he asserted that the only way to form a new council to replace the CIC would be to stress the *regional* character of the program within which the demands for *racial* change could be shaped. The continuing joint committee accepted this and in Atlanta, in November, established the Southern Regional Council, effective January 1, 1944. Howard Odum and Charles Johnson were appointed cochairmen; the board was almost equally black and white. The SRC's goal would be to seek to change "economic, civic, and racial conditions in the South . . . to attain through research and action programs the ideals and practices of equal opportunity." It was a restatement of the Johnsonian research-advocacy role, with all its value and limitations. Minimally, it was better than the CIC.

Yet the dilemma remained for years. The SRC would not declare against segregation; its strategy was a progressive gradualism. The resulting conflict, according to Raymond Gavins, "split the liberals' ranks, spread doubt among black spokesmen, and exposed the racial limitations of regionalism."[23]

Will Alexander knew this position could not stand. He had come a long way from New Deal days and his support of Roosevelt's conciliation of the southern Democratic bloc and the segregationists to provide critical economic aid to Negro Americans. In 1945 he wrote that the SRC must come clean—"abandonment of the old patterns of segregation." But not so for many others still professing to be outspoken southern white liberals but who were in fact still persuaded of the Negro's "inferiority" (even if social, not biological, and even if susceptible to improvement) and who were still totally committed to segregation. A classic case is William T. Couch, director of the University of North Carolina Press, whose pathetic version of white liberalism was published in 1944.[24] As for Charles S. Johnson, who hailed the formation of the SRC in *Into the Main Stream*, published in 1947, without mentioning the failure to carry the Durham Statement on "compulsory segregation" into the SRC creed, there is no doubt of his anger and frustration over this issue. But Johnson being Johnson, he did not let his unwavering opposition to segregation interfere with his other role priority, "research . . . and action" against race prejudice and racial discrimination. The council was organized for that purpose; he stayed with it, on the board and executive committee. He supported the appointment of Ira De A. Reid as associate director. Hancock, too, remained on the board and executive committee, expressing his disappointment in private letters to Ames. Publicly, he would only say that for the time being getting something done would be better than getting something said (about segregation). But the issue could not be laid to rest. The new executive director, Guy B. Johnson of the North Carolina Odum group—Odum remained as SRC president—wrote to Odum in 1945, "We've got to dispose of the segregation dilemma as soon as possible, or it will keep on blocking the future of the Council."[25] The white liberals had to do something.

Eventually they did, after six years of wavering. In 1951, when the tide had already turned and the Truman civil rights program was four years old, the SRC proclaimed in its journal, the *New South* that, indeed "segregation must go." Thereafter, it was far more effective in both aspects of its program—research and action. And after 1954 it could work within an entirely new framework, the Supreme Court decision in *Brown*; the highest tribunal in the land had, in effect, ratified the Durham Statement. From the perspective of the 1990s this complex black-white and white-white controversy seems dated and dusty. Why did not Johnson simply resign or, like Lillian Smith and J. Saunders Redding, refuse to join? It is not difficult to be judgmental. Yet if we are concerned with drawing a balance sheet on Johnson's conception of the role of regional advocacy, we are at least given pause in comparing the short, sad history of the SCHW with that of the SRC. The SCHW put racial integration at the core of its agenda for socioeconomic and racial change in the South. It was destroyed. The SRC tried to be a middle-way voice for liberal whites and blacks seeking to promote equality of opportunity for blacks and promote a greater measure of tolerance among whites. For strategic reasons it postponed for some years confronting the central problem of abolishing racial segregation and demanding racial integration in the South. It survived to live another day and do some good. Their histories are integral to an understanding of the changing South, still debating the economic, social, and political consequences of the racial question. Charles S. Johnson was a central part of the two histories.

The third dimension of Johnson's role of research-advocacy, the effort to connect with Washington and national public policy on race relations, requires a much briefer discussion for the 1940s than for the 1930s. The Great Depression had a direct bearing on Johnson's two preoccupations in the South, the depressed state of the southern rural population (white and black) and the oppressive racial system constricting the lives of black Americans. The New Deal proposed to deal massively and directly with the first and, indirectly, through its economic policies, to make the second a little less oppressive. Moreover, there was in Washington a small but important group of southern white liberals and black middle-level New Dealers who were committed to both economic and racial change. They had worked with Johnson, he had worked with them; together, they could press for racial justice in everything from persuading Harold Ickes to desegregate the Interior Department cafeteria to achieving the passage of the Bankhead farm tenancy legislation.

For the period from the defense boom to the end of World War II, half the decade, however, the dominating problem was the mobilization of the war effort, and the plans of the Washington group had to be subordinated to that, whatever the force of "double V for victory." In addition, Johnson and his approach did not have a central part to play in the small-scale but militant protest movement that *did* arise, led by Randolph and others, whose aim was confrontational strategy to compel the Federal government to insist on obtaining real equality of opportunity in industry and in the vast military structure. Consequently, for those five years, Johnson continued to conduct more research surveys, to pursue advocacy in regional terms in the SCHW or SRC, and to write general books on race relations which outlined what must be done once the war was over and African Americans, his two sons included, came home.

Then, only a year after the end of World War II and demobilization he was appointed president of Fisk University. After twenty-four years as a preeminent black sociologist at the Urban League and Fisk, presiding as chief of the major—some would say the only—social science research center devoted entirely to race relations, he would now have a rather different kind of position, quite broad and general in character.[26] Although he kept a strong hand in the race relations work, in the annual institutes in particular, he would become a statesman of higher education in the 1950s, a voice government and the foundations could turn to when important considerations of race relations impinged on the future of education in the nation at home and in Africa and Asia abroad. How should the more than one hundred historically black colleges make the transition when, inevitably, desegregation of southern higher education arrived? How would a distinguished black educator view the emergence of dynamic new educational changes among "the nations of color" of the Third World?

In early 1946, before the Fisk presidency, he was appointed to the U.S. Advisory Commission on Japanese Education by William Benton, assistant secretary of state. Later that year Benton named him to a national commission on participation in UNESCO and then Benton chose him to be in the delegation to the first UNESCO conference in Paris in November 1946 just when he was named president of Fisk. He was also appointed to national advisory committees for UNICEF, the United Nations children's organization, and to attend the Interior Department's conference on international resources and the U.S. Office of Education council on international education. He served on the Board of Foreign Scholarships (the Fulbright program). He played an important part in the support group the American Association for the United Nations. He was a leading figure at the first assembly in 1948 in Amsterdam of the World Council of Churches. One result was his only book in the 1950s, *Education and the Cultural Crisis* (1951), a collection of essays on the new, changed international context of education. The basic theme was familiar, broadly expressed, written in a rather pedestrian style, but still worth stating: the need for searching, sociological cross-cultural study and interpretation of educational systems wherever they may be found in the world.[27]

In all this activity in the late 1940s only the experience in Japan, and perhaps to some degree in UNESCO, had substantive significance. In Japan, the occupation force under General Douglas MacArthur had the daunting task not simply of rebuilding Japanese education but of democratizing it so that it no longer served as a primary agent of socialization of the young into glorious Japanese nationalism and imperial expansion. On the surface this may have seemed an arrogant and presumptuous mandate to have handed to the twenty-seven-member commission, which spent March and April of 1946 in Japan. Yet, realistically, it falls to the conquerors, not the conquered, to begin the task of restructuring the social order of the defeated nation. In the Japanese case, however, to the surprise of critics of Western ethnocentrism and chauvinists interested solely in punishing Japan for its aggression, the commission charted a sensible course. The recommendations on decentralization, democratic administration, curriculum, and academic freedom did not overturn Japanese education but were grafted to it. Not all the reforms outlasted the occupation; many did. The *Report of the U.S. Education Mission to Japan* exemplified what Johnson would reiterate in his book: the conqueror in ruling the conquered must take into account the sociocultural context of the defeated people, a lesson no less important for being obvious.

Johnson was one of many in the American delegation to the first UNESCO general conference; others included the journalist Anne O'Hare McCormack, the educators George Stoddard, George Shuster, and Milton Eisenhower (Stoddard had chaired the Japanese mission), and Chester Bowles and Anna Rosenberg, representing the liberal, internationalist tradition in the Truman administration. Benton, and the poet Archibald MacLeish chaired the delegation.[28] Essentially, what Johnson did in Paris and at subsequent conferences was to provide that perspective, that sociological cross-cultural view of nations (in particular, the "nonwhite" world of Asia and Africa) which had been with him since the days of the Liberian inquiry. In addition, he found fascinating the complicated, convoluted political maneuvering that made even the high-minded UNESCO activity sometimes resemble the battle over segregation inside the Southern Regional Council.

Johnson without a doubt liked his new role in international education. He found most rewarding and enjoyable his talks with Jawaharlal Nehru in 1949 where race relations figured in the agenda along with educational problems. But, in truth, with the presidency, the continued work in regional advocacy, and the ongoing supervision of the Race Relations Department (though he turned the directorship over to Herman Long), he could not commit heavily to these international organizations.

From 1947 into the next decade Charles Johnson's base in Nashville would be centered on his Fisk presidency, although he maintained a good many of his regional and national activities that gave him his standing in the general and the black communities in America. Critics soon began to say that these other roles were sometimes played out at the expense of his Fisk obligations, a charge that later had some substance. But on the whole he took his responsibility very seriously and set about making something distinctive of the position. Much of the work was routine, however, and that he could delegate to his able associates and assistants, though it was said that he kept too many decisions to himself.

What was not routine was the process of his selection. As celebrated as was his research and advocacy beyond Nashville, at Fisk his administration of the Social Science Department and Race Relations Department was not considered an unmitigated success by everyone. His teaching, when he taught, was not inspired, was average at best. And the day-to-day running of the departments hardly benefited from his frequent absences. Still, over the years, it had to be acknowledged that he had built a strong research and teaching structure and, above all, that he knew how to recruit outstanding social scientists, black and white, as visiting stars and permanent faculty. All the same, in 1946 he could say truthfully, with candor, that he did not think he would be on the final very short list of contenders.

The process got under way in 1945. Long before that colleges had expressed interest in Johnson; he was not interested in them. In 1930, when Frazier and Johnson were on cordial terms, Frazier informed Johnson that Shaw, a private Baptist college in Raleigh, North Carolina, wanted him for its president. He received other offers after that. Late in 1945, Thomas Elsa Jones, a Quaker, who had given twenty years of dedicated service to Fisk, decided to resign and take the presidency at Earlham College, a Quaker institution in Indiana. By the summer of 1946 he was already at his new post and when Johnson became president at Fisk wrote to him, "It is a great joy to know of your being my successor."[29]

In the search to replace Jones, it was clear from the start that Fisk should choose a Negro; that decision was long overdue. But as important as race was the future of Fisk. Jones had been outstanding as president, raising the school's standards, building a good library and expanding the physical plant, doubling enrollment, recruiting an interracial, internationally known faculty, whose racial balance was about two-thirds black, one-third white. Some Fiskites liked to call it "the Negro's Harvard in the South"—a claim disputed by Morehouse in Atlanta. It was the first black school ever to be rated Class-A by the regional accrediting association. If all that were to continue, the next president would have to be a Negro, but he—in 1946 the interracial Board of Trustees would not even think of considering a black woman— would also have to be a man of splendid accomplishment and remarkable organizational talent. Johnson fit the bill.

So did Charles Wesley. The board spent most of 1946 in meetings, at times acrimonious, winnowing the list to the two men. Du Bois worked hard to block Johnson's nomination, and he had influence as Fisk's most distinguished alumnus. (Fisk always had the integrity to do what it wanted to do whatever the outside perception of it; in 1938 it had awarded Du Bois an honorary degree.) Wesley, too, had excellent credentials. A Fisk alumnus, he was president of Wilberforce University in Ohio and had been dean of the graduate school at Howard. He had a doctorate from Harvard, had written extensively about American Negro history, and possessed as many honorary degrees as Johnson. He was somewhat narrower than Johnson as a scholar and like him had been described as a "moderate." Finally, in October 1946 the Board of Trustees chose Johnson. Wesley accepted the presidency of Central State University, down the road from Wilberforce. He lived a long and active scholarly life until his death at ninety-six in 1987.[30]

The battle of the board, lasting for months, was intense, unseemly, and highly partisan along racial lines. Du Bois, for all his greatness, in this affair was excessively combative. He was allied with a black trustee, Dr. Ernest Alexander, and with the president of the Fisk Alumni Association, in behalf of Wesley. Brownlee, Wood, and most of the other white trustees were determined to have Johnson—who was himself determined to get the job (whatever he said publicly to the contrary). Only Wesley seems to have behaved honorably, simply submitting his résumé and agreeing to be nominated; but even he got caught up eventually in Du Bois's strategy. Du Bois threatened publicly in the *Nation* to accuse Johnson, who knew what the social sciences meant for Fisk's national standing, of threatening to resign if Wesley, and not he, were appointed. (Du Bois's article did get printed in the *Nation* on September 7, 1946.) In the end Du Bois accepted defeat with equanimity, despite his anger at the white trustees who he said really wanted a white president but "settled" for Johnson. A week after the battle ended, he wrote to Dr. Alexander (November 5, 1946): "The attitude of those who preferred someone else should be that of complete neutrality and silence. I do not think we should undertake any campaign of ouster. . . . Moreover, there is a possibility that he will make a good president for Fisk. I doubt it, but it may come true. He has the ear of the foundations and will probably get the money that Fisk so sorely needs. He will probably build the university physically and may be able to get a faculty about him of the sort of teacher that Fisk needs. At any rate, the only thing we can do now, it seems to me, is to keep still and give him a chance." Though he waged an equally political fight for the presidency, Johnson was not as manipulative as Du Bois. And five years later, when Du Bois was unjustly indicted on the flimsy charge of failing to register as "the agent of a foreign power," Johnson did not hesitate to take a public stand on his behalf.

It is important to contrast Du Bois's attitude toward Johnson with that of A. Philip Randolph, who was just as militant as Du Bois. He would not call Johnson "reactionary," and he had regarded him as a friend since the days of *Opportunity* and the *Messenger*. But he recognized that the research-advocacy role could not contribute much when militant action was called for. In 1949 he was lining up support for his Committee Against Jim Crowism in the Military. He was very angry, as "the Army told Mr. Johnson [Lewis Johnson, secretary of the army] that it is not eliminating segregation." He foresaw a strong fight in the Congress to get the military desegregation bill passed and, if that failed, another march on Washington. Responding, Johnson pledged his firm support for the congressional fight but doubted the effectiveness of mass marches. If he had lived to witness the 1963 March on Washington he might have changed his mind and come to view mass demonstrations as valuable, along with research-advocacy, in getting things done.[31]

Johnson at least said he was not completely certain he wanted the job. According to Patrick Gilpin, Johnson knew very well that his position in the Social Science and Race Relations departments was in some ways better for him than the presidency. Still, a change might energize him and move him in a new direction. Gilpin's Fisk respondents presented three additional reasons: his wife, Marie, wanted it intensely, as much for herself as for him; a different president might not be as willing as Jones to give Johnson the remarkable autonomy and resources he presently enjoyed; and as president Johnson could strengthen his advocacy role regionally and nationally. Though he remained on the board of the SRC, he left the SCHW. And when the civil rights movement got under way in the 1950s he was wholly supportive but not in a leadership role. At all events, when the board presented the offer, Johnson accepted with alacrity and enthusiasm.

For the remainder of the 1940s the Johnson presidency proceeded with reasonable competency and efficiency. Later there would be difficulties. At a dinner in New York in February 1947, in his honor, he observed that he "had no designs on such a post" up to the moment of nomination. The next morning, a friend, meeting him on the street in New York, said, "Well, this is an interesting break with tradition in the style and content of college presidents. It will be worth watching." Probably so, Johnson agreed. And by the time of the February 1947 dinner he had even arrived at a broad set of goals, not exactly a response to what everyone was asking, "What is your program?", but a kind of guide to his future agenda. It did not differ greatly from what he had said and done for years as a sociologist: he was an "educational realist"—he moved ahead firmly and as swiftly as possible, once the facts were known and the strategy for change was adopted. He believed in the strength of character and moral fiber of young people without losing sight of their problems. He believed, above all, in democracy in education and life, which meant opposing the barriers that inhere in caste, class, race, sex. He knew that any college must connect with, could not be isolated from, community in the widest sense of that term. Interdependence in the world was a fundamental fact. He believed in freedom to conduct scientific inquiry and to choose religion (which he did) or not choose it. And he said that it was necessary to be pragmatic in reaching for these goals at Fisk; method should follow the lead of that professor of engineering who teaches students to build railroads by building railroads.

These were not platitudes; they were Johnson's values. In the actual practice of directing a Fisk education in the late 1940s, however, they translated into some fairly conventional changes and some continuities. He got foundation help to try to decentralize education, establishing little centers of learning around the campus. He continued to attract faculty of excellent caliber. He worked vigorously to maintain the innovative African and Caribbean studies programs and the fruitful exchange relationship with Haiti, although these programs eventually faltered. He built new buildings, substantially expanded the budget and endowment, instituted an honors program, and got for Fisk a chapter of Phi Beta Kappa. And in still keeping a strong hand in the celebrated Fisk social science machine, the research surveys, the Institutes of Race Relations, and the field placements, he helped younger colleagues now directing the work to retain Fisk's national standing as research center and clearinghouse on race relations.

Johnson took up his presidency in the fall of 1946, but it would be nearly a year before he would be officially installed. November 1947 was the time for the inauguration. Given Johnson's national reputation and the friends and associations he had made from Chicago to Harlem to Nashville, the presidential investiture was bound to be impressive. And it was. Congratulations poured in from the highly placed to ordinary families: Randolph, Bethune, Walter White, Hughes, Myrdal, Frazier, William Benton, President Truman, Alexander, Mrs. Roosevelt ("Dear Charlie"), Van Vechten from Renaissance days, as well as the children of the Sunday school of his father's pastorate, the Lee Street Baptist Church of Bristol, Virginia. For an entire week the festivities went on. There were seminars on a wide variety of subjects, a gala concert (Roland Hayes sang at fabled Ryman Auditorium to an unsegregated— a first—audience), an evening of poetry (with Langston Hughes, Arna Bontemps, Bette Lattimer, and Robert Hayden), a reception that packed the Johnson house to the rafters. Johnson was immensely pleased that so many friends who had shared with him the work on race relations and the research-advocacy came to his inauguration: Embree, Brownlee, Reid, Odum, Louis Wirth, Ralph Bunche, Frank Horne, William Hastie (now governor of the Virgin Islands), L. Hollingsworth Wood of the Urban League and the Fisk board. Charles Houston, Percy Julian, Robert Redfield, and Myrdal received honorary degrees. With Houston there it seemed appropriate that on the very day of the inauguration, November 7, a federal judge in Louisiana ruled against a school district paying a black school principal $505 annually while a white teacher with similar credentials was getting $1,575. Finally, Johnson could summon up the names of the many men and women of the Social Science Department, like the Valiens, Lewis Jones, and Eli Marks, whether present at the inaugural or not, who did the statistics and the interviews that created the books.

In his inaugural address Johnson decided not to talk about race and civil rights; that was left to the seminars. Instead, he said what he had said in New York: "I believe in work, justice, freedom, and moral power."

After the ceremony came the work. For exactly ten years he would be president of Fisk. He would be tested as an educator and social scientist in the 1950s, a time we now know was not as bland as first thought. But folded into the new challenge would be the remembered experience of Chicago in 1919, Harlem in 1925, and Macon County, Alabama, in 1933.

VII

FISK: RACE AND
THE SOUTH

Charles S. Johnson lived through some three-fifths of the decade of the 1950s and surely realized that his core theme, continuing change toward equality of opportunity in a democratic society, was still reasonably alive and well. That era has been characterized as one of conservatism, of static tranquillity, if not stagnation. It was called an "age of conformity" dominated by the establishment, with the younger "silent generation" concerned mainly with getting ahead and the working class with getting by. Neither leaders nor followers appeared to have an abiding interest in the grave economic, social, and political problems—including race—facing the nation, the unfinished agenda left by FDR's New Deal and Harry Truman's Fair Deal. Freedom, it was argued, meant *personal* freedom, to climb the job mobility ladder, to escape the trouble of inner city, to move to the suburbs, to have family in a home of one's own.

If the American people worried, it was unnecessarily about some vague "communist menace" abroad and not enough about the disturbing trend toward severe repression of those at home who contended all was *not* well and who tried to say so through political dissent. (The cultural dissenters, the "beats" and rebels with long hair and different lifestyles, fared not much better—but they could get away to subcultural enclaves.) Du Bois, fellow traveler and apologist for Stalinism though he was, could still deliver the proper rebuke on the racial aspects of the anticommunist hysteria. "We want to rule Russia and we cannot control Alabama. We who hate 'niggers' and 'darkies' propose to control a world full of colored people."[1] Such were the asserted dimensions of the age of conformity.

In fact, the reality, in both general conditions and the question of civil rights for racial minorities, was, as Johnson well knew, somewhere between the view of those super-Americans who said about the country "love it or leave it" and the gloomy critics who found American society hopelessly reactionary and socially vacuous, "the bland leading the bland." Johnson, who kept on keeping on with the steady work he had been doing in race relations, saw a degree of positive change early in the decade. Two significant events were symbolic: the Supreme Court was steadily inching away from a misguided effort to get the states to put "equality" seriously, with precision, into "separate and equal" and was moving toward the momentous *Brown* decision declaring racial segregation unconstitutional. And Martin Luther King was developing his nonviolent direct action strategy that would, in 1955, sustain the Montgomery bus boycott started by Rosa Parks and E. D. Nixon. In the picture Johnson drew of the racial situation at mid-decade, after *Brown* and just after Montgomery, however, he cited the continuing high level of violence in the South, the formation of white Citizens Councils all over the region, the murder of Emmett Till in Mississippi, the intimidation of Negroes seeking to register to vote, the massive resistance in the South, despite *Brown,* to desegregation of schools and public accommodations, and the slowness with which employment opportunities were being opened to blacks in an economy that was relatively prosperous and expanding. We now see, in the view of revisionist historians—and history is always being revised—that racism, urban poverty, and repression of political dissent were as much a part of the 1950s as suburbanization and the search for personal happiness.

For Johnson in this context of change and resistance to change, the 1950s were hardly a period of uneventful calm. Beneath the placid surface, Johnson detected a growing determination in the Negro population, a restlessness and anger in particular among younger blacks, that could presage further, more dramatic changes in the 1960s, though he would not live to see them.

Changes would occur not just in race relations. As David Halberstam has observed a social ferment was already at work in the mid-1950s which would transform economic and social life in the next decade and produce tumultuous political conflicts and deep social fissures. Dan Wakefield has expressed this ferment in broad terms: "The time from Ike's election to the coming of the Beatles was a decade in which the taste, politics, mores and culture of our society underwent a deep change, one that not only unleashed the tidal wave of the sixties but formed the patterns from which future decades would flow, shaping the way we live now in the closing years of what began as 'the American century.' "[2]

In sum, the 1950s were more eventful and the conflict over civil rights deeper and more extensive, than we think. It is only because the 1960s were even more eventful that we imagine the previous decade to be a gentle prelude to the storms that came later. It is sometimes forgotten that the first great test of racial integration in the armed forces, the "breakthrough on the color front" as it was called in military metaphor, occurred in battle, in Korea, in 1950–51 at the very start of the decade. In was in 1951, as well, that *Brown* v. *Board of Education* was filed in Topeka, Kansas. Oliver Brown, a black welder, did not understand why his daughter should walk twenty-one blocks to the Negro school when the white school was seven blocks away; he tried to register her, was turned away, then sued. And again, early in the decade, the mountain of research data that Johnson and other social scientists had spent a lifetime compiling began to reach the public more forcefully via the press, which for decades had given race so little play, and especially via television. Now people could *see* the difference between the Robert E. Lee High School on one side of town and Booker T. Washington on the other. There were pictures of the towns where the alleged killers of Emmett Till and Mack Parker in Mississippi lived, and there were pictures of the hooded Klansmen in Alabama, burning their fiery crosses.[3] The fall of the southern bastion, the system of white supremacy, was already under way in the last years of Johnson's life, foreshadowing the further crumbling in the 1960s. As James MacGregor Burns has rightly said, "The storm that gathered during the 1950's was . . . over a transcendent moral and ideological issue. This was freedom for southern and other Negroes."[4] In Washington the battle lines would soon be formed on segregation in the schools and voting rights in the South. President Eisenhower, elected in 1952, and unlike Harry Truman unwilling or unable to change his provincial attitudes about race, resisting mightily, was finally drawn in when, in 1957, he reluctantly sent federal troops to Little Rock, Arkansas, to open Central High School to Negro children blocked from entering by Governor Orville Faubus.

Indeed, the Eisenhower presidency (1952–60) presents a revealing perspective on race relations, illustrating at once the benign and placid side of the 1950s and the decade as a not sufficiently understood era of social action and political conflict. In a sense this contradiction is personified by Dwight Eisenhower himself.[5] Mostly he wanted to do the right thing. But nothing in his early socialization in Kansas, his long career in the military, or his presidency prepared him to relinquish his deep-rooted belief that to end racism, evil though it might be, nothing could be done from Washington; it must occur voluntarily in local communities: "The final battle against intolerance is to be fought, not in the chambers of any legislature, but in the hearts of men," he said in a celebrated speech given at the Hollywood Bowl on October 19, 1956.

His attitude is not surprising; he was insulated from the problem. At West Point, between the Civil War and World War I, thirteen Negroes attended, of whom three graduated. In Panama, where he served, the infamous "gold" and "silver" caste system governed for Panamanians. After World War II, as chief of staff, he testified vehemently against desegregating the military. To his credit, he got passed the Civil Rights Act of 1957, weak and emasculated though it was, the first since Reconstruction, which established the Civil Rights Commission. He saw to it that his special assistant Maxwell Rabb fully implemented the desegregation of Washington restaurants. But at bottom he was not interested. Even at Little Rock his concern was not equal educational opportunity but the challenge to his mandated authority to carry out the law and uphold the Constitution.

To historians of the 1950s the contrast between Eisenhower and the chief justice of the Supreme Court, Earl Warren, is instructive. Warren had been a competent attorney general of California, a man of integrity and fair-mindedness without much concern for civil rights and civil liberties. He had carried out efficiently President Roosevelt's executive order sending Japanese-Americans, citizens and aliens alike, to detention camps, although there was no evidence that they were a threat to national security. (Later, he deeply regretted his involvement in what he realized was an exercise in racism. Once, apologizing yet again to Japanese-Americans for what had been done to them, he burst into tears.) Eisenhower did not really know Warren. At a White House dinner, Eisenhower, noting that John W. Davis, a southern lawyer and counsel for the board of education in the forthcoming *Brown* case before the Court, was also present, addressed the issue. These are good people in the South, he told the chief justice. "All they are concerned about is to see that these sweet little girls are not required to sit in schools alongside some big overgrown Negro." Such barracks humor did not sit well with Warren. In any case, Warren worked energetically to produce a consensus and then unanimity. And he did. In May 1954, the Court held, nine to zero, that racial segregation in public schools was in violation of equal protection in the Fourteenth Amendment. *Brown* v. *Board of*

Education was one of the most momentous cases ever decided in the history of the Court. Eisenhower's comment was characteristic: "The decision set back progress in the South at least 15 years."

Thus, almost squarely at the halfway mark of the 1950s, there was set in motion the change in the South that would redefine forever the race relations of the region and of the nation. "It was, therefore," Halberstam has written, "perhaps the single most important moment in the decade, the moment that separated the old order from the new."[6] The dominion of *Plessy* v. *Ferguson* was over. (Justice John Marshall Harlan's famous dissent in the eight-to-one decision—"our Constitution is color blind"—would be vindicated.) It would be tempting to imagine that when Charles Johnson heard the news he thought of Homer Plessy. In 1892 that black man boarded a train from New Orleans to Covington, Louisiana, in a deliberate test of segregation and was arrested. He claimed his rights under the Fourteenth Amendment were violated—curiously, he also claimed nonapplicability, being "only one-eighth African blood"—but Judge John H. Ferguson ruled against him. Or perhaps Johnson who, among others, helped Thurgood Marshall with background material for the legal brief in *Brown,* remembered that moment when he and his mother, visiting the local pharmacy in Bristol, Virginia, for their weekly ice cream soda, were told that henceforth they would not be served. It is more likely, however, that the king of pragmatists set about immediately making plans for monitoring the desegregation process and for analyzing in his books both the "best practices" and the massive, often ugly and violent resistance that would be part of the South's racial transition, its mid-century passage "into the mainstream."

In view of the eight long years of the Eisenhower administration, with its relative indifference to civil rights, it is not surprising that Johnson's research-advocacy role at the national level was much more limited than in the New Deal era or the Truman period. This is evident in the difference between his participation in the White House Conference on Children and Youth (1950) and in the White House Conference on Children in a Democracy (1940). The report on the 1940 conference, though silent on segregation, is comprehensive in its recommendations on curbing child labor and treating poverty in the minority child population; the 1950 report is more perfunctory, even though this was during the liberal Truman administration. In 1951 the president appointed him to the President's Commission on Health

Needs of the Nation (PCHN). Johnson worked on a small subcommittee on how social science research could show the dimensions of the problem, exactly his research-advocacy role. But given the political conflict over government and health care—the American Medical Association launched a bitter attack against PCHN as taking the nation down the road to "socialized medicine"—the final report, *Building America's Health* (1953), fell far short of recommending minimal requirements to strengthen the nation's health. After the 1952 election, as might be expected, Johnson did not receive any major assignments from the federal government.

From 1948 on, however, he was involved in a major controversy at the national level, fueled by House and Senate investigating committees concerned with civil liberties rather than his central preoccupation, civil rights. The committees, in the name of 100 percent Americanism and the need to ferret out "commies," "subversives," and anyone else guilty of "un-American activities" whatever that might mean, soon found in the universities and colleges a vulnerable target for subversive cleansing. Johnson, in public statements in the 1940s, in responses to the state and national committees, and in private correspondence, did not hesitate to denounce these witch-hunts as much more un-American than the un-American activity being pursued. That is what he told the Tenney Committee, whose official name was Joint Fact-Finding Committee on Un-American Activities, State Senate of California. This mini-version of HUAC had been looking into the "dangerous" movement in the state to organize the farm workers, an extraordinarily difficult task attempted years before Cesar Chavez mounted his challenge in the 1960s. Johnson was a vice-chairman of the National Sharecroppers Fund (NSF) and still a leading member (though no longer on the board) of SCHW, both supportive of this effort and both said to be "communist fronts." NSF had the usual mix of black social scientists, southern white liberals, the Washington group, and northern activists: Johnson, Randolph, Reid, Arthur Raper, Bethune, Frank Graham, Norman Thomas. In his prepared statement to the committee in 1948, Johnson defined the committee itself as "un-American in principle." In this climate of political harassment and loyalty oaths, Johnson was pained to receive messages from friends and colleagues who were being hounded. Ira De A. Reid wrote to him in 1951 with a very unfair complaint. He, Johnson, "one whom I have called friend," must have deliberately sabotaged Reid's application for a State Department assignment by informing the department that Reid was not a good risk. Ridiculous, Johnson responded: "Are you sure this is not a hoax, a bad dream, perhaps an extra glass of beer?" But he was very disturbed. St. Clair Drake, writing to him for a letter of reference for a third Fulbright grant in 1953, told Johnson he feared he would not get it owing to his old membership in the National Negro Congress, now on the attorney general's list of subversive organizations. Again, Johnson felt depressed.[7]

This was his general commendable position. In 1951 the Subcommittee on Internal Security of the Senate, chaired by Senator James Eastland of Mississippi, held hearings in Memphis and alleged that two former communist teachers and a communist student had been at Fisk years ago. Johnson calmly pointed out the meaninglessness of "former," went on to say there were no communists at Fisk presently, and added that unfounded charges by SISS's chief informant were "just another example of smearing" the good name of Fisk. ("No Commies on Fisk Staff, Johnson says," was the headline in the *Nashville Tennessean* the next day, October 27.) Yet he could waver, not out of timidity, he told close friends, but because he feared he might lose vitally needed financial support for Fisk. When Du Bois was indicted in 1951 on the flimsy charge of not registering as an agent of a foreign power (he was easily acquitted less than a year later), he said that worse than the ordeal of the trial was that "most Americans of education and stature did not say a word or move a hand." Johnson *did* speak out publicly against the indictment and in praise of Du Bois. He was the only one of fifty Negro college presidents whom Du Bois knew "who publicly professed belief in my integrity before the trial." But he did not sign the petition circulated nationally, presumably because it was sponsored by a national left-wing association that accepted communists as members. Possibly, he could have worked more strenuously in behalf of this man whom he had called, on the occasion of his eightieth birthday, "the elder brother of the whole colored family." He did not join the handful of other nationally prominent college presidents, such as Robert Hutchins, formerly of Chicago, and Nathan Pusey of Harvard, in openly challenging Senator Joseph McCarthy and the whole phenomenon of McCarthyism. And in one particular instance, the Lorch case, he caved in to pressure, betraying the principle that the political opinions of faculty outside the classroom are protected as part of their academic freedom and cannot be cause for dismissal.

For all his forcefulness in addressing the Tenney Committee, there were intimations that Johnson might not always be willing to defend vigorously civil liberties and academic freedom. In 1949, at a Paris peace conference sponsored by Soviet-front groups, the renowned singer and pro-communist activist Paul Robeson had said that people of color all over the world (including American Negroes) would not be likely to fight in a war against the Soviet Union. The statement was unexceptional in general terms; a number of national black leaders were saying something close to that—the "in spite of" thesis advanced by Johnson and other moderates during World War II was totally inadequate to express their anger over racial injustice everywhere, especially in the military. In coupling this sentiment with an expression of solidarity with the Soviet Union, however, Robeson outraged members of the House Un-American Activities Committee. At subsequent hearings, national Negro leaders were summoned to denounce Robeson and affirm the loyalty of black Americans, which they dutifully did. Alone among them, Jackie Robinson, the great baseball star and the first to integrate the major leagues, chose to instruct the committee on the true problem. Robeson's political views were naive, to say the least, he said, but communism had nothing to do with the real issue, the right of every American, black or white, to denounce the pervasive system of racial discrimination. (His testimony given, Robeson had to return to New York because Washington hotels would not admit Negroes for an overnight stay.)

Johnson, called to testify on alleged communist infiltration into the historically black college system, could have emulated Robinson. Instead, he limited himself to a perfunctory statement that there was no evidence communists were attempting to "impregnate" (infiltrate) these schools. And although he and Eslanda and Paul Robeson had been good friends, he did not defend their First Amendment rights. Nor did he lecture the committee, as did Robinson, on the actual un-American activity, the system of racial discrimination about which he was one of the country's leading authorities.

At about the same time, HUAC turned its attention to a group of young scientists at the Radiation Laboratory at the University of California at Berkeley, a major center for atomic research. Outside the laboratory their politics were on the left, but they had no connection with what HUAC termed "an atomic spy ring." Among those called to testify was Ross Lomanitz, who had left the laboratory to complete a doctorate at Cornell and who had just been hired by Fisk as an associate professor of physics without tenure. Like many others, Lomanitz refused to answer questions under the protection of the Fifth Amendment and was cited for contempt. Johnson then informed Lomanitz that because the contempt charge was still not resolved he would be offered another year's work but it would have to be without a contract. Lomanitz would not accept this condition and left Fisk. In effect, the "offer" was an invitation to resign.[8]

Lee Lorch was a brilliant mathematician and committed teacher who had been dismissed previously from New York University and Pennsylvania State University not only for his leftist political activism but for vigorous denunciation of racist practices. At New York University, for example, he led the fight against Metropolitan Life's exclusion of Negroes from its celebrated development, Stuyvesant Town, where Lorch and his family rented an apartment. He was, by several accounts, exasperating and difficult as a person, but as Justice Oliver Wendell Holmes noted, and Johnson should have realized, it is the difficult cases, not the easy ones, that truly test our resolve to preserve freedom of expression. Johnson, however, gave him a chance when no other school would touch him. (First-rate radical teachers and researchers, blacklisted from jobs in the North, were willing to go South—but obviously not to the "white South." And a few historically black colleges, in need of good faculty, were willing to hire them despite the risk.) Lorch came to Fisk in 1950, quickly rose in the ranks, and became chairman of the mathematics department. On September 15, 1954, the HUAC road show came to Dayton, Ohio, its members described by one writer as "bigots, racists, reactionaries, and sheer buffoons." Lorch was summoned to testify under subpoena. He stated he was not a Communist party member at Fisk but properly took the Fifth Amendment of self-incrimination with respect to previous membership and invoked the First Amendment on HUAC's repression of freedom of speech. The next day, Johnson's statement, released to the press, contended that Lorch's refusal formally to deny past or present membership in the Communist party "is for all practical purposes tantamount to admission of membership" and "under such circumstances Fisk University would have to take prompt steps to release the person." Lorch then had to appear before the Board of Trustees in New York, where he repeated his Dayton statement that HUAC was really interested in shutting down protest in behalf of Negro rights. The hearing and appeals process dragged on, but finally the board voted not to renew Lorch's contract in April 1955. Much later the American Association of University Professors censured Johnson and the board for procedures "lacking in the proper safeguards of academic due process."

The battle then moved to the Fisk campus, where Nelson Fuson of physics and Vivian Henderson of economics (later to become president of Clark University in Atlanta) organized a movement, to no avail, to get Lorch reinstated. The local press and the power elite of Nashville lost no time in initiating a campaign of criticism of Fisk, publicly for "radicalism," actually for being a tribute to interracialism in the midst of a segregated community. Eventually, in Dayton federal district court in November 1957, Lorch was acquitted of contempt, the judge criticizing HUAC's frivolous fishing expeditions. Lorch left to teach at an obscure Negro college in Arkansas and eventually went into exile in Canada. The red-baiting of HUAC and SISS played itself out in the 1950s, as it had in the 1920s and 1930s. McCarthy went down in disgrace and quickly drank himself to death. But the price was high in the incalculable damage done to those whose careers were ended and whose lives were ruined. The stain on the country was indelible.

Johnson knew he had not acted altogether honorably. He felt that to protect Fisk he had no alternative. At the very start of the decade he had written to his old friend, now judge, Hubert Delany: "Some time ago I was invited before the House Committee on Un-American Activities to say something about the feeling of Negroes on the matter of communism. It was prompted by Paul Robeson's remarks which created great concern, in fact, consternation in various quarters. I was impressed by the abnormal hysteria over communism and the inability to distinguish between communism and basic human aims which were condemned because they were akin to Soviet statements of policy. It required a strong character and a clear mind to stay reasonably clear of this hysteria."[9] Judge Delany had written Johnson earlier in the year about a similar hysteria, the curious charge that the sedate, middle-road NAACP had sold out to the communists. In dismissing Lorch, Johnson did not lose his strong character and clear mind—one page does not make a whole volume. But in this case he did not stand up squarely, and he realized it. To Fuson, who with others on the faculty offered to take a cut to make up a salary for Lorch, he admitted Lorch was wronged and repeated that he had to do it for Fisk. Vivian Henderson agreed it was not defensible. "It was out of character for him to handle it as he did. . . . It was one of those things that contributed to his death . . . He brooded over it."[10]

Forty years later it is futile to grade the political integrity of all those caught up in McCarthyism, though it is instructive even now to have before us the roll call of who named names and who refused to speak of anyone except themselves.[11] Johnson decided on a compromise with HUAC; others took an uncompromising position of resistance. The play is now closed, the players gone. Still, it might be in order to print an excerpt from the eloquent statement of Myles Horton, a good friend of Johnson's and a founder of the Highlander Folk School in Tennessee, a labor-affiliated interracial training center and encampment where Martin Luther King lectured and Rosa Parks learned the doctrine of nonviolent direct action before boarding the bus in Montgomery:[12]

Connection with Hearings
Before Subcommittee on
Internal Security of the Senate
Judiciary Committee
New Orleans, Louisiana
March 18, 1954

I do not intend to invoke the 5th Amendment . . . I do not believe that anything I say about myself could possibly incriminate me in a court of law. . . . [However], I shall not and will not engage in any discussion before this Committee with respect to my opinions on people or issues. I will not talk about other people who are not here to protect themselves. I believe . . . the Constitution of the United States protects me in the position I have taken. Congress has no authority to legislate concerning the opinions and beliefs of private citizens. . . . This Committee has no authority to inquire into the opinions and beliefs of private citizens.

Communism has never tempted me because I believe in democracy, a powerful concept worthy of mankind the world over. You know, if you have made any effort to find out, that I have never been a member of the Communist Party. . . .

De-segregation and integration of the public schools would spectacularly refresh the democratic thesis everywhere. The inspiration of such an event would reach into the remotest corners of Asia, and Africa—and Mississippi, and truly would be heard "round the world." For lack of any evident reason, I am compelled to ask whether it is because I have expressed these views and have acted on these principles that I am now hailed before this Committee. . . . But, as an American, I am unwilling to assume that a legislative group bearing the authority of my Government represents the dark and dismal outlook that justified slavery in the dead

154

past and which today equates the fight for the full democratic rights of all men, including Negroes, with Communism.

Johnson's application of the research-advocacy role to racial problems in the South involved a very different controversy from the 1940s into the 1950s not centered on anticommunist hysteria. For now, it became clear that racial segregation itself, and not simply the battle to reduce racial discrimination in education or voting, would be the fundamental focal issue. For Johnson this meant two specific challenges, one under way even before *Brown,* the other following in the wake of the Court's decision. The first concerned the Southern Regional Council, the second the Southern Education Reporting Service (SERS). That other important southern advocacy group in which Johnson was highly placed, the Southern Conference for Human Welfare, had been devastated by HUAC's inquisition and by disruptive internal conflicts, and its successor, the Southern Conference Education Fund, formed in 1947, would have little impact. Its president, the outspoken southern white liberal and New Dealer Aubrey Williams, whose nomination to be head of the Rural Electrification Administration was defeated in the Senate for the usual bogus reasons ("communist sympathies," "race mixing"), retired to a farm near Montgomery, Alabama, to publish a successful magazine, *Southern Farm and Home,* and to try, unsuccessfully, to hold together in the 1950s a militant advanced guard of the southern white liberal coalition.[13] His life, like Johnson's, remains testimony to the South's dying but tenacious grip on its racial system.

Aubrey Williams, unlike some southern white liberals, took an uncompromising position on the segregation question from the start. Born in Springville, Alabama, he came from a family whose earlier generations were slave owners. His family, fallen on hard times, moved to Birmingham, where his father ran a blacksmith shop. He worked from an early age, bypassing school until adulthood. As was true of so many other southern white liberals, the poverty and racism he witnessed turned him away from conventional southern thinking. After attending Maryville College in Tennessee, he went to Europe, serving during the war, first in the Foreign Legion and then with American forces. After finishing college at the University of Cincinnati, he became a social work administrator and activist in Madison, Wisconsin. He came into the New Deal in 1933 as Harry Hopkins's deputy in FERA, the federal relief agency, and then joined the WPA. He was appointed to head the

NYA in 1935. There he and his deputy, Mary McLeod Bethune, pressed their fieldworkers hard (among them the young Lyndon Johnson) to distribute jobs to young blacks as well as whites in the South. But his vigorous stand for integration and civil rights legislation alienated the southern bloc in Congress, and he was forced out in 1943. From the farm in Alabama he helped direct first SCHW and then SCEF. Because he took a different path from the Odums and Alexanders, he encountered great hostility in Alabama. After SISS under Senator Eastland subpoenaed him, as it did Horton, Lorch, and others in 1954 and charged him with promoting "Communism in agriculture," his political influence in behalf of racial integration was effectively over, though he had a role in the Montgomery bus boycott. Sometimes irascible and dogmatic, he was yet honored by some in the South for his political courage. His is the portrait of the prophet who tries to make a region go faster than it wants to go.

The basic problem at SRC was how, if ever, it could become a real force for racial change in the South instead of continuing as an essentially uplift organization devoted to educational programs for improving intergroup relations and promoting interracial cooperation. Nothing could be done until the SRC faced up to the need to challenge segregation directly which was finally accomplished at the very end of the 1940s. This must have been a source of satisfaction for Johnson, who kept silent but hated a situation in which prestigious "progressive" white moderates like Virginius Dabney and Mark Ethridge lent their support to interracial cooperation on the condition that segregation not be on the agenda. (At one juncture, Dabney, the influential editor of the *Richmond Times-Dispatch* suddenly, inexplicably, proposed that transportation be integrated, then quickly withdrew the proposal in the face of opposition.) Now there would be less hypocrisy; ultimately the Dabneys would either have to withdraw or commit to integration, as another white southern liberal, Ralph McGill, editor of the *Atlanta Constitution*, eventually did after much soul searching. Dabney, a southern white liberal, more or less, before *Brown*, ended up close to endorsing "massive resistance," so outraged was he by *Brown*, a case of outsiders "forcing doctrine" on the South. "Southern people," he said on many occasions, "can be persuaded but they can never, under any circumstances, be driven." Predictably, he left the Southern Regional Council.

At the outset, this issue did not trouble the SRC's plans for specific projects. For example, funded substantially by the General Education

Board (the Rockefeller Foundation), the funding worked out by Jackson Davis of the board, and by the Rosenwald, SRC initiated a successful major program that ran from 1945 to 1947 and stayed within segregation boundaries. Eight black men and one white, returning veterans, were sent round to communities in the South to inform returning black soldiers of benefits they could obtain under the GI Bill and Veterans Administration. But by 1947, as racial conditions worsened in the South, SRC began to edge toward opposing segregation. As usual, Johnson pointed the way. In the May 1947 issue of SRC's journal, *New South*, he wrote bluntly, "For the Negro to accept segregation and all its implications as an ultimate solution, would be to accept for all time a definition of himself as something less than his fellow man."[14] But under the new director, George S. Mitchell, who replaced Guy Johnson, SRC still tried to tread a middle path. Denial of rights to black people is the fundamental question, it said, not "dating and use of swimming pools." But denial of job and vote were part of the same problem as exclusion from the library and the hotel room. So, finally, the SRC bit the bullet in 1949. Segregation "in and of itself constitutes discrimination and inequality of treatment," stated the *New South* in May 1949. As the decade of the 1950s ended, the SRC found itself increasingly marginal, its middle way increasingly irrelevant, as the growing civil rights revolution directly confronted the coalition of interest groups committed to "massive resistance."

With the gauntlet laid down by *Brown*, membership dwindled; many so-called white progressive moderates no longer were active. Dabney quit and moved to the other side. Odum, who died just six months after *Brown*, thought the decision unwise, an attempt to hurry social change; he urged measured compliance and confessed himself not up to participating in the process.[15] Alexander, though committed to the desegregation decision, had retired to his farm in North Carolina and he, too, mainly watched from the sidelines. The SRC went on for some years more and issued some important studies. But its founders, including Johnson, recognized that after 1954 its day was basically done. It had been overtaken by events.

SERS, coming later, illuminated as did SRC why the most astute students of the 1950s are right to see in that era the seeds of change as well as the firmament of order and stability. In the months before *Brown*, journalists, educators, foundation directors, and social scientists came together in conference. They established a biracial body, Southern

Education Reporting Service, which would have the critical function of reporting, with scrupulous objectivity, how school desegregation was proceeding in the South, state by state, month by month. The field reports would be brought together in the monthly *Southern School News*. Funding came from the Ford Foundation Fund for the Advancement of Education. Ford had already developed experience in this area, having supported Harry Ashmore, editor of the *Arkansas Gazette* and a genuine southern white liberal with no problem accepting desegregation, in studies of the early stages of transition. The model contemplated was obviously Charles Johnson's well-known *Monthly Summary* of race relations in the South during the 1940s so he would play a strategic role. Naturally, he expected Negro reporters would be employed along with whites and that his associate Bonita Valien would be a key coordinator. Shortly before *Brown* came down, SERS was organized in Nashville, the work to be shared by Fisk, Vanderbilt, and Peabody College of Education. Colbert McKnight, later editor of the *Charlotte Observer*, was chosen as executive director and the board included Dabney, Ashmore, Harvey Branscomb, chancellor at Vanderbilt, Gordon Blackwell of the University of North Carolina, Thomas Waring, editor of the *Charleston News and Courier*, P. B. Young, Phillip Coombs of Ford, and Johnson. Valien was employed as coordinator. SERS performed a valuable service and lasted from 1954 to 1972.

But as with SRC, so with SERS. Both organizations waited too long to confront the segregation issue directly. Johnson, as always maintaining his credo of research in the service of social change, did not see a contradiction between strictly objective reporting and implementation of desegregation, the two functions, of course, related but strictly separated in print, according to the journalistic canon. Dabney, Waring, and other more conservative white "liberals" on the board, assuming segregation would be maintained and, in fact, defending it strenuously in their editorial pages, defined SERS as a strictly neutral vehicle of information. The question of SERS's direction was far more important than technical differences of opinion about journalism. What it came down to, as in the case of SRC, was whether distinguished southern white men and women, of some influence, with the power to reach and teach, were going to help sustain the region they professed to love by coming to terms with a necessary social change or would hold the (crumbling) fortress intact. Ashmore, McGill (later), Frank Graham, and others, in the deepest tradition of southern white liberalism, and its capacity to shape itself to social change, readily accepted the future and continued to work with Negro leaders such as Johnson and Young, as they had before *Brown*. Dabney, Waring, and those of like mind could not. Neither could great numbers of others in state legislatures, governors' offices, and executive suites. Nor could thousands of ordinary white southerners, reared since childhood in the everyday world of separate schools and restaurants in the South.

Frank Porter Graham exemplified the tradition of the more forthright of the southern white liberal group. Born in Fayetteville, North Carolina, he took his undergraduate and law degrees at the University of North Carolina. After further studies in England he returned to the university as professor of history and became president in 1932. Like Johnson, he served on many commissions for the New Deal. At the university he fiercely defended academic freedom, and in the South he earned the extreme hostility of the white supremacists for his work in associations attempting to deal with farm tenancy, race relations, and other social problems. Serving after the war on President Truman's Committee for Civil Rights, he was instrumental in making that report a landmark for its time. In 1949 he was appointed to the Senate to fill out an unexpired term. But when he ran again, he was defeated in the Democratic primary. His enemies had bided their time. The campaign they conducted against Graham, using the racial issue viciously, was said to set a new low in political campaign history. But Graham survived and ended his days as a venerated liberal statesman of the South.[16]

The results of this division between the Grahams and the Dabneys of the South were predictable, as seen in the extensive Johnson correspondence in just the two years between the formation of SERS and his death. He had, from the start, made his view perfectly plain. "The walls of segregation are crumbling," he said in 1954, perhaps too optimistically, in his address "How Soon Will Southern Schools Be Integrated?"[17] So he was not surprised, only further wearied, when he was already wearing down, by all the letters. From Norfolk, P. B. Young wrote to Dabney in Richmond, resigning from the board: "Each board member has a perfect right to take the position his conscience dictates on the matter of racial segregation, but when . . . this leads in the direction of open revolt against the government's highest judicial tribunal, I do not think this can be dissociated in the public mind from the board itself."[18] Johnson wrote at great length to Coombs that Bonita Valien, sociologist-coordinator at headquarters, was not being paid what a white in a comparable position would get; she was eased out eventually for not being sufficiently "objective," despite Johnson's "Dear Phil" letters. In a letter to Claude Barnett, director of the Associated Negro Press, in June 1956, Johnson disagrees with Young about resigning and goes on to restate his own familiar position as a social scientist, a position roundly criticized year after year by more militant Negro leaders but to which he adhered firmly until the very end:

> I am a sociologist with a conscience about factual rectitude and a conscience about keeping the channels of communication open in an increasingly tense situation. Although it is costly in time and gets scant approval in the Negro press, I felt it important to do my fighting in the council chamber where policy is made, and where, if I cannot affect the most extreme member of the council, I can at least influence, with incontrovertible fact, the opinions of others and the resultant output in the publication, that to thousands of persons is received as objective recording. I can see enough effect of this position to make it seem to me something approaching the desertion of an ideal to withdraw from this opportunity. . . . It would be much more pleasant and heroic . . . to be off the Board than on it. But I would rather not run from this fight, unless it convinces me that it is hopeless.

On the other side, T. R. Waring had to take P. B. Young's route, white differing with black, for opposite reasons. A copy of his letter to the editor of the *Augusta* (Georgia) *Courier*, in June 1954, was sent to Johnson. SERS had barely started, but the other editor asserts that "its real purpose is to coordinate the activities of various groups and organizations which seek an end to public school segregation." At that early juncture, Waring responds. He takes it for granted that SERS will remain nonpartisan, strictly factual, not espousing "either point of view." In any case, SERS has nothing to do with the intention of his *News and Courier* to campaign "with all the vigor we possess, to prevent the end of segregation by whatever means may be deemed useful." Vigor or no, however, Waring, Dabney, et al. were already being consigned to history. And SERS, like SRC, would be overtaken by events.

If neither national nor regional research-advocacy retained their previous significance for Johnson between 1950 and 1956, then the Fisk presidency would have to place the final stamp on his life's work. To be sure, the celebrated national role as chief mediator for the grants and the money continued apace. Embree had closed out the Rosenwald Fund in 1948. There was less to do with the Rockefeller, but now the Ford Foundation and the new John Hay Whitney Foundation occupied his attention. Even so, the work now with the philanthropic foundations had to be fitted to the presidency, not the other way around.

The assessment of the opening years of the presidency, 1947–50, had been generally favorable, mixed with some criticism, as noted in the previous chapter. Johnson thought he had done a commendable job in the late 1940s, and he continued to think so in the 1950s. His evaluation seems to have been reasonably correct, although the balance changed to a degree, with some increase in criticism. His strengths remained— the building up of the physical plant and the financial endowment, the establishment of special programs for freshmen and honors students, the comprehensive courses in the social sciences. Although the African and Caribbean programs foundered later and had to be reinforced and restructured, there is no doubt that they constituted an achievement, especially in view of the fact that it would not be until the 1960s that other schools, large and small, discovered the Third World and the richness of African American culture. The annual Institutes on Race Relations continued to have a real impact in Tennessee and beyond. Herman Long was now director; Johnson could still be depended upon to bring in the stars. And consistently, as he had done in the 1930s and 1940s within the framework of the social sciences, he succeeded in attracting some outstanding faculty and, as usual, substantial financial support from the foundations.

He was an asset to Fisk, nationally and internationally, wherever he went. For example, on the eve of his inauguration he was in Paris, delegate to the first UNESCO conference; naturally, he sought out physical and social scientists possibly interested in coming to Fisk. As a result, the French physical chemist Marie-Louise Josian arrived. Percy Julian, distinguished chemist, business leader, and a trustee of Fisk, persuaded her to undertake infrared spectroscopy research. This led to the Fisk annual institute in spectroscopy which year after year attracted international attention. Similar recruitments happened more than once. Johnson was good at it. Fisk's mission was his mission.[19]

But problems increased along with the accomplishments. Many were externally caused, not of his making, for example, the Nashville problem and the perception of Fisk by the community. The mayor and the governor were honored guests at Johnson's inauguration. But in the more than a quarter of a century of his tenure at Fisk and in the twenty years since E. Franklin Frazier dared to attend a Chicago alumni luncheon in the Vanderbilt University cafeteria, to the consternation of the assembled whites, it is astonishing that so little change occurred in the relationship of Fisk to the white community and to Vanderbilt University, only a short distance away, a half hour walk from Fisk but for years not ready to invite him socially to the campus.[20] And, of course, segregation of facilities downtown, lasting into the 1950s reminded Johnson and faculty and staff families, black and white, that *Brown* notwithstanding, it was still the South. Even in the 1970s, after desegregation, in casual conversation, whites in Nashville would say, when race came up, "you know, they really want to be with their own, that's all, just like us." As older faculty members reminded me, leaving the campus in Nashville in the 1940s and 1950s was like entering another world. On occasion a white professor would ride the bus in back to be with peers. All this meant that however famous he was in New York and Chicago, Johnson did not have in Nashville the necessarily important bond with the white establishment that went automatically to Vanderbilt in support of its library and football stadium.

Administratively, however, some problems were internal and at least in part attributable to Johnson's style. A few complaints carried over from the 1940s: he was away too much (less true in the last years), he was too distant and sometimes haughty, he let mundane but necessary day-to-day details slide, he did not sufficiently honor departmental autonomy and especially the need for a cooperative relationship with chairpersons. Even Embree, the closest of friends, with immense respect for Johnson (which was reciprocated), needed on occasion to get beyond his usual comment that Johnson must be doing things right because conservatives thought him too radical and radicals too conservative. Addressing the matter in the late 1940s, Embree conceded that perhaps Johnson might work too closely with "powerful white interests," but how else should he get the resources to do important studies? He drove his staff too hard—they knew the man's integrity and remained fervently loyal. He was too serious, unbending, but he was not compulsively driven, stayed calm in crises, and made sure his family got plenty of unhurried time. To Johnson's friend and colleague of the 1950s, Leslie Collins of the English Department, author of a comprehensive study of the Harlem Renaissance, however, he seemed indeed too distant and remote, with little trace of the amiable man of the Renaissance who loved jazz at the clubs.[21] Part of this was no doubt because of his forbidding secretary ("Johnson's guard dog") and his assistant Bonita Valien ("Johnson's dragon"), who overprotected him. Part was his own inclination.

To these administrative difficulties was added a somewhat nettlesome relationship with the trustees, some of whom felt he had too much freedom on the budget, carried over from social science days, and was not effective enough in raising money and raising buildings, despite evidence to the contrary. A few faculty, resentful of his national standing and what they felt to be his neglect of internal problems, allegedly had the ear of the trustees. The board had trust in Johnson but wanted him to be more of an on-campus president of Fisk.

Whatever the justice of these complaints and rumors of complaints, Johnson was not deterred from shaping the presidency as he saw the challenge. When he was cut off prematurely at sixty-three he was in the process of working out ideas to energize Fisk and the presidency anew. At the end in 1956, though fatigued physically and not thrilled with the routinized aspects of college bureaucracy, he still continued to look ahead. He still appreciated, he said, Daniel Burnham's blueprint for the turn-of-the-century Chicago World's Fair: make no little plans. And he still considered that he was an effective president of Fisk University.

Besides, as before, he had his circle of friends and family to sustain him. The mountain of personal correspondence in the 1950s was no less than in the previous decade; much of it displayed a tone of warmth and affection that very few were allowed to see in the presidential office on campus. His note to Gordon Hancock on the occasion of his retirement was as gracious as President Truman's to him when he was inaugurated. The oldest and most trusted friends, like Aaron Douglas and Arna Bontemps, were, of course, at Fisk, but others from Renaissance days, like Langston Hughes, continued to visit and write, as in the 1940s. In 1945 he had written an engaging letter to "Charles" from "Langston." *Sewanee Review*, the staid southern literary review put out by Allen Tate and other southern "Fugitives," had established a literary contest and had asked Johnson to recommend Negro writers from the South. Hughes did not know if he qualified geographically but would send some names. Then he remembered Tate's reply to an invitation to a party to be given in Nashville following a poetry reading by Hughes and James Weldon Johnson in the 1930s. Tate said that "perhaps he might attend such a mixed party in New York but never in the South as such things were simply not done there."[22]

A decade later, Lillian Smith wrote from her Clayton, Georgia, home, thanking him for inviting her to Fisk, touched and grateful for the Johnsons' hospitality: "I got much more than I gave. I loved every minute of it." Severely ill with cancer, she still wants to lay out "our northern liberal friends" who say that now *Brown* has come down, we should go easier, we should understand and sympathize with the "poor white southerners having to go through the 'ordeal' of change." How about the poor colored southerners, she asks, and their ordeal? She is even harder on the southern white liberals of the SRC group who accept the inevitability of desegregation and integration but think it should come about more slowly, by "erosion," not by the courts. Then she writes:[23]

> At Emory Hospital, in the Winship Cancer Clinic where I seem to spend a large portion of my time, there is a corridor where we cancer patients sit. It is lined with all those people, some almost dead, all sick, all worried even though trying to be tremulously hopeful. There we sit: malignant human beings. And down the corridor, a few steps, there is a drinking fountain with a sign over it *For Whites Only*. There is not a Negro patient in Winship. Yet that sign is up. And we cancer patients, gnawed on by our disease, sit there looking at each other and every once in a while one of us gets up and walks over to the drinking fountain for a sip of water. I wonder how many of them take pleasure in seeing that sign. How many of them, facing their dread disease, care now about white supremacy. I want to ask them, Do you care? Does it make any difference to you now? We are levelled down pretty low by this cancer business, do you still think you are superior because you have a white skin? But if I said it, I suspect the Emory authorities would think I had lost my mind and should not be there. Ah . . . what a world we live in. What a world.
>
> My very warm regards to you, to Marie, and to all the nice people I know at Fisk.
>
> Sincerely,
Lil

Not all the friends were still there. Nearing and then passing sixty, we think of our own mortality as older friends begin to go. Park died in 1944; Johnson wrote the tribute. But Park was one generation back. Embree, as close a friend as Johnson ever had, died in 1950. Again, Johnson wrote the tribute, prefacing what he wrote substantively with that familiar, moving line: "So many virtues joined in him as we can scarce pick here and there in history." "No man in America," he said, "has shown greater understanding and zeal for democracy. . . . It was this understanding and zeal, aided by personal courage, that carried him into the tangled emotional area of race in America."[24] And as one would have expected, Johnson repeated a favorite anecdote of both men. They were in Gee's Bend, Alabama, way out in the country, an all-black little community, trying to explain to an old man why they were there, to work on *Shadow*. Embree and others spoke, "but he just looked blank. Then, seeing Doctor Johnson, his face lighted up and he called: 'Mistuh Johnson! Mistuh Johnson! Come on over hyar and understan' 'em fer me.' That was the highest tribute I ever heard paid to a sociologist. 'Understan' 'em fer us' is just what Dr. Johnson has spent his life doing."[25] Odum died in 1954, shortly after *Brown*, and Johnson chose to remember not the excessive caution in delaying coming out against segregation until so late but rather the basic honesty and decency of the man, the many sociological ideas they shared, and the way they both worked to bring general concept to research fruition. Alexander died in January 1956, just nine months before Johnson; his death brought to an end the odyssey of a historic trio—Johnson, Embree, Alexander— each different in personality, all committed to biracial work and the battle against discrimination for forty years and more. Speaking at the dedication of the new library at Dillard University in 1961, named for "Dr. Will," Robert Weaver might have had all three men in mind when he said Alexander was seeking the key "to unlock so many doors of opportunity for southerners of both races and all conditions."

Through the years in the social sciences and then in the presidency, family was always the rock, the solid foundation for his work and career. He had seen the children through; now even the youngest, Jeh Vincent, had gone off to college; he would go on to the Columbia School of Architecture and the practice of architecture. They were all adults by this time. Charles, the oldest, had tried Virginia Union, his father's school, for a year but did not do well—the family joke was that he became E-d-d-i-e, renamed for his grades—returned to Nashville and Fisk and did very well there and at Meharry Medical School, across from the Fisk campus. He moved to Dayton, Ohio, to practice medicine, married, and had two children. Robert (Bobby) had his difficulties, but, with therapy, struggled through valiantly. His father was proud of his career choice, not only sociology but race relations in particular. He completed his doctorate at Cornell; his research was original, his articles well-written. But there were bouts of depression. With his excellent credentials he had a choice of research positions. In 1954 he was working for the American Friends Service Committee, which was fine for him because the position combined sociological research with his commitment to the Friends' spiritual philosophy, "what altruistic love is all about," as he wrote to his father. In that letter he asked for advice about his career. He had a Russell Sage grant, and the foundation wanted him to stay on. Thurgood Marshall at the NAACP had offered him a job in research in the field, and he was part of the strategy team assembled by the NAACP to decide how *Brown* should be implemented. Professionally and personally Bob was caught up in the excitement: "I personally want to know a lot more about whether you desegregate schools gradually or immediately . . . how you make desegregation an occasion for maximal new learning and growth."[26] He moved ahead in his career, but, sensitive and vulnerable, he could maintain only a fragile psychological balance. In the early 1960s he married again and started a teaching career in sociology at Central State College (now University). He died there in 1965; he was only forty-three.[27]

Patricia, the only girl, chose Fisk too. After college she started in the social work field, married a doctor, and settled in Philadelphia. There were three grandchildren; Johnson often described the joyous visits to Philadelphia. Basically, Patricia Johnson Clifford saw herself as wife, mother, and social activist. A handsome, dynamic woman, she was fulfilled in working with community organizations in Philadelphia and participating in the Germantown historic preservation project. For years she was a strong force in the Fisk Alumnae Association.

Marie, Johnson's wife, had now been at his side for more than thirty years. For all the criticism of her regal airs, her "imperial" personality as Fisk's first lady, there is no doubt of the strength of their long partnership together, the closeness of the Johnson family life. As Embree said, she gave full meaning to the old folk word, "helpmeet." She presided skillfully over an extremely busy household; always there were visitors. G. Franklin Edwards, who worked in the Johnson home as did other students, has described the stream of visitors and the challenging conversation that went on. (The home was expanded in the early 1950s when Julia Johnson, Charles's sister, a social worker and schoolteacher who had been living in Tuskegee, became ill and had to be moved to Nashville. Independent, never married, and a lively storyteller, her favorite story about Charles concerned his birth. She claimed he was rushed up to the third floor to fulfill the old folk myth that an infant held very high will be "high" in achievement later in life.) Busy as Johnson was, "his wife and his three sons and one daughter get more easy fellowship from him than many families where the father doesn't do a thing," Embree said.[28]

It is surprising, then, that a brief period of intense strain in the 1950s, at one point nearly breaking up the marriage, represented a sharp divide in the story of a long, happy marriage and family life. There was no reason to anticipate this trouble. Always, when he was away, Charles would write or call, at times daily, using terms such as "My dear lovely lady" and "my dear you." After describing details of boring or interesting people and places, he would add, "I would be infinitely happier if you were with me." At the plenary session of the first UNESCO conference in Paris in 1946, when his big moment arrived, his speech to the delegates "representing the entire arsenal of the social sciences," he could scarcely wait to write to Marie: "Dearly beloved, the presentation came through in very good form. Archibald MacLeish said it had the elements of poetry as well as the dynamics of determined action."[29]

In the fall of 1952, however, Marie inexplicably seemed to become obsessed with what had always been his normal work pattern—late hours at the office, frequent travel on Rosenwald, AMA, or Whitney business, commitment to research projects, conferences, and meetings across the country. Why was all that frantic activity necessary? Could it even be there might be infidelity? Where was he on certain days and what was he doing? Why Marie should have turned on him, in near-paranoia, for a work pattern she had shared amicably with him for years is uncertain. Perhaps, with the children grown and away, she found life too constricting, even as the wife of the president of Fisk. In Chicago, at the outset, she was the dynamic one, correcting the prose style in the Chicago race relations report, teaching the shy young social scientist how to dance with verve. Then she had willingly given up her own possible career in music, theater, and education. Whatever the explanation, it was a deep and serious rift.

The accusations were not true. Just the same, Johnson was bewildered, upset, and uncharacteristically, at times, very angry. Why did she think his activity at the office and in New York and Chicago was anything other than ordinary routine? Why did she continue her irrational skepticism? In October 1952, he wrote of being "impatient and riled. Why must I, in the midst of very active large events that make heavy demands, have to stay on my knees pleading for tolerance regarding things that have never entered my life and never will." Even so, he writes, she should never doubt "my worship, my admiration, and my love." He considers that "the roots of this disturbance are not entirely in my own life" and adds his own possible explanation: "I have failed in some way to do proper honor to your career as an individual. This I hope to correct, God helping me. Good night, my love, Charles." Clearly, Marie Johnson was having a late midlife identity crisis, and Charles Johnson did not know how to handle it, except to promise he would understand and love her for her own self and not simply as his wife and mother to their children.

Johnson being Johnson, even these emotional, heartfelt comments were accompanied by the usual running accounts of his activity as social scientist, mediator between foundation and research body, national and regional advocate for Negro civil rights. On the road the demands on him were as heavy as at home. He writes on the train from Memphis to Birmingham that the Nashville American Legion is mounting a campaign to prevent Langston Hughes from giving a poetry reading. "My answer to them is of course that Langston Hughes appears and reads his poetry as scheduled." He writes about research and how sister Julia is doing at Tuskegee, from "the empty and rather soiled 'colored' waiting room in Anniston, Alabama, the station for Talladega College." From Washington, D.C., where he will be at a meeting of the National Conference of Christians and Jews, he writes that he is extremely worried by the Republican presidential victory. Even though more money might possibly be distributed as a salve for the conservative conscience, "the cause of racial integration is endangered." Writing from New York, where he has seen Jeh at school, he is very hopeful of obtaining $150,000 from the Ford Foundation and $25,000 more from the General Education Board in support of various experimental programs at Fisk. Having to be away at Thanksgiving prompts a warm letter to "Dear Mother and Children" on how grateful he is for his family, important, as they know, "beyond the turkey and the cranberry sauce."

In Atlanta, looking for money from the white establishment, he writes that he is not letting himself build up his hopes for the Supreme Court on *Brown*. But if and when it comes, as he thinks it will in the near future, "it will be time for a buildup," a mobilization for a great new challenge. Back in Washington in late 1952 he hears that the president-elect "may have an important appointment for me in his apron pocket, as a person skilled in human relations." Nothing came of this, as Johnson surely should have expected. John Hay Whitney had recommended him, and the president reportedly responded that the two Negroes he was going to rely on most heavily were Ralph Bunche and Charles Johnson. It is possible that Johnson may have been derailed by his association with the Ford Foundation—sponsored Fund for the Republic in Pasadena (later the connection was severed) and Clarence Faust and the Ford Foundation in New York. The know-nothing committees in the Congress had now gone after the foundations as subversives with money. Just as well, Johnson might have thought. Frederick Morrow, an able and amiable man of that rare species, black Republican, had been appointed as "the Negro" in the administration. As it turned out, he could not get an apartment in Washington until the administration intervened at the highest level, and he wound up with a limited, minor position at the White House.

At the end of the year 1952, the brief but intensely emotional storm had blown over and Johnson could return in his letters to the regular traveling routine, searching for grants, organizing committees in behalf of civil rights, and trying to figure out how a Negro gets a meal in the dining room of such hotels as the Biltmore in Atlanta. His "hello, ma honey" was no longer followed by words of angst and pain. On the eve of Christmas 1952 he wrote to Marie, from Charleston, West Virginia, "When there is no news to report I can always settle down to the eternal verities and my favorite verity is you and the cord that unites us in one circulation system of a very beautiful passion . . . living with you adds up to something both great and grand." And he recognized at last some justice in what she had been saying. "Lord! Lord! *I am full-up of advocacy.* I want the chance to relax and be a person and a solicitous and loved husband, out of the swift channels of trade." In the end their brief crisis was a catharsis for both, showing them how to weather inevitable strains that could, paradoxically, make the bond between them stronger and more enduring.

In the three years left to him, 1953–56, Johnson did indeed endeavor to strike a better balance between work and home. He reduced to a degree the innumerable connections to national and regional associations. He still undertook the many, many journeys, but he could work into his itinerary family visits and play with the grandchildren in Philadelphia and Dayton. It was especially gratifying that Robert came to the 1954 Institute of Race Relations ("Dad, I wouldn't miss it") to participate and to discuss with his father a subject about which Johnson had vast experience: how to implement social change after *Brown*. The Supreme Court decision reenergized Johnson and set him to new tasks of research and advocacy. It would take two years of "massive resistance" in the region, of continuing brutal assaults on Negroes, of a dragging of heels on the part of some of his lifetime allies, the southern white liberals and moderates in the struggle over desegregation, to diminish his optimism and increase his pessimism.

The letters to Marie Johnson from "your devoted husband" were, as before, a reflection of all this. Johnson kept among the associations a firm participation in the national Congregational Christian church and the American Missionary Association, the "parent" of Fisk, Talladega, and other Negro colleges. He needed AMA support for putting up the new social science building to be named for Park. He announced to her he was now sure of the grants from Ford and Whitney. The Institutes of Race Relations in 1953 and 1954 were especially fruitful. At the 1953 institute, she would be pleased to hear, Johnson wrote, that Thurgood Marshall told him "Bobby had made a great impact on the sociology department at Cornell," a place, Marshall could not help pointing out, "that did not want Jews around, much less Negroes, some ten years ago."

Late in 1953 Marie Johnson had to undergo a serious operation in Philadelphia (chosen because Dr. Clifford and the family were there). Johnson was obliged to remain in Nashville, but he wrote to her almost daily, expressing both his concern and his love: "I am in love with an awful pretty gal who means so much to me." Without her he feels like "the separated twin with the top of his head cut off." To encourage Marie and cheer her up he summons his old friend-adversary: "Brother Du Bois, I recall, had lots of pruning and sewing done about 25 years ago and here he is barging toward 90." Johnson, perhaps still smarting from the punishing campaign Brother Du Bois conducted against him over the Fisk presidency, cannot help adding a scalding postscript, though Du Bois had been tried and acquitted of the foolish foreign-agent charge some two years before. "Incidentally, he just won't stop playing in the mud. He was awarded the Stalin Peace Prize, I understand, and was a chief mourner at the funeral of the Rosenbergs. (The latter is all right if he knew them.)" This was, sadly, the Johnson of the Lorch case speaking, not the Johnson who laid into the Tenney Committee.

With Mrs. Johnson returning—and able to help him straighten out the work of the secretaries—Johnson resumed his busy schedule, though not at the old pace. (He had air-conditioning put in the house as a surprise coming-home gift for her.) But then there is a shock; at the end of 1953 there was a recurrence of her psychological problems, an emotional upheaval even more intense than before. There were periods of calm, but then she would be caught up again in what Johnson called her "terrible sickness." He told himself he would have to be even more understanding, "to fill out the emptiness of the children gone." He faced up to "two inescapable alternatives: absence on a trip under a cloud of horrifying and humiliating suspicion of uninviting and indecent behavior . . . and at home together under constant petulance, checking of words, accusations and indifference, selfishness, and shortcomings." He even wondered whether it might be better if the charge of "faith-lessness" were actually true instead of false; at least it would allow her "the right to martyrdom."

There was something more. In a way it transcended Mrs. Johnson's erratic and disturbing behavior and had to do with him. When Mrs. Johnson wrote that she might possibly get a job and leave home and coupled that with venting her fury against the Whitneys and the Whitney Foundation, one reason for so many trips to New York, Johnson realized what was at stake, the bridging role with the foundations he had played so long and so well that it was practically second nature to him.

Funding from the Whitney Foundation was vital to his plans for Fisk and for himself and Marie in the retirement years after Fisk. Having "neither solvency nor savings," he needed assistance for the last years "if I live that long." That demanded, however, not only long discussions at the office in New York but a good deal of socializing as well. For "Jock" Whitney, who was more than willing to give money, wanted also to talk at length after hours—about life and the meaning of life and what he could do to make the rest of his more meaningful. He was happy to be asked to give the commencement speech at Fisk, but that was incidental to making some deeper commitment with all his money. Johnson could help him to shape that. He had wasted too many years, put too much money into things that had no deeper purpose. Now, Johnson wrote to his wife, Whitney told him the foundation "had given him a real reason for living." A lasting contribution to education, to interracial education, and human relations could be his legacy. He wanted more for Johnson, too, in the process. That helps to explain "the Eisenhower thing."

Jock Whitney was an interesting and complex businessman-publisher of the *Herald Tribune* and a philanthropist, with considerable political influence in the Republican party. (He later was appointed ambassador to Britain.) Close to the president, Whitney was high in his praise for Johnson; he spoke to Eisenhower of his own new direction and how much a part of it Johnson was. His strong praise for the president of Fisk was communicated directly to the president of the United States. At the end of 1952, Johnson wrote to his wife, "The President-elect was both surprised and interested in the concern of the person to whom he was most indebted for the election." An exaggeration, certainly, but Whitney did have the essential access to power. Johnson looked for a possible result. It never came.

Yet the question of the Whitney, and Whitney himself, needs consideration from the point of view of Mrs. Johnson as well. For too many years she had watched him travel back and forth, and back again, working matters out with the Rosenwald and the AMA; now the Whitney and the Ford were taking up large amounts of his time and energy. It infuriated her when he reported that after an immense amount of work and, he admitted, a certain amount of flattery, it looked as if *they* were winning. Their stock in the strategic Whitney family was now "high." It could go higher, with more time and effort. He and Whitney were good friends, though each in a way was using the other. He needed only three or four more years to make the Fisk presidency truly outstanding; to do it required this kind of breakthrough.

All his life, especially in the exhilarating Harlem days, Charles Johnson had functioned well in the bridging and negotiating role. It was important, and he did it. He still needed to, for just a short time more. Would she have him stop traveling to New York, he asked her? Would she have him resign from the presidency? "I do not want to give up the job, but the choice is rapidly approaching a crisis." If she left him, he would not be able to carry on the difficult work in Nashville and New York. But nothing had really changed for him: now "my love and my constancy have their greatest test. At 60 I believe I deserve better. If you are unhappy . . . it can only be because you want to be something different from your role as my wife, and this I cannot help. I can only be the best husband I know how to be."

Happily, the second storm ended as the first, in reconciliation and the resumption of a good life at home. Still, it had taken something from him—a certain zest (controlled though he might have been), a spring from his step, a greater reluctance to make those journeys by train that he had once taken in stride. If he was content again, he knew nonetheless he would write no more general books on race relations nor oversee complex research projects. His pride and joy, the Race Relations Department, was functioning adequately in new hands; that would have to be enough. At the start of 1954 he was already complaining of fatigue and periodic exhaustion. In Memphis, his speech to the Negro Secondary and College Association seemed to him "the most impassioned laying out of facts and philosophy that I have achieved in one presentation." Yet afterward he felt totally drained—"can't keep this up." (Interestingly, the parallel white association was meeting at the same time down the way. The "white group shut itself in the Peabody Hotel" and would not even consider the idea of a joint session.)[30] Increasingly tired though he was, however, he was buoyed by the pleasures of good home life once again. In July 1956, just three months before he died, he wrote to Marie of his "profound tiredness," yet he preferred to dwell on the warm memories of thirty-six years of "going steady." "You have no idea of how delightful you can be when you want to be and that is often enough for my happiness." Life, once again, was in balance. He could work, he could go home, and Mary Jane Hatfield, who cooked so well for the Johnsons, for "the Virginia Gentleman at Home," could prepare his favorite—old-fashioned Virginia steak with biscuits and stewed tomatoes.

In the last two years, despite the physical problems and the fatigue, he felt his stewardship as Fisk president was proceeding well. He had increased the endowment once more, brought in the foundation support once more. Some of the faculty criticism might be acknowledged privately; the irritations and certain difficulties in the relationship with the Board of Trustees would be dealt with in time; Heritage House and the residences could use further refurbishing. But none of this was major. Fisk University remained among the best of the Negro colleges and could certainly invite comparison with mainstream schools of its type and size. The twenty-seven years of work from the Nashville base had produced a substantial contribution in the form of research-advocacy. The Whitney consultantship was achieved at good pay. No matter he didn't get paid anything for working with Thurgood Marshall on the preparation of the argument for *Brown* two years before. A truly great decision! He had his wry humor ready for that one: "I got satisfaction out of this," he wrote to Marie, "although perhaps the only non-paid documenter."

173

Well prepared, as usual, he boarded the train at Nashville for the meeting of the Board of Trustees in New York. At Louisville, changing trains, he died on the platform. It was October 27, 1956. A week later, in the *New York Amsterdam News*, Lester Granger, executive director of the Urban League and an old friend, wrote: "We are saddened by the loss of skilled leadership and persuasive diplomacy at the very time when the national racial scene demands these qualities most desperately. There are still those who sneer at the art of persuasion as something weak-kneed. And so it can be, of course. However, in the case of Charles Johnson there could never be any such suspicion. He had all of the normal man's ambition, naturally, but the main purpose of his life's work was always clear; it was to dissipate the ghost of social superstition by letting the light of social facts stream in."[31]

VIII

THE VOYAGE OF
CHARLES S. JOHNSON

The voyage was over from Bristol to Richmond to Chicago to New York to Nashville. Charles S. Johnson died at sixty-three, a tired man, tired especially of all the traveling, but still looking ahead and making plans. He wanted three or four years more of the Fisk presidency, then a semiretirement, perhaps principally with the Whitney, as consultant. Research-advocacy in national public policy would certainly continue. He intended to resume the writing that had been reduced by the presidency. He would be at home more. He would keep all this going.

The family would miss him greatly. Mrs. Johnson had much to do, working on his papers, planning with Fisk faculty the Charles S. Johnson Memorial Lecture and Award, continuing her community service. But there was an immense void. She wrote to Mrs. Jock Whitney ("Betsy") in February 1957, "I feel painfully adrift in many ways . . . an unusual disintegration in my life and the life of people around me has followed Charlie's going."[1] She kept busy, however, and the family rallied round her. She made arrangements for Arna Bontemps to do the biography "since he has known him as patron, friend, and coworker since the early twenties," though it did not materialize; Bontemps died in 1973.[2] She asked Johnson's dearly beloved friend Fred Brownlee, who had retired from the AMA and was living in North Carolina, to evaluate the Johnson papers, in collaboration with Robert Johnson (now research director for the National Conference of Christians and Jews) and Preston Valien. With Lewis Jones, Bontemps, and others Mrs. Johnson brought together thirteen volumes of speeches and addresses, which they presented to the Social Science Department in April 1959.

Robert Johnson, in 1956, had been going through one of his difficult periods. Now he was confident once more in his professional and personal life and wrote to his parents that he would "again be a whole and wholehearted person to both of you." A few months after his father died, he wrote a touching, candid letter to his mother, asking for her "unconditional love" and support. His depressions had their own sources, of course, but he was cognizant of that perennial problem, how children of a famous parent who enter the same profession cope. "I cannot and will not be a carbon copy of Dad, but I am going to build on the magnificent family traditions that have been bequeathed to me." There was, happily, before Johnson died, a new understanding, after many difficulties in their relationship. "It took me 30 years to find Daddy, but I'm glad that we did find each other, if only for a brief time." Sadly, his buoyancy did not last. Reading his excellent sociological study drawn from his dissertation and his perceptive letters to his parents makes one all the more regretful that he died so young, at forty-three.[3]

Johnson fully expected that his great contributions to Fisk and to the tradition of sociological research in race relations, embodied in the Social Science Department and the Race Relations Department, would go on. Indeed they did, as did the annual Institutes of Race Relations, which lasted well into the 1960s. Without his presence, however, the departments and the institutes eventually began to diminish in importance. Although the studies continued, the research center seemed not to have the same luster as in the 1940s and early 1950s. No longer would Edgar Thompson of Duke University, who had been evaluating centers of sociological research in the South, be able to assert, as he had previously, that Johnson's center at Fisk and Odum's at Chapel Hill were, coequally, the best in the region. (To be sure, this new situation was a result of the rapid growth of other centers and institutes and of a striking expansion of mainstream universities in the South in the 1960s and 1970s.) Fred Brownlee exaggerated in saying in 1957, in a letter to Marie Johnson, that "it looks as if the Social Science Department has been shot to pieces." "Eventually diminished" is better phrasing. But Brownlee did recall that when he asked Johnson why he accepted the Fisk presidency, Johnson replied, "One reason is that I might save the Department I spent 18 years in producing."[4] Brownlee contended that Johnson had made the Fisk center one of the most distinguished in the world. At least, that was true in national and regional terms.

The work of the departments, the countless studies, the huge Johnson correspondence, his personal library, the manuscripts of his and other books—all that was finally organized, with help from a Whitney grant, and was presented to the Fisk University Library in April 1959. The principal invited speaker was Clarence Faust of the Ford Foundation, described by Arna Bontemps as Johnson's "most understanding friend of his later days." Mrs. Johnson was unhappy with the slowness of the cataloging after that, with the decline in Fisk's standing, with the new president, Stephen Wright, and with many other aspects of the post-Johnson era. Obviously, she had a familiar, wholly understandable reaction, a continuing proprietary interest in her husband's legacy. What she failed to take into account was that her perception of her husband's presidency did not altogether match that of many on the faculty. She was not willing to accept the view: "A very good president in external terms, a very poor president internally."[5] She did not have the full picture of the convoluted, byzantine political maneuvering that went on at Fisk (as it does on most campuses), the factions set off against one another. She may not have been fully aware of Johnson's brusque and impatient way with subordinates, of his not brooking rivals who might challenge him. It did Johnson no good to try to present his ten-year governance of Fisk as a kind of golden age, followed by mostly chaos and mediocrity. A spouse's judgment is not always a good measure.

In fact, after the memorial services and the presentation of one's papers to the library, after the tributes and the memorial lectures in one's honor, the standing and reputation of a man and woman must be left to time and to biographers who can be detached in their analyses and yet have a great liking, respect, and sympathy for their subject. Biographers do not have the closeness of spouses or children. They do have the distance, the objectivity, to see the subject whole and in historical and social context. In those terms it is possible to draw up, at the end, a balance sheet of Charles S. Johnson's life and work, a judgment gladly open to other students and contrary opinions.

First, Charles Johnson, with others, built a tradition of sociological research by black sociologists. In this development Johnson was a prime mover. From the research of Du Bois at the turn of the century, his Philadelphia study and the Atlanta monographs, down to the work of Johnson, Frazier, Reid, Cayton, Drake, Locke, Allison Davis, Oliver Cox, Miller, Haynes (to mention the most prominent) from the 1930s to the 1950s, a solid body of sociological and historical work on race relations was achieved against great odds. The point may seem obvious. It is not. These men—unhappily, there were no women in the group, for black male social scientists in this early period were as unconcerned as their white counterparts about the lack of females in the field—

were focused on race relations because it was woven into their personal lives and challenged their intellectual interest as well. They had to do their work almost entirely within the Negro college structure or within various Negro social service agencies because they were not invited to take professorships in the mainstream system even though their talents and degrees obviously qualified them to be there. If they worked in the South in particular, as did Johnson and many others, the problem of segregation and discrimination constantly impinged on them, whereas white social scientists could take the surrounding community and culture for granted. Often, they had to work in isolation, even in the larger southern cities with flourishing sociology departments on nearby campuses. The colleges that supported them in most cases were not comparable to white institutions in resources, salaries, teaching loads, and other characteristics critical to doing research. They did not in any sense succumb to these constrictions; they conducted their research, subject to peer reviews and countervailing hypotheses, from the same social science ethos as their white peers. That was a distinctive achievement. Johnson was central in their number. His achievement is one with theirs.[6]

It is true that this work, with few exceptions, did not make permanent significant contributions to the mainstream of general conceptual and theoretical sociology. The black sociologists could readily have done so; they were prepared to do so. But their main task, their urgent task, was to document, describe, analyze, and demonstrate the significance of the historical evolution of race relations and the black community in the United States. For that they drew on such concepts as class, caste, marginality, role conflict, subculture, social change, normative values, and so on, as they needed them. Du Bois and Oliver Cox did adopt a neo-Marxist theoretical orientation, but their attention was still directed to data on race relations, to a revisionist view of Reconstruction or whether the concept of color caste was applicable to the South. Thus Frazier on the Negro family, Johnson on the black sharecropper, Reid on the Negro immigrant, Cayton and Drake on black Chicago retain their great value as studies, even if the conceptual framework is conventional, not strikingly innovative. The studies add up to a vital and important body of work; they express a deep tradition in the sociology of race relations.

The question is sometimes raised, Why did not the succeeding generation of black sociologists produce a comparable body of work and achieve the same stature? This may not be a fair question because the racial climate has changed so dramatically with reference to careers in the social sciences. Today, though still underrepresented statistically, there are many excellent African American sociologists, some specializing in race relations, some not, some men, some women, the ablest of them in the mainstream universities, not in what are now called the historically black colleges. Because the numbers are relatively greater and because these sociologists are to be found in many institutions, South and North, a particular study by a particular sociologist is less likely to stand out in the way that *The Philadelphia Negro* did at the turn of the century or *Black Metropolis* in the 1940s. Nonetheless, from this larger pool there will emerge unquestionably in the future another young and gifted Frazier or Johnson. In fact, several are already here.

Second, Charles Johnson and his associates at the Fisk center provided something of great value in southern regional terms. Du Bois's Atlanta monographs apart, there had been nowhere near enough research on the racial system and the black community in the South, and much of what there was had been conducted by white social scientists. In the studies of black culture, of black youth, of black family life, in selected counties across the South, the Johnson group made a distinctive contribution. The richness and subtlety of this material, the view of racial oppression from those experiencing it rather than those responsible for applying it added a very important dimension to the conventional histories and sociological studies of the region. Additionally, Johnson developed further a methodology, the ethnographic case study and the use of the human document that produced innovative results. The seeds were sown in his early research in Chicago, in his work with Park, who, as newspaperman and writer, knew how vivid enhancement is given to the description and the statistical table when ordinary people address their problems in their own words. It is these thoughts spoken by the respondents that give both edge and depth to the chapters in both *Shadow of the Plantation* and *Growing Up in the Black Belt,* and some of these men and women have been quoted in preceding chapters. The county was exactly the right dimension for this cultural anthropology of the South. Objectively, yet with deep awareness of the injustices inflicted by the class-color system of the region, Johnson and his associates introduce us to portraits of Macon in Alabama, Johnston in North Carolina, Greene in Georgia, Coahoma in Mississippi, Davidson in Tennessee—sharing certain characteristics, differing in others. In this way the sense of a single region is dispelled, the diversity that southerners know is evoked. In the brief introduction to *The Statistical Atlas of Southern Counties* Johnson writes of "the bayou dwellers of Louisiana, and the bristling aggressive farmers of North Carolina—the Southern highlanders who live in the lower reaches of the Appalachians and the Texas farmers who flourish in the black waxy land that is the new hope for cotton." The black and white relationship cuts across regions, subregions, economic areas, the urban-rural line; many Souths are seen within the South.

To the development of a tradition of race relations research by a group of black social scientists and of a regional county case study and a comparative methodology in the rural South, we need to add a third aspect of Johnson's work. This is his distinctive deployment of the research-advocacy role as a strategy of change, as a means of persuasion to induce the makers of public policy to act more decisively to combat racial discrimination, to end racial segregation. The premise was always his conviction that in a democratic society social change is always possible, even in the face of the persistence of the most appalling forms of racial oppression. Obviously, playing this role brought severe criticism down on his head. He had to endure the label of "ultra-conservative," the accusation of toadying to the white establishment, of placing too much faith in the even more cautious southern white liberals. But that is how he chose to practice advocacy and activism. It can be defended in its own terms.

It has been argued that Johnson worked so closely with the white philanthropic and government establishment that he could never bring himself to a dramatic challenge in print or in action against the real white power structure that functioned behind the facade of an American Missionary Association or a New Deal Farm Security Administration and sanctioned the system of racial discrimination. Less harshly, it has been said that the years of service on the research councils, the foundation boards, and the government commissions simply reinforced his basic conviction that persuasion in the Urban League style, based on research, would work best for him. Johnson firmly believed in the scholarly role *in itself* as a powerful instrument of advocacy. The more thorough the work on the scope and depth of the problem of lynching or desperate farm poverty, the more the majority community, the white community, would be stirred to anger, outrage, and—what counted most—action in the form of public policy and law. Lewis W. Jones, first Johnson's brilliant student and then his close friend, had the most apt term for this—a strategy of "indirection." The young Jones, when student editor of the Fisk paper, showed Johnson a furious editorial he had just written. "This piece says you are angry," Johnson told him, "that is not what you are after; you want to make other people angry." The impact of *Shadow* and *Growing Up* is in the anger they provoke in us, not in any anger within the texts themselves. Reviewing *Patterns of Segregation,* Henry Lee Moon noted, "Whatever fury the author may have experienced in the preparation of this volume, he has effectively sublimated in his writing. The result is a coldly logical documentation of race relations in America today."[7]

Johnson's dedication to the creed of social science, his humanism, his balanced humor, his understanding of the white community (its entrenched racism as well as its potential for remedial action) could not have produced any other than the research-advocacy perspective and the bridging role described fully in the preceding chapters. Indirection was for him a strategy, not a failing or a want of courage. Given this strategy, self-chosen to be sure, he then did not have the freedom of a Du Bois in his later period (outside the system and able to defy it in tracing the roots of racism to predatory capitalism) or an Oliver Cox (inside the academy at Lincoln University but so marginalized, even in the Negro college network, that his very important work on race, class, and capitalism could be safely ignored). Unlike Du Bois and Cox, Johnson, committed to the bridging role and the strategy of indirection, was bound to make the "law firm" of Rosenwald, Rockefeller, Whitney, and Ford essential to his research.

Frazier may be placed somewhere in the middle. "He never played the game," insists his colleague of many years at Howard G. Franklin Edwards.[8] Frazier was scornful of Johnson's gradualism, his excessive deference to the white philanthropic and government establishment, and the playing out of the cooperative strategy with the white southern liberals. Not incidentally, Frazier could point out that he, the more forthright and direct, and not Johnson, was the first Negro to be elected president of the American Sociological Association, in 1949. But Frazier oversimplified; he was pleased to participate with Johnson in the American Youth Commission studies, and his contribution, *Negro Youth at the Crossways* (1940) equals Johnson's *Growing Up* as a solid sociological study. In the writing, Frazier, like Johnson, "effectively sublimated the fury." Nor did he argue in 1940, as Cox and Du Bois might have, that the racial situation of Negro youth could only be an expression of class domination under capitalism. This said, he was obviously far more militant than Johnson and obviously not a partisan of the school of indirection.

The question of the research-advocacy role, and the criticism of that role, is central to an understanding of Charles Johnson's life and work. Other negative assessments, though not to be discounted, are relatively unimportant in drawing up a full and fair balance sheet. August Meier, who was Johnson's research assistant for a year in the mid-1950s, has contended that Johnson should be faulted for appropriating the research of others under his own name. "How little of Johnson's later work was actually his own," he has written.[9] Meier is one of the most distinguished scholars of the history of race relations in America, and his work on black leadership has been invaluable. But here he is simply being disingenuous. If the asserted deception involves only the "later" work, then early and middle stages—when Johnson's best research was produced—are not included. Further, Meier cites specifically only one actual instance of appropriation—his own draft article on the Negro for the *Encyclopedia Americana*. He elevates his one unhappy experience into a generalization. As Irving Howe once observed, "for example, is not a statement." Set against Meier's contention is a large amount of material in the Johnson Papers showing the generous assistance he gave to countless younger scholars. And in cooperative ventures he usually credited his associates and assistants on the title page. Johnson did not conceal his practice of "farming out" research. But the charge of appropriation seems to lack substance.

Butler Jones and others have raised a different, related issue, Johnson's bureaucratic control of the channels of resources and research. This criticism is usually preceded by praise for the quality and quantity of his research as well as the productivity of the "Fisk machine." "The community of black sociologists has freely admitted its indebtedness to him for his work in maintaining at Fisk a center for the education and training of blacks in the intricacies of sociological research."[10] But the praise is accompanied by a litany of criticism. "He was the new Booker T. Washington," controlling the race relations research territory available to blacks, exercising suzerainty over fellowships and grants, resisting the efforts of other black social scientists to establish centers of graduate study for blacks comparable to Fisk's, all of this leading to "professional jealousies and feuding" in the black sociological community.[11] There were indeed conflicts and controversies involving

Johnson's research-advocacy and bridging role in presiding over the "Fisk machine." But there is no evidence to indicate this activity was above and beyond the usual maneuvering and countermaneuvering characteristic of the academic world. In all probability it was made more intense within the Negro college network because, owing to the terrible injustices of the racial system, internal resources were far more limited, and external support much more problematic. That does not, however, make Johnson a "new Booker T. Washington" if only because Johnson's generation, coming later than the master of the Tuskegee Machine, was not as hemmed in and narrowly defined by white power. Like his father before him, Charles Johnson negotiated with the white world; he did not surrender his integrity and self-respect. He practiced what Andrew Young liked to call the high art of how to get power from the powerful and share it with the powerless.

There is reason to believe that the attempted downsizing of Johnson's accomplishment, the dimming of his star, is a consequence of the 1960s and the civil rights revolution. Teaching at Hampton University in the 1960s and spending research time at many other campuses in the historically black college system, many times I heard from young men and women: "We would not have to be doing these sit-ins, these marches to the courthouse for voter registration, if our parents had fought harder for civil rights in their time." There is some truth to that, and we can suppose that the present generation of young black men and women is well aware, or should be well aware, of how much more some of their parents achieved in the 1960s in the battle against racial injustice. Still, the implication that Johnson and his peers were missing the critical capacity to resist, to fight back, finally, to overcome, in Malcolm X's words "by any means necessary," does a disservice to those Negro leaders (and some white liberals as well) who did their best with what they had under the conditions that governed from the 1930s to the 1960s.

In other words, the life of Charles S. Johnson, whether in Bristol, Virginia, in 1900 or in Nashville, Tennessee in 1940, must be seen in context, in *historical* context. Johnson and many a Negro citizen of Bristol and Nashville resisted or tried to resist, but they had to do so in the era of segregation when even the prospect of real change seemed to be realizable, at least for the near future, only within the hard confines of "separate and equal." The proverb asserts that history does not repeat itself. That is not necessarily true. But history does connect then to now. Charles S. Johnson, preparing to draft the statement in Durham, North Carolina, in 1942, which would for the first time come out directly against racial segregation, was *for that time* evoking a spirit of nonviolent combat akin to that of the four black students who, in Greensboro, North Carolina, in 1960, seventy miles down the road from Durham, prepared their sit-in at Woolworth's lunch counter to protest denial of service.[12] The Durham Statement and the Greensboro sit-in connect in the evolution of the question that has been at the heart of southern history since slavery: race.

Charles Johnson died fourteen years after Durham, four years before Greensboro. Had he lived on, he would have reflected on both his career, past to present, and the prospect for change in the future in the area that had absorbed him for a lifetime, race relations. He could take a measure of pride in what he had done. In Chicago, where he had formed his lifelong association with Park, he had designed and carried through the most comprehensive study of a race riot and its roots in urban conditions ever done to that date. The study had shown him what would be his metier, his forte for years to come—the dispassionate, systematic analysis of the way race is built into the social structure in all the institutional manifestations. The study had exemplified his fundamental belief—that the prelude to changing the deplorable condition of racial discrimination would have to be as complete and knowledgeable a review as possible of the bedrock facts of the situation. Then, with the material ordered in terms of accepted sociological concepts, the recommendations to the policy makers would have the force of proven social science as well as the moral imperative to seek justice.

The 1920s in New York were alive in Johnson's memory long after the events themselves. The work as research director for the National Urban League represented continuity with Chicago, and the editorials written under his editorship at *Opportunity*, the league's journal, gave him the chance to construct a second role, research-advocacy, in which he could use the power of the pen not only to study change but possibly to effect it, however modestly. More than that, living in Harlem, vital and lively for all its social problems, was an exhilarating time for Charles and Marie Johnson. From that time he remembered the nurturing of the Harlem Renaissance writers and artists, the extraordinary night of the New York dinner when *Opportunity* brought Langston Hughes, Zora Neale Hurston, Countee Cullen, Frazier, Sterling Brown, Eric Walrond, and all the others together with leading critics, publishers,

184

writers from the world downtown. Three hundred sixteen people had come to the Fifth Avenue Restaurant to the first awards ceremony to listen to a series of distinguished speakers and to hear James Weldon Johnson read Hughes's first-prize poem, "The Weary Blues." That was a memorable night, for the writers who went on to fame and for those whose light burned brightly for a time and then faded out. He had been the "entrepreneur" and "midwife" of the Renaissance—but credit must go to Alain Locke for his part in it.

And then came the long, productive sojourn in Nashville, at Fisk. He was sure the fruits of those more than twenty-five years would still be there after him, the Social Science Department, the Race Relations Department, the Institutes of Race Relations, the reports on racial and socioeconomic conditions in towns and cities across the South. And from the Nashville base he had been able as well to do something in his national advocacy role, from the service on President Hoover's White House Conference on Housing, to the behind-the-scenes activity in behalf of the Bankhead Farm Tenancy Act, to the work with the National Manpower Council in the 1950s, to the appointment by Truman to UNESCO and the Commission on Postwar Japanese Education. The regional advocacy role had achieved some success, perhaps measured best in the Durham Statement, but he had to acknowledge that neither the CIC nor the SRC had fulfilled his hope for an eventual frontal assault on segregation. He recognized that too many southern white liberals had waited too long before challenging directly an archaic and unjust racial system, and he was impatient with them. As for the Fisk presidency, he would stand by his sense that his tenure had been effective, although some aspects did merit the criticism that circulated—too much attention given to the national and regional advocacy role, too unbending in managerial style, and so on. In any event, there was still the future, the years ahead to plan better innovations at Fisk.

As for the future and future change in race relations, Johnson still retained at the end that realistic, tempered optimism, that sense that in a democracy like ours there is direction, progress toward the achievement of equality of opportunity. But the line is often wavering, progress halted, even a trend of regression occurs often in the cycle. He had called the Supreme Court decision in *Brown* in 1954 possibly the most important turning point for Negroes since emancipation. Just two years later, in his article for the *New York Times Magazine,* he lamented the viciousness and the violence with which southern state legislatures and their constituencies initiated the campaign of "massive resistance."

On the progress side, had he lived on into the 1960s he would have hailed the strategy and the achievement of the civil rights movement, in particular the passage of the Civil Rights Act of 1964 and the Voting Rights Act of 1965, the culmination of the enormous work and the sacrifices (above all the loss of lives) required of the movement in the 1960s. He always believed in the importance of public policy and legislation and in the contribution of sociological research as well as nonviolent direct action to that end. He never accepted the Sumnerian view that stateways cannot change underlying mores. He would have been a firm supporter of affirmative action on the grounds that increasing the proportion of minority group members' access to jobs and higher education is not a "quota system" but a constructive effort to bring people through the door once the door (of opportunity) has been legally opened. And he would have been a firm opponent of the black nationalism—black power movement of the late 1960s and 1970s. He would have certainly understood and analyzed sympathetically the psychological sense of frustration in this movement, the rage, the impatience with the entire system and its racism, just as he had done with the forerunner, Garveyism. He would have condemned the brutal repression of the Black Panthers by the Federal Bureau of Investigation. But as a serious economist, he would have shown the idea of a powerful economically self-sufficient entity to be illusory, the idea of a completely separate political power base built without regard to interdependence with progressive coalition interest groups and the Democratic party equally illusory. Beyond that, he would have been shocked and saddened to see the attention given to the early Black Panthers with their suicidal determination to challenge "the system" with their guns, in the streets.

Perhaps it is most symbolically appropriate in considering in this final summation Johnson's preoccupation with social change and how he might have viewed the future, to turn at the end to the site of his best book, *Shadow of the Plantation,* to the place where he developed so insightfully his methodology of case study and human document—to Macon County, Alabama, and to Gee's Bend in Wilcox County nearby where the old gentleman, having trouble with the words of Embree and others as to what they were doing in central Alabama, called on the distinguished sociologist: "Mistuh Johnson! Come on over hyar and understan' 'em fer me."

From 1932, the year of the study, until the year of Johnson's death, a quarter of a century later, change was slow in Macon County, economically and racially, although, as Johnson predicted, the feudal plantation economy of owner and sharecropper would fall into decline. In the late 1950s and early 1960s change began to accelerate, not because of any transformation in the white community of central Alabama but of combined external pressure from the federal government and its courts, from the civil rights movement and its "invasion" of Alabama. Subsequent research in the 1970s showed an improved but still mixed picture: the "racial gap" in occupation, income, health, and completion of education was less, but it was still wide. Politically there occurred a remarkable rise in the black vote in Alabama, though, again, owing to their proportion in the lower income levels, Negro nonvoting remained a problem. In this period blacks assumed political control of Greene County, blacks were elected mayors in Tuskegee and Pritchard, and—Johnson would find it hard to believe—Macon County elected a black sheriff. The power of the arch-segregationist governor George Wallace would begin to wane, and then he would recoup in the 1980s. Realist as he was, he abandoned segregation and made his direct populist appeal for black votes. By the beginning of the 1980s white candidates for the Congress could no longer win with the old emotional, primitive campaigns of "nigger-baiting." By the mid-1970s there were more than three hundred black students at the University of Alabama in Tuscaloosa, compared to the two, Vivian Malone and James Hood, who, through the decisive intervention of the federal courts and the Kennedy administration by Attorney General Robert Kennedy, broke the color bar in 1963 after months of dismaying indecision. Most of all, the very places Johnson observed and studied in 1932 commenced to ring with a new resonance, the result of the movement. Selma, Montgomery, Birmingham, Damascus Baptist Church, Gee's Bend—these connoted resistance to racial exploitation as they once connoted, in Johnson's study, accommodation of what he called "black peasantry" to the twin forces of racial and economic exploitation. Many problems remained in the 1970s—they still do in the 1990s—but in Johnson's terms, had he been there, there was palpable hope for change in 1972 where there was little or none in 1932.

There is a little-known footnote to the story of the celebrated march from Selma to Montgomery in 1965, at the height of the civil rights revolution. Within the overall conflict and confrontation, there were complicated internal disputes between the older black leaders in the Southern Christian Leadership Conference, including Martin Luther King, and the younger, more militant leaders of the Student Non-Violent Coordinating Committee.[13] In the midst of all that, Martin Luther King came over from Selma to Gee's Bend, Alabama, population seven hundred, all black, still poor, as when Embree and Johnson had stopped by so many years before and the old man had asked Johnson to "understan' 'em fer me." Martin Luther King said:

> "I came over here to Gee's Bend to tell you, you are *somebody* . . . you are as good as any white person in Wilcox County."
> The old ladies [in the church] with head scarves knotted in front nodded, and said, "It's so. It's so."[14]

Charles S. Johnson would have liked that.

NOTES

Preface

1. Richard Robbins, Supplement 6 "Charles S. Johnson," *Dictionary of American Biography* (New York: Scribner's, 1980).

2. James Baldwin, *Notes of a Native Son* (Boston: Beacon Press, 1955), p. 8.

Chapter I

1. An excellent analysis of Park as theorist and applied sociologist is in Lewis Coser, *Masters of Sociological Thought*, 2d ed. (New York: Harcourt Brace Jovanovich, 1977), pp. 357–84. Park's wide-ranging important work in race relations is restored to stature in James B. McKee, *Sociology and the Race Problem: The Failure of a Perspective* (Urbana: University of Illinois Press, 1993), esp. pp. 105–13. Most sociologists concentrated on assimilation, thus missing Park's insistence on the significance of initial conflict of the kind that came to be the hallmark of the great civil rights struggle of the 1960s. See also Fred R. Mathews, *Quest for an American Sociology: Robert E. Park and the Chicago School* (Montreal: McGill-Queens University Press, 1977). Mathews views Johnson, despite his advocacy of liberal reform—anathema to Park—as a true Parkean in the sense that he was a "hard-headed realist" who understood that the results of his research might never find expression in actual public policy. Winifred Raushenbush, *Robert E. Park: Biography of a Sociologist* (Durham: Duke University Press, 1979), emphasizes the friendship and mutual respect between Park and Johnson. Park's general influence on Johnson can be seen in Charles S. Johnson "Race Relations and Social Change," in Edgar T. Thompson, ed., *Race Relations and the Race Problem* (Durham: Duke University Press, 1939), pp. 271–303. Frazier, whom Everett Hughes described to me as "Park's most complete student," made some use of Park's concepts but went far beyond the mentor in analyzing racial conflict in a worldwide setting. See Stow Persons, *Ethnic Studies at Chicago, 1905–45* (Urbana: University of Illinois Press, 1987), chap. 8. Park's ideas on race are set out in Robert E. Park, *Race and Culture* (Glencoe, Ill.: Free Press, 1950).

2. St. Clair Drake, Introduction to Charles S. Johnson, *Growing Up in the Black Belt* (1941; rpt. New York: Schocken, 1967), p. xi.

3. On the assessment of Johnson as far too conservative see Herbert Aptheker, ed., *The Correspondence of W. E. B. Du Bois* (Amherst: University of Massachusetts Press, 1978), 3:306–7. On Du Bois's self-definition as a "propagandist," his account of his trial, and his expression of gratitude to Johnson for publicly supporting him, see *The Autobiography of*

W. E. B. Du Bois (New York: International Publishers, 1968), esp. pp. 367–72, 394–95. Frazier was even more outspoken than Johnson in behalf of Du Bois.

4. John H. Stanfield, *Philanthropy and Jim Crow in American Social Science* (Westport, Conn.: Greenwood Press, 1985), p. 100. See also Edwin R. Embree and Julia Waxman, *Investment in People: The Story of the Julius Rosenwald Fund* (New York: Harper, 1949).

5. Stanfield, *Philanthropy*, p. 134. Chapter 6 is a valuable commentary on Johnson's research and advocacy.

6. The classic statement is Everett C. Hughes, "Dilemmas and Contradictions of Status," *American Journal of Sociology* 5 (March 1945).

7. Quoted in Patrick Gilpin, "Charles S. Johnson: An Intellectual Biography" (Ph.D. dissertation, Vanderbilt University, 1973). I am greatly indebted to Gilpin for material used in this biography.

8. August Meier, the noted scholar of black history, raised this issue in an essay-review in 1977 of a book in which I had a chapter on Johnson and did so again in a book published in 1993. Meier is strongly critical of me for not treating the charge that Johnson took over the work of others in his own name. Indeed, I should have dealt with this matter. But Meier is himself seriously in error in asserting this to be Johnson's general practice. Meier writes, "How little of Johnson's *later work* was actually his own" (emphasis added). Meier was at Fisk for only three years in the 1950s, one of them as Johnson's assistant. He cites only one instance, an article of his own, which he claims Johnson appropriated intact in his name. Over against this is a great amount of material in the Johnson Papers showing that he did everything possible to get young scholars published in their own names. Further, if the charge involves only "later work," then all the works written earlier are "actually his own." It is disingenuous for Meier to translate one instance, his own unhappy experience, into a blanket indictment. See August Meier, *A White Scholar in the Black Community* (Amherst: University of Massachusetts Press, 1993), 14–18, 73–87; Richard Robbins, "Charles S. Johnson," in James Blackwell and Morris Janowitz, eds., *Black Sociologists* (Chicago: University of Chicago Press, 1974). The controversy is treated more fully in Chapter 8.

9. On the great significance of *Brown* see Richard Kluger, *Simple Justice, The History of Brown v. Board of Education* (New York: Vintage, 1977). Thurgood Marshall emphasized the value of Johnson's contribution in preparation of the case before the Supreme Court.

10. Charles S. Johnson, "A Southern Negro's View of the South," *New York Times Magazine,* September 26, 1956. With other prominent leaders Johnson established the Southern Education Reporting Service to monitor school desegregation and the resistance to it. Reports were issued monthly in *Southern School News.*

11. Gunnar Myrdal et al., *An American Dilemma: The Negro Problem and Modern Democracy* (New York: Harper, 1944). A twentieth anniversary edition (Harper & Row) appeared in 1962. Neither Johnson nor any other Negro was considered to head the definitive study of the "Negro problem" although Johnson's entire career was premised on his ability to carry out large-scale research with scrupulous objectivity, the very basis for selecting a distinguished Swedish economist for the post. The story of Myrdal's appointment, his tour of the South with Jackson Davis of the General Education Board, and the selection of a white sociologist, Arnold Rose, to direct research and coauthor the study, is told in Stanfield, *Philanthropy*, chap. 7. The enormous, encyclopedic study was overpraised for years, then criticized perhaps too severely. It still has value, for all its faults, especially for its historical analysis of the race question and the roots in slavery. And the American Creed framework, for all its limits, is still a relevant context for conflict-of-values sociology. See, for example, Robert K. Merton, "Discrimination and the American Creed," in R. M. MacIver, ed., *Discrimination and National Welfare* (New York: Harper, 1949). The best study of the entire Myrdal enterprise is Walter A. Jackson, *Gunnar Myrdal and America's Conscience: Social Engineering and Racial Liberalism: 1938–1987* (Chapel Hill: University of North Carolina Press, 1990). See also David W. Southern, *Gunnar Myrdal and Black-White Relations: The Use and Abuse of "An American Dilemma"* (Baton Rouge: Louisiana State University Press, 1987). McKee, *Sociology and the Race Problem*, chap. 6, "An American Dilemma," emphasizes the agreement of Johnson and Myrdal that central planning by the federal government was the essential key to racial change. Ralph Ellison's trenchant comment is from his *Shadow and Act* (New York: Random House, 1953), p. 365.

12. The list of those close to Johnson is from Gilpin, "Charles S. Johnson," chap. 15. It is consistent with my own interviews with Johnson's younger colleagues.

13. Charles S. Johnson, "A Spiritual Autobiography" (undated), typescript, Johnson Papers, Special Collections, Fisk University Library, Nashville, Tennessee.

14. Interview, *Boston Globe*, January 16, 1995. John Egerton, *Speak Now Against the Day: The Generation Before the Civil Rights Movement in the South* (New York: Knopf, 1994). His book is the most incisive and thorough treatment of the coalition of southern black leaders and white liberals that tried in the years from the 1930s to the 1950s to change the racial climate of the South—"Yesterday's South in the Throes of Change."

Chapter II

1. On the different dimensions of southern Appalachia see Charles R. Wilson and William Ferris, eds., *Encyclopedia of Southern Culture* (Chapel

Hill: University of North Carolina Press, 1989), "Appalachians," p. 418; "Appalachians, Black," pp. 139–42; "Appalachian Myth," pp. 1128–29. The celebrated WPA Guides compiled by the Federal Writers' Project in the 1930s on Virginia, Tennessee, and West Virginia are still useful but deplorably thin on black history. See, for example, *Virginia: A Guide to the Old Dominion* (New York: Oxford University Press, 1940), "The Bristol area," pp. 435–42, "The Negro," 350–57. See also Jean Gottmann, *Virginia in Our Century* (Charlottesville: University Press of Virginia, 1968).

2. Charles J. Harkrader, *Witness to an Epoch* (Kingsport, Tenn.: Kingsport Press, 1965), pp. 33–37, 77.

3. Charles S. Johnson, "A Spiritual Autobiography" (undated), typescript, Johnson Papers, Special Collections, Fisk University Library, Nashville.

4. I am indebted to Rev. W. Alexander Johnson (no relation), pastor of the Lee Street Baptist Church, and to several older members of the congregation for interviews in 1975. The Moore Street home was sold by Charles S. in 1945 for $2,700. In 1943, Johnson arranged a family "mass migration" to Bristol to unveil a portrait of his father in the church. As always, they faced segregation when deciding where to stay. A longtime friend and agent for the house, Warren Brown, finally found them lodging with families.

5. The defining study is Rayford W. Logan, *The Negro in American Life and Thought: The Nadir, 1877–1901* (New York: Dial, 1954). For an excellent compact account see John Hope Franklin and Alfred A. Moss, Jr., *From Slavery to Freedom: A History of African Americans,* 7th ed. (New York: McGraw-Hill, 1994), chaps. 5, 13, 14, and 15. See also Howard M. Rabinowitz, *Race Relations in the Urban South, 1865–1890* (New York: Oxford University Press, 1966). Essential reading is C. Vann Woodward, *The Strange Career of Jim Crow,* 3d ed. (New York: Oxford University Press, 1974). The connection between the arrival of the Jim Crow system and what happened to Charles and his mother in their daily lives in Bristol was not atypical; it was happening to Negro families all over the South. The young sisters in the famed Delany family had exactly the same experience, Jim Crowed on the trolley, turned back at the drugstore, at about the same time in Raleigh, North Carolina. See the witty, warm, but tough-minded memoir by the sisters, both of whom lived to be over one hundred years old: Sarah Delany and A. Elizabeth Delany with Amy Hill Hearth, *Having Our Say* (New York: Kodasha International, 1993), pp. 65–68.

6. On myth and reality about race in Appalachia see John M. Stanfield, "The Sociological Roots of White-Black Inequality in Urban Appalachia," in Williams H. Turner and Edward H. Cabell, eds., *Blacks in Appalachia* (Lexington: University Press of Kentucky, 1985). This book reprints Carter Woodson's classic essay "Freedom and Slavery in Appalachian America" (1910). An affecting memoir of a later period in this region is Henry Louis

Gates, Jr., *Colored People: A Memoir* (New York: Knopf, 1994). Gates warmly evokes black community family life as well as the persistence of discrimination in Piedmont, West Virginia, in the 1950s. After *Brown* and desegregation there were changes; children got into "the white school," but some distinctive, deeply held black community institutions were lost.

7. Joseph H. Cartwright, *The Triumph of Jim Crow: Tennessee Race Relations in the 1800's* (Knoxville: University of Tennessee Press, 1976). See also Allen W. Moger, *Virginia: Bourbonism to Byrd, 1870–1925* (Charlottesville: University Press of Virginia, 1968); Charles E. Wines, *Race Relations in Virginia, 1870–1902* (Charlottesville: University Press of Virginia, 1961); Lester C. Lamon, *Black Tennesseans, 1900–1930* (Knoxville: University of Tennessee Press, 1977); Vernon I. Wharton, *The Negro in Mississippi* (Chapel Hill: University of North Carolina Press, 1947). Joel Williamson, *The Crucible of Race: Black-White Relations in the South Since Emancipation* (New York: Oxford University Press, 1984), brilliantly portrays this period and the preoccupation with race.

8. Federal Writers' Project, Hampton Institute, sponsor, *The Negro in Virginia* (New York: Hastings House, 1940), p. 242. In the Virginia of Johnson's youth nonsoutherners sometimes were confused by caste rules. The French author Andre Chermand used the same trolley line on a visit to Washington's tomb in 1906. Refusing to surrender his "colored" seat, he was arrested, then released. Enraged, he cried out, "Jeem Crow? I do not know zee name!"

9. Gunnar Myrdal et al., *An American Dilemma: The Negro Problem and Modern Democracy* (New York: Harper, 1944), p. 740.

10. There is a very extensive literature on accommodationism/militancy and the two protagonists Du Bois and Washington. John Hope Franklin and August Meier, eds., *Black Leaders of the Twentieth Century* (Urbana: University of Illinois Press, 1982), provides rounded portraits of these two leaders as well as of Thomas Fortune, Ida Wells-Barnett, Marcus Garvey, A. Philip Randolph, and others. Du Bois describes the conflict in his first autobiography *Dusk of Dawn* (1940; rpt. New York: Schocken Books, 1968). Two useful biographies are Elliott M. Rudwick, *W. E. B. Du Bois: Propagandist of the Negro Protest*, 2d ed. (New York: Atheneum, 1969); and Francis L. Broderick, *W. E. B. Du Bois, Negro Leader in Time of Crisis* (Palo Alto: Stanford University Press, 1959). The defining biography of the younger Du Bois is David Levering Lewis, *W. E. B. Du Bois: Biography of a Race* (New York: Henry Holt, 1993). The most incisive analysis of Washington is in August Meier, *Negro Thought in America* (Ann Arbor: University of Michigan Press, 1963). See also Louis Harlan's comprehensive two-volume biography, *Booker T. Washington: The Making of a Black Leader, 1865–1901* and *Booker T. Washington: The Wizard of Tuskegee, 1901–1915* (New York: Oxford University Press, 1972, 1983). See also Hugh Hawkins, ed.,

Booker T. Washington and His Critics (Lexington, Mass.: D. C. Heath, 1962). Williamson, *Crucible of Race,* pp. 70–78, effectively contrasts the positions of the two men.

11. See W. E. B. Du Bois, *The Philadelphia Negro: A Social Study* (1899; rpt. New York: Schocken Books, 1967), p. 194, for his early expression of a Johnson-like research-reform strategy. The quotation on abandoning scientific detachment is from his *Dusk of Dawn,* p. 51. A judicious selection of Du Bois's sociology is Dan S. Green and Edwin D. Driver, eds., *W. E. B. Du Bois on Sociology and the Black Community* (Chicago: University of Chicago Press, 1978).

12. Charles S. Johnson, "The Social Philosophy of Booker T. Washington," *Opportunity,* April 1928, pp. 102–5.

13. David Levering Lewis has described Johnson's subsequent key role in the Harlem Renaissance: "If the road to the ballot box and jobs was blocked, Johnson saw that the door to Carnegie Hall and the New York publishers was ajar" (*When Harlem Was in Vogue* [New York: Knopf-Random House, 1981], p. 48).

14. This phrase, in a sense linking Johnson closer to Washington than to Du Bois, is from Richard Bardolph, *The Negro Vanguard* (Westport, Conn.: Negro Universities Press, 1959), and is meant as a compliment. In private correspondence Johnson was always forthright in denouncing racial segregation, but in public he sometimes argued for holding off temporarily on the segregation issue in the interest of short-term objectives such as an antilynching law. In the 1930s this meant for him, as Raymond Gavins says of Gordon Hancock, "living with ambiguity." But by 1942, when he played the leading role, with Hancock, in drafting the Durham Statement (see Chapter 6), his position was clear and forthright: racial segregation must be addressed and attacked directly and openly. See Raymond Gavins, *The Perils and Prospects of Southern Black Leadership: Gordon Blaine Hancock, 1884–1970* (Durham: Duke University Press, 1977), p. 187. Hancock, a well-known sociologist and leading proponent of Negro economic development as a wedge for racial change, was the prime figure, along with Johnson, in shaping the Durham document.

15. Arna Bontemps, *One Hundred Years of Negro Freedom* (New York: Dodd-Mead, 1963), pp. 224–25.

16. See Charles S. Johnson, "How Much Is the Migration a Flight from Persecution?" *Opportunity,* September 1923, pp. 272–74, and "The Negro Migration and Economic Interpretation," *Modern Quarterly* 2 (1925). There has been a recent revival of scholarly interest in this issue. See Florette Henri, *Black Migration: Movement North, 1900–1920* (New York: Doubleday, 1975). See also Alferdteen Harrison, ed., *Black Exodus: The Great Migration from the American South* (Jackson: University Press of Mississippi, 1991). William Cohen, "The Great Migration as a Lever of Social

Change," in the same volume provides a thoughtful critique of Johnson's research and describes how Emmett Scott, then special assistant on Negro affairs to the secretary of war, obtained the Carnegie funding in 1917. The second great wave is described in moving personal stories in Arna Bontemps and Jack Conroy, *Anyplace but Here* (New York: Hill & Wang, 1966). The same approach is employed by Nicholas Lemann, *The Promised Land: The Great Migration and How It Changed America* (New York: Knopf, 1991).

17. E. Franklin Frazier, *The Negro Family in the United States* (Chicago: University of Chicago Press, 1932), p. xiii. Johnson did adopt a modified version of Park's cycle thesis in *Patterns of Negro Segregation* (New York: Harper, 1943). In Park's view, race tensions are a necessary stage of development in which ethnic-racial groups are eventually absorbed into a common cultural "community of purpose and action." See Robert E. Park, *Race and Culture* (New York: Free Press, 1950). The basic inadequacy of Park's race relations cycle thesis is demonstrated in Stanford M. Lyman, *The Black American in Sociological Thought: Failure of a Perspective* (New York: Putnam, 1972), chap. 2. Park's sociological thought on race is perceptively criticized in Patrick Gilpin, "Charles S. Johnson: An Intellectual Biography" (Ph.D. dissertation, Vanderbilt University, 1973), chaps. 3 and 4. Johnson knew nothing of Park on arriving at the university, though he already was aware, while at Virginia Union, that the best sociology was there. He was deeply impressed by Park's course "Crowd and Public." "It dawned on me that I was being taken seriously and without the usual condescension or oily patronization of which I had seen too much" (quoted in Winifred Raushenbush, *Robert E. Park: Biography of a Sociologist* [Durham: Duke University Press, 1979], p. 181).

18. St. Clair Drake and Horace R. Cayton, *Black Metropolis* (1945; rpt. New York: Harper & Row, 1962), Vol. 2. In this edition the authors prophetically predicted widespread urban violence if racial discrimination was not addressed. See also William J. Wilson's introduction to the third edition of *Black Metropolis* published by the University of Chicago Press in 1993.

19. See Arthur W. Little, *From Harlem to the Rhine: The Story of New York's Colored Volunteers* (New York: Covici Friede, 1936). See also Jack D. Foner, *Blacks and the Military in American History* (New York: Praeger, 1974); Franklin and Moss, *From Slavery to Freedom*, chap. 16.

20. *The Negro in Chicago: A Study of Race Relations and a Race Riot* (Chicago: University of Chicago Press, 1922). A valuable analysis of the commission's formation and report is Martin Bulmer, "Charles S. Johnson, Robert E. Park and the Research Methods of the Chicago Commission on Race Relations, 1919–22: An Early Experiment in Applied Social Research," *Ethnic and Racial Studies*, July 1981. Bulmer emphasizes the innovative survey and case study research techniques developed by Park and Johnson.

And he cites Park's celebrated statement on research that was absorbed by Johnson and the other graduate students. As Ernest Burgess remembered it, Park told them there were already enough crusaders and reformers ("do-gooders"). Rather, "their role was to be that of the calm, detached scientist who investigates race relations with the same objectivity and detachment with which the zoologist dissects the potato bug." Burgess is quoted in R. H. Turner, *Robert E. Park on Social Control and Collective Behavior* (Chicago: University of Chicago Press, 1967), p. xvi. See also Martin Bulmer, *The Chicago School of Sociology* (Chicago: University of Chicago Press, 1984). The report was highly praised by successive generations of leading sociologists, including Seymour Martin Lipset and Morris Janowitz. Park himself, reviewing the book (*New Republic,* April 11, 1923), called it not only "probably the first complete, authentic and unbiased account of a race riot" but a pioneering work in the social psychology of the crowd and mob.

21. Typical among many statements is the following: "For the Negro to accept segregation and all of its implications as an ultimate solution would be to accept for all times a definition of himself as something less than his fellow man" (*New South, the Journal of the Southern Regional Council,* 2 [May 1947], p. 8).

22. *The Negro in Chicago.* The best account of the ghetto before the riot is Allan H. Spear, *Black Chicago: The Making of a Negro Ghetto, 1890–1920* (Chicago: University of Chicago Press, 1967). He shows how "in a thirty-year period a relatively fluid pattern of race relations gave way to a rigid pattern of discrimination and segregation" and how "Negro leaders . . . veered away from the militant abolitionist tradition and adopted a policy that basically accepted separate Negro community life" (p. ix). See also William M. Tuttle, Jr., *Race Riot: Chicago in the Red Summer of 1919* (New York: Atheneum, 1972), and Arthur Waskow, *From Race Riot to Sit-In, 1919 and the 1960's* (New York: Doubleday, 1966). Stow Persons, *Ethnic Studies at Chicago, 1905–1945* (Urbana: University of Illinois Press, 1987), pp. 64–67, discusses the background of the riot and report and the difficulty in fitting this and other ethnic studies to Park's race relations cycle thesis.

23. Langston Hughes, *The Big Sea: An Autobiography* (1940; rpt. New York: Hill & Wang, 1975), p. 91.

Chapter III

1. Harlem, "Negro capital of the world," in Claude McKay's words, has long been studied in both histories and literary work, the Harlem of shadows and sunlight. James Weldon Johnson's *Black Manhattan* (New York: Knopf, 1930), describes the early period and provides a lively view of black musical theater. Claude McKay, *Harlem: Negro Metropolis* (New York: Dutton, 1940), is at once acerbic and affectionate about Harlem. Perceptive contemporary books are Gilbert Osofsky, *Harlem: The Making*

of a Ghetto, 1890–1930 (New York: Harper & Row, 1968), and John Henrik Clarke, ed., *Harlem: A Community in Transition* (New York: Citadel, 1964). Jervis Anderson, *This Was Harlem, 1900–1950* (New York: Farrar, Straus & Giroux, 1982), is a fine integration of social history and literary analysis.

2. Osofsky, *Harlem*, p. 187.

3. Clearly, though anchored to the same white philanthropic base as the Urban League, the NAACP, in its emphasis on battling discrimination in the courts and legislative halls, was the more assertive organization. The best account of the early years is by Du Bois himself in the first autobiography, *Dusk of Dawn* (New York: Harcourt, Brace and World, 1940), chap. 4. Du Bois dedicates the book to Joel Spingarn, "knight and scholar," with whom he was very close. See also Mary W. Ovington, *And the Walls Came Tumbling Down* (New York: Harcourt, Brace, 1947), chap. 4, and Walter White, *A Man Called White* (1940; rpt. New York: Ayer, 1969). See also B. Joyce Ross, *J. E. Spingarn and the Rise of the NAACP* (New York: Atheneum, 1972).

4. The background on Jones, Wood, and Haynes comes from Guichard Parris and Lester Brooks, *Blacks in the City: A History of the National Urban League* (Boston: Little, Brown, 1971).

5. Nancy Weiss, *The National Urban League, 1910–1950* (New York: Oxford University Press, 1974), p. 217. See also Ralph L. Pearson, "Charles S. Johnson: The Urban League Years" (Ph.D. dissertation, Johns Hopkins University, 1970).

6. *The Negro Population of Denver, Colorado: A Survey of Its Economic and Social Status* (New York: National Urban League, 1929), p. 46. The same theme of interrelatedness is found in Reid's survey of Albany, New York.

7. Ira De A. Reid, *The Negro Immigrant* (New York: Columbia University Press, 1939).

8. Quoted in Weiss, *National Urban League*, pp. 219–20. The Hill statement is from a NUL memorandum, February 11, 1928.

9. This paragraph is based on a content analysis of issues of *Opportunity* and the *Crisis* between 1923 and 1928, Johnson's years at the league. The *Messenger* was sampled at regular intervals during the same period. See also Theodore Kornweibel, *No Crystal Stair: Black Life and the Messenger, 1917–1928* (Westport, Conn.: Greenwood Press, 1968).

10. When Boas presented this persuasive thesis at Atlanta University in 1906, Du Bois was deeply impressed and decided to work even more intensively on African culture, pan-Africanism, and the liberation of African people from colonialism. In later years both he and E. Franklin Frazier devoted much of their work to the fundamental theme that racial oppression in the United States and Western imperialism dominating and exploiting

colored people in Africa and Asia were expressions of the Western "white" capitalist world system.

11. All references in these paragraphs except to Boas are to interpretive essays in Alain Locke, ed., *The New Negro: An Interpretation* (New York: Boni & Liveright, 1925).

12. All these interpretive sociological essays are in Charles S. Johnson, ed., *Ebony and Topaz* (New York: National Urban League, 1927).

13. The great upsurge in the 1960s in interest in black studies and literature sent scholars and readers back to the Harlem Renaissance. In 1983 I was a participant in a seminar on Alain Locke and the Renaissance at Atlanta University, funded by the National Endowment for the Humanities. I am grateful to Richard Long, the seminar director, for his analysis of the Renaissance and Charles Johnson's role in it. Three contemporary books cite Johnson's role. David Levering Lewis, *When Harlem Was in Vogue* (New York: Knopf, 1981) is a brilliant study, at once scholarly and entertaining. Anderson, *This Was Harlem,* places the Renaissance in historic continuity, 1900–1950. Nathan Irvin Huggins, *Harlem Renaissance* (New York: Oxford University Press, 1971), is a balanced, incisive interpretation of the contribution and the limits of the Renaissance in the context of American social history. See also, for a conspectus of opinion, Arna Bontemps, ed., *The Harlem Renaissance Remembered* (New York: Dodd, Mead, 1972). Nathan Huggins, ed., *Voices from the Harlem Renaissance* (New York: Oxford University Press, 1976), covers many of the writers. A recent comprehensive anthology is David Levering Lewis, ed., *The Portable Harlem Renaissance* (New York: Viking, 1994).

14. See Jervis Anderson, *A. Philip Randolph: A Biographical Portrait* (Berkeley: University of California Press, 1986).

15. McKay's searing defiance of racism caught everyone's attention. During World War II, Winston Churchill, addressing a joint session of Congress, cited the poem as defining Britain's heroic resistance to Nazism.

16. A fourth review, the *Liberator,* deserves at least a footnote. Founded by Max Eastman, this socialist magazine took on McKay as writer-editor with a mandate to write freely of Negro life. McKay published poetry by Jean Toomer as well as his own work. But Eastman and Michael Gold clashed with him. McKay quit his editorship and went into European exile, first in the Soviet Union.

17. Anderson, *This Was Harlem,* p. 214.

18. These opinions about Johnson are all quoted in Lewis, *When Harlem Was in Vogue,* p. 125.

19. Alain Locke, "The New Negro," in Locke, ed., *The New Negro,* p. 9.

20. See Richard Robbins, "From Home to HBCU's (Historically Black Colleges and Universities)," in John H. Stanfield, ed., *A History of Race Relations* (Newbury Park, Calif.: Sage, 1993). The first part of this memoir

recounts growing up white, Jewish, and library-addicted in Brooklyn in the 1930s.

21. John Hope Franklin and Alfred A. Moss, Jr., *From Slavery to Freedom*, 7th ed. (New York: McGraw-Hill, 1988), chap. 18.

22. Hurston's last years were spent in Eatonville, Florida, her childhood home and source of many stories. Even in the Renaissance years she was never one to be weighed down by what she called "tragedy of color" thoughts. In her own inimitable phrasing anyone who would discriminate against *her* could not be worth very much. A discerning biography is Robert E. Hemenway, *Zora Neale Hurston: A Literary Biography* (Urbana: University of Illinois Press, 1977). See also the Hurston anthology, Alice Walker, ed., *I Love Myself When I'm Laughing* (New York: Feminist Press, 1979). See also S. Jay Walker, "Hurston, Zora Neale, 1901(?)—1960," *Dictionary of American Biography*, Supplement 6 (New York: Scribner's, 1980). By chance, thanks to the alphabet, my own entry in the *DAB*, "Johnson, Charles S., 1893–1956," follows in the next pages. In 1995 the Library of America issued an anthology, *Hurston: Novels and Stories* (New York: Library of America, 1995).

23. Those who disliked Johnson for his formal, reserved personality did not see this side of him. He well understood the deeper meaning of the blues and wrote: "Stark full of human passions [the blues] crowd themselves into an uncompelled expression, so simple in their power, that they startle" (quoted in E. Franklin Frazier, *The Negro Family in Chicago* [Chicago: University of Chicago Press, 1932], p. 78).

24. See the fine biography by Thadious Davis, *Nella Larsen: Novelist of the Harlem Renaissance* (Baton Rouge: Louisiana State University Press, 1994). Davis contends that Johnson had an antipathy to women writers such as Larsen and Fauset. His "anti-feminist, behind-the-scenes work was calculated and manipulative" (p. 160). This could well be, though Johnson did praise Larsen for her depth of knowledge in literature. I could find no evidence of this attitude in Johnson's later years at Fisk.

25. Charles S. Johnson, "After Garvey—What," *Opportunity*, August 1923, pp. 231–33. Johnson warned: "The sources of this discontent must be remedied, effectively and now, or this accumulating energy and unrest, blocked off from its dreams, will take another direction" (p. 233).

26. Huggins, *Harlem Renaissance*, pp. 306–7.

27. Langston Hughes, "The Negro Artist and the Racial Mountain," *Nation*, June 23, 1926, reprinted in Lewis, ed., *Portable Harlem Renaissance*, pp. 91–95. One should cite as well the poet Sterling Brown (1901–89), a prizewinner in the essay category in Johnson's *Opportunity* contest. He went on to write in just the way Hughes advised. Educated at Williams and Harvard, he taught briefly at Fisk, then in 1926 went to Howard where for forty years he taught literature to a new generation of writers. In his own

work, spirituals, blues, and work songs are often woven into the verse. See Sterling Brown, *The Collected Poems*, selected by Michael Harper (Chicago: Another Chicago Press, 1990).

28. Arnold Rampersad, "Introduction," *The New Negro* (reprint. New York: Atheneum, 1992), pp. xxii–xxiii.

29. Charles S. Johnson, "The Negro Renaissance and Its Significance," Annual Spring Conference, Social Science Division, Howard University, Washington, D.C., April 22, 1955, reprinted in Lewis, ed., *Portable Harlem Renaissance Reader*, pp. 206–18.

30. On the transition from Renaissance to Fisk see Patrick J. Gilpin, "Charles S. Johnson, Entrepreneur of the Harlem Renaissance," in Bontemps, ed. *Harlem Renaissance Remembered*. The entire chapter is a perceptive summary of Johnson's role in the Renaissance.

Chapter IV

1. On the discussions between Jones and Johnson see Patrick Gilpin, "Charles S. Johnson: An Intellectual Biography" (Ph.D. dissertation, Vanderbilt University, 1973).

2. See Raymond Wolters, *The New Negro on Campus: Black College Rebellions of the 1920's* (Princeton: Princeton University Press, 1975), chap. 2, "W. E. B. Du Bois and the Rebellion at Fisk University." Wolters describes major protests at Howard, Hampton, Lincoln (Missouri), and Wilberforce. The students were basically integrationist; they fought against their exclusion from mainstream higher education. But the wave of rebellions foreshadowed the more militant black student rebellions of the 1960s.

3. Joe M. Richardson, "Fisk University," in Charles Wilson and William Ferris, eds., *Encyclopedia of Southern Culture* (Chapel Hill: University of North Carolina Press, 1989), p. 283. See also Joe M. Richardson, *A History of Fisk University, 1865–1946* (University, Ala.: University of Alabama Press, 1980).

4. John Hope Franklin, a distinguished alumnus and trustee, to Richard Robbins, July 8, 1975. Franklin, with other trustees and alumni, was instrumental in saving Fisk. He wrote, "We will have to tighten our belts if we are to recover." Fisk did.

5. These data are mainly from Boxes 228 and 229, Johnson Papers, Special Collections, Fisk University Library, Nashville. The statistics provide only a faint clue of what it meant for blacks to live daily with segregation during the 1930s. Horace Cayton, a bright young sociologist, came to teach in Johnson's department. After a year at Fisk in "rigidly segregated" Nashville, "I finally made up my mind that I could never live in the South, no matter how important a job might be offered me" (*Long Old Road: An Autobiography* [Seattle: University of Washington Press, 1963], p. 234).

6. Joseph P. Lash, *Dealers and Dreamers: A New Look at the New Deal* (New York: Doubleday, 1988), p. 418. Walter White, director of the NAACP, once tried a different approach. He asked Roosevelt's personal maid to intercede with the president to persuade him to speak out against the filibuster of the antilynching bill. Roosevelt said no but added he would send Mrs. Roosevelt to sit in the Senate gallery to show where they both stood, and he denounced lynching publicly as "a vile form of collective murder." The number of lynchings was sharply increasing; more than sixty took place between 1930 and 1934. In 1935, when the antilynching bill failed, a lynching was taking place every three weeks. Roosevelt was appalled but noted, "We knew we did not have the votes."

7. Quoted ibid., p. 415.

8. Arthur M. Schlesinger, Jr., *The Coming of the New Deal*, Vol. 2 of *The Age of Roosevelt* (Boston: Houghton Mifflin, 1958), p. 374. See also Roger Riles, *The South and the New Deal* (Lexington: University Press of Kentucky, 1994).

9. See John Kirby, *Black Americans in the Roosevelt Era: Liberalism and Race* (Knoxville: University of Tennessee Press, 1980), for a general assessment. Kirby concludes that Negro gains under the New Deal were real but necessarily limited. Johnson saw New Deal reform as an opportunity for Negroes to win a greater degree of economic and social inclusion. The quid pro quo was not to press the segregation issue. At the same time, Johnson argued against Du Bois's new position of racial separatism. As Kirby summarizes, "He [Johnson] did not want to change the American system; he simply wanted to see barriers eliminated and a situation created that would aid black people's entrance into that system." (p. 199). On the general political question of Negroes and the New Deal, see Ralph Bunche, *The Political Status of the Negro in the Age of FDR* (Chicago: University of Chicago Press, 1970); Nancy Weiss, *Farewell to the Party of Lincoln* (Princeton: Princeton University Press, 1983); Harvard Sitkoff, *A New Deal for Blacks*, Vol. 1 (New York: Oxford University Press, 1978); Robert S. McElvaine, *The Great Depression* (New York: Times Books, 1984), pp. 187–95.

10. "The Economic Foundation of Race Prejudice," Address, Cleveland, July 27, 1929, Box 161, Johnson Papers. He anticipated here as well Robert Merton's celebrated comment on stereotypes, that is, that Lincoln was admired for "Yankee thrift" while Jews were denigrated as "misers." The Japanese in California, Johnson wrote, "whose great offense was that they were actually as thrifty as Benjamin Franklin thought Americans ought to be," were targets of severe racial discrimination. See also Charles S. Johnson, "The Economic Basis of Race Relations," in Alain Locke and Bernhard J. Stern, eds., *When Peoples Meet* (New York: Progressive Education Association, 1942), pp. 217–31.

11. Charles S. Johnson, Edwin R. Embree, and W. W. Alexander, *The Collapse of Cotton Tenancy* (Chapel Hill: University of North Carolina Press, 1935), p. v.

12. Ibid., p. 66.

13. Lewis Jones, Johnson's student and friend, argued that because Mrs. Roosevelt placed the *Collapse* study on FDR's nightstand, and he read it, Johnson could fairly be said to have had a direct hand in farm tenant policy.

14. William E. Leuchtenberg, *Franklin D. Roosevelt and the New Deal, 1932–1940* (New York: Harper & Row, 1963), p. 141. For a perceptive summary of the significance—and the limits—of the FSA program, see John Egerton, *Speak Now Against the Day: The Generation Before the Civil Rights Movement in the South* (New York: Knopf, 1994), pp. 91–98. On the striking FSA documentary photographs, an important FSA achievement, see Nicolas Natanson, *The Black Image in the New Deal: The Politics of FSA Photography* (Knoxville: University of Tennessee Press, 1992). When Negroes received less than a fair share in some New Deal programs, racial discrimination was the most important, but not the only, reason. Raymond Wolters contends that at least with respect to NRA and AAA, private black civil rights organizations were also culpable in failing to mobilize sufficiently the black community into a "powerful political and economic interest group that government could not afford to ignore" (*Negroes and the Great Depression: The Problem of Economic Recovery* [Westport, Conn.: Greenwood Press, 1970]).

15. See Wilma Dykeman and James Stokely, *Seeds of Southern Change: The Life of Will Alexander* (New York: Norton, 1976).

16. On Odum's long, productive career, see Rupert B. Vance and Katherine Jocher, "Howard W. Odum," *Social Forces* 33 (March 1955). On the inadequacy of Odum's regional thesis and on his evolving, somewhat more liberal views on race, see Daniel J. Singal, *The War Within: From Victorian to Modernist Thought in the South, 1919–1945* (Chapel Hill: University of North Carolina Press, 1982), chap. 5. Odum's convergence theory proved out, though more slowly than anticipated. Ten years after his death in 1954, the socioeconomic "southern lag" had been reduced but was still there, and on some indices Negroes were nearly as disadvantaged as before. See John C. McKinney and Edgar T. Thompson, eds., *The South in Continuity and Change* (Durham: Duke University Press, 1965). On Odum's stewardship of the Institute for Research in Social Science, a parallel to Johnson's at Fisk, see Guy B. Johnson and Gion B. Johnson, *Research in Service to Society* (Chapel Hill: University of North Carolina Press, 1980). Odum's maneuvering in behalf of Johnson is described in Ida Harper Simpson, *Fifty Years of the Southern Sociological Society* (Athens: University of Georgia Press, 1988). John Shelton Reed's studies and essays on the sociology of southern regionalism carry on the Odum tradition. His work is informed by

wit and style rare in sociology. See Reed, *The Enduring South* (Chapel Hill: University of North Carolina Press, 1986), and *One South* (Baton Rouge: Louisiana State University Press, 1982).

17. Anthony Platt, *E. Franklin Frazier Reconsidered* (New Brunswick: Rutgers University Press, 1991), p. 99.

18. This imposing record is well summarized in Gilpin, "Charles S. Johnson," chaps. 10–13.

19. See D. S. Dykes, "Bethune, Mary McLeod," *Dictionary of American Biography,* Supplement 5(New York: Scribner's, 1970).

20. Charles S. Johnson, *The Negro in American Civilization* (New York: Henry Holt, 1930), p. 468.

21. Charles S. Johnson, *Bitter Canaan: The Story of the Negro Republic,* Introductory Essay by John H. Stanfield (New Brunswick: Transaction Books, 1987).

22. Charles S. Johnson, "Liberian Centennial Broadcast," CBS-London, July 26, 1947, quoted in Stanfield, introductory essay, *Bitter Canaan,* p. xiv. On the bloody civil war, in which fighting among various tribal-regional factions caused some three hundred thousand in killed and wounded and induced the flight of possibly a million refugees, see Jeffrey Goldberg, "A War Without Purpose in a Country Without Identity," *New York Times Magazine,* January 22, 1995.

23. Johnson, *Bitter Canaan,* pp. 216–17.

Chapter V

1. Charles S. Johnson, *Shadow of the Plantation* (1934; rpr. Chicago: University of Chicago Press, 1966).

2. H. Jack Geiger, in a review of the definitive study, James H. Jones, *Bad Blood: The Tuskegee Syphilis Experiment* (New York: Free Press, 1981, rev. ed., 1993), in *New York Times Book Review,* June 21, 1981. A shorter but thorough analysis is Allen M. Brandt, "Racism and Research: The Case of the Tuskegee Syphilis Study," *Hastings Center Magazine,* December 1978.

3. Johnson, *Shadow of the Plantation,* p. 126.

4. Ibid., p. 212. On this complex and cruel system, as it developed in two black belt counties, Greene and Macon, in the rural South, see Arthur F. Raper, *Preface to Peasantry* (Chapel Hill: University of North Carolina Press, 1936). See also Arthur F. Raper and Ira De A. Reid, *Sharecroppers All* (Chapel Hill: University of North Carolina Press, 1941).

5. See Johnson, *Shadow of the Plantation,* pp. 3 and 33–46, and E. Franklin Frazier, *The Negro Family in the United States* (Chicago: University of Chicago Press, 1939), pp. 3–26. Herskovits's critique of both is in his *Myth of the Negro Past* (New York: Harper, 1941), chap. 1. A balanced view of these controversies may be found in James B. McKee, *Sociology and the Race Problem* (Urbana: University of Illinois Press, 1993), chap. 5.

6. Richard Bardolph, *The Negro Vanguard* (Westport, Conn.: Negro Universities Press, 1959), p. 238.

7. Willis D. Weatherford and Charles S. Johnson, *Race Relations: Adjustment of Whites and Negroes in the United States* (Boston: D. C. Heath, 1934), p. viii, E. Franklin Frazier, "Good Will, Bad Science," *Nation*, July 10, 1935.

8. Charles S. Johnson, *A Preface to Racial Understanding* (New York: Friendship Press, 1936), p. 192.

9. Charles S. Johnson, *The Negro College Graduate* (1938; rpr. New York: Negro Universities Press, 1969).

10. Charles S. Johnson, *Growing Up in the Black Belt* (1941; rpr. New York: Schocken Books, 1967).

11. Letter to Charles S. Johnson from Harry Stack Sullivan in Greenville, Mississippi, undated, but probably spring 1939. Unprocessed Boxes, Section 5, Johnson Papers.

12. Johnson, *Growing Up in the Black Belt*, p. 274.

13. Harry Stack Sullivan, "Memorandum on a Psychiatric Reconnaissance," ibid., pp. 328–33.

14. Ibid., p. 327.

15. On this issue see Wilson Record, *The Negro and the Communist Party* (New York: Atheneum, 1971). Frazier had no problem in the 1930s, the progressive New Deal era. But in the 1950s he, too, was engulfed by right-wing anticommunist hysteria. See Anthony M. Platt, *E. Franklin Frazier Reconsidered* (New Brunswick: Rutgers University Press, 1991), chap. 19.

16. The characterization of Johnson's role at the conference is by Raymond Gavins, *The Perils and Prospects of Black Leadership: Gordon Blaine Hancock, 1884–1970* (Durham: Duke University Press, 1977), p. 125.

17. Jacqueline Dowd Hall, *Revolt Against Chivalry: Jessie Daniel Ames and the Women's Campaign Against Lynching* (New York: Columbia University Press, 1978). This is an eminently fair-minded, sympathetic assessment of Ames's necessarily "conservative" strategy in race relations as part of her stance as a southern white liberal. See also John Shelton Reed, "An Evaluation of an Anti-Lynching Organization," *Social Problems* 16.2 (Fall 1968), pp. 172–81.

18. There is a discerning biography, more literary than sociological, Anne C. Loveland, *Lillian Smith: A Southerner Confronting the South* (Baton Rouge: Louisiana State University Press, 1986). See also Margaret Rose Gladney, ed., *How Am I to Be Heard: Letters of Lillian Smith* (Chapel Hill: University of North Carolina Press, 1993).

19. John Egerton, *Speak Now Against the Day* (New York: Knopf, 1994), p. 134. This is the definitive portrait of the major figures of southern white liberalism, early and late. Morton Sosna, *In Search of the Silent South: Southern Liberals and the Race Issue* (New York: Columbia University Press, 1977), is an earlier study of the region the white liberals both loved and rebelled against.

20. On the criticism of the CIC as too cautious see Harvard Sitkoff, *A New Deal for Blacks: The Emergence of Civil Rights as a National Issue*, Vol. I (New York: Oxford University Press, 1978).

21. Charles S. Johnson, *Into the Main Stream: A Survey of Best Practices in Race Relations in the South* (Chapel Hill: University of North Carolina Press, 1947), p. xii. In view of the latter-day charge that Johnson did not give proper credit to his colleagues and assistants, it is worth noting that the title page reads "by Charles S. Johnson and Associates, Elizabeth L. Allen, Horace M. Bond, Margaret McCulloch, Alma Forest Polk."

22. Linda Reed, *Simple Decency and Common Sense: The Southern Conference Movement, 1938–1963* (Bloomington: University of Indiana Press, 1991), p. 187. The book discusses fully the many weaknesses of SCHW and SCEF but pays tribute to the idealism and courage of its founders. Others contend the 1930s groups were far too limited to serve as models for the civil rights movement of the 1960s.

23. See the biographical sketch, ibid., pp. 10–11.

24. Charles S. Johnson, "More Southerners Discover the South," *Crisis*, January 1939, pp. 14–15. See J. Egerton, *Speak Now Against the Day*, for a vivid description, "Revival in Birmingham," pp. 195–97.

25. On the ever-increasing preoccupation of the New Deal administration with the challenge from abroad, see William E. Leuchtenberg, *Franklin D. Roosevelt and the New Deal, 1932–1940* (New York: Harper & Row, 1963), chaps. 12–13.

26. For many examples in the war time period see Doris Kearns Goodwin, *No Ordinary Time: Franklin and Eleanor Roosevelt: The Home Front in World War II* (New York: Simon & Schuster, 1994), pp. 161–76, 247–53.

27. On the march controversy see John Hope Franklin and Alfred A. Moss, Jr., *From Slavery to Freedom*, 7th ed. (New York: McGraw-Hill, 1994), pp. 435–38.

28. Although the president acted only after pressure from the protest movement, once he did so he was prepared, as he was not in the past, to take on the southern conservative Democratic bloc that bitterly opposed federal intervention in race relations and during the 1930s was wholly successful in blocking legislation to repeal the poll tax and end lynchings. See Frank Friedel, *F.D.R. and the South* (Baton Rouge: Louisiana State University Press, 1965), chap. 3. Friedel calls Roosevelt's position in that earlier period one of "benevolent neutrality."

29. Du Bois regarded Johnson as much too accommodative to the white establishment and too conservative in general. As Fisk's most famous alumnus he led the opposition to Johnson's nomination to be Fisk's president in 1946 (see Chapter 7). In 1950, when George Padmore, the radical writer and anti-colonialist, wrote to him as to whether he, Padmore, should seek Johnson's help in getting his book, *The British Empire in Africa*, published in America, Du Bois responded that it would not hurt to write Johnson but

would probably be fruitless. "He is, if not reactionary, certainly very cautious." See Du Bois to Padmore, March 17, 1950, in Herbert Aptheker, ed., *The Correspondence of W. E. B. Du Bois*, Vol. 3 (Amherst: University of Massachusetts Press, 1978), p. 281.

30. Egerton, *Speak Now Against the Day*, p. 285.

Chapter VI

1. Chester Himes quoted in Nancy Weiss, *Farewell to the Party of Lincoln: Black Politics in the Age of FDR* (Princeton: Princeton University Press, 1983), p. 296. Weiss, like the majority of New Deal scholars, holds that the economic lift given to blacks in a desperate time outweighs the fact that racial discrimination did not lift very much, if at all. I agree. For a dissenting view from the left see Barton J. Bernstein, "The Conservative Achievements of Liberal Reform," in Bernstein, ed., *Towards a New Past: Dissenting Essays in American History* (New York: Random House, 1968), pp. 279–80. Himes actually did not take quite so grim a view of FDR.

2. John Hope Franklin and Alfred A. Moss, Jr., *From Slavery to Freedom*, 7th ed. (New York: McGraw-Hill, 1994), p. 436. See also John Morton Blum, *V Was for Victory: Politics and American Culture During World War II* (New York: Harcourt Brace Jovanovich, 1976), chap. 6, which is especially useful on the failure of the Roosevelt administration to support the FEPC and its vigorous chairman, Malcolm Ross, and on the organization of CORE, the Congress of Racial Equality, during the war by A. Philip Randolph, Bayard Rustin, and A. J. Muste. CORE pioneered in nonviolent civil disobedience, including the sit-in, which became the model for the civil rights movement of the 1960s.

3. Humphrey, only thirty-seven then, got a roaring response from the convention floor when he said at the end of this historic speech, "The time has arrived for the Democratic Party to get out of the shadow of states' rights and walk forthrightly into the bright sunshine of human rights" (quoted in David McCullough, *Truman* [New York: Simon & Schuster, 1992], p. 639). Senator Strom Thurmond, the Dixiecrat leader, will always be remembered for his response, "All the laws of Washington, and all the bayonets of the army, cannot force the Negro into our homes, our schools, our churches." Years later, with the passage of the voting rights act, he suddenly saw the light and actively sought black votes.

4. Ibid., pp. 588–89. On Truman's mixed record see William Berman, *The Politics of Civil Rights in the Truman Administration* (Columbus: Ohio State University Press, 1970). In the words of one Truman official, civil rights strategy sometimes amounted to "backtrack after the bang." On Truman's bigotry and racial stereotyping see Alonzo L. Hamby, *Man of the People: A Life of Harry Truman* (New York: Oxford University Press, 1995), pp. 364–66.

5. This assessment is based partly on extensive interviews with those who worked closely with Johnson, including G. Franklin Edwards, Guy Johnson, Herman Long, Leslie Collins, Nelson Fuson, and Albert Whiting.

6. See Stanley Smith, "Sociological Research and Fisk University: A Case Study," in James E. Blackwell and Morris Janowitz, eds., *Black Sociologists* (Chicago: University of Chicago Press, 1974). I am not sure why the editors felt impelled to add an editors' note to this article. They do so, they say, to emphasize that Fisk was the one important exception to the modal pattern of research at the historically black institutions. Everywhere else the colleges had to contend with terribly inadequate support from foundations and with very inadequate resources on campus, to say nothing of the hostility in the surrounding community and region. Moreover, to cover the curriculum, faculty had extremely heavy teaching loads, precluding time for research.

7. Quoted in Patrick J. Gilpin, "Charles S. Johnson: An Intellectual Biography" (Ph.D. dissertation, Vanderbilt University, 1973), chap. 11, p. 474.

8. Box 1, Johnson Papers, Special Collections, Fisk University Library, Nashville.

9. "Unwritten History of Slavery #1," p. v, Box 210, ibid.

10. *Louisiana Education Survey*, Vol. 4, 1942, Box 182, ibid.

11. Johnson Papers, not boxed.

12. Gilpin, "Charles S. Johnson," chap. 13. Programs and lists of participants may be found in Box 37, Johnson Papers.

13. Gilpin, "Charles S. Johnson," chap. 13.

14. Charles S. Johnson and Associates, *Statistical Atlas of Southern Counties* (Chapel Hill: University of North Carolina Press, 1941); Charles S. Johnson and Associates, *To Stem This Tide: A Survey of Racial Tension Areas in the United States* (Boston: Pilgrim Press, 1943); Charles S. Johnson, *Patterns of Negro Segregation* (New York: Harper & Bros., 1943); Charles S. Johnson and Associates, Elizabeth L. Allen, Horace M. Bond, Margaret McCulloch, Alma Forrest Polk, *Into the Main Stream: A Survey of Best Practices in Race Relations in the South* (Chapel Hill: University of North Carolina Press, 1947).

15. Johnson and Associates, *To Stem This Tide*, p. vi.

16. Ibid., p. 105.

17. The best and most comprehensive analysis is Walter A. Jackson, *Gunnar Myrdal and America's Conscience: Social Engineering and Racial Liberalism, 1938–1987* (Chapel Hill: University of North Carolina Press, 1990). David W. Southern, *Gunnar Myrdal and Black-White Relations* (Baton Rouge: Louisiana State University Press, 1987), effectively analyzes the many controversies since publication. See also John H. Stanfield, *Philanthropy and Jim Crow in American Social Science* (Westport, Conn.: Greenwood Press, 1985), chap. 7, and Walter A. Jackson, "The Myrdal Study," unpublished paper presented at State University of New

York (SUNY), Buffalo, February 6, 1978. The late Bernhard J. Stern, of Columbia University, a Marxist sociologist with whom I worked in the late 1940s, was initially a consultant with the Myrdal group. He told me angrily that Myrdal at first took a tough-minded conflict-power approach to the Negro problem but changed it to the "softer" conception in accord with the moral values of the white middle class because of Carnegie Corporation sponsorship.

18. I met Cayton first on one of his tours after he wrote his fascinating autobiography, *Long Old Road* (New York: Trident Press, 1965). He could have been a major figure in sociology; his work was brilliant, if often fragmentary. But his unstable personal life, his drinking, and his three marriages and divorces often left him distraught, and many projects could not be completed. He died in Paris, at work on a biography of Richard Wright. Johnson supported him strongly in good times and bad.

19. Johnson, *Patterns of Negro Segregation,* p. 234.

20. Johnson et al., *Into the Main Stream,* p. 313.

21. See Linda Reed, *Simple Decency and Common Sense: The Southern Conference Movement, 1938–1963* (Bloomington: Indiana University Press, 1991). This is an excellent study, but Reed underestimates the power of the communist faction to destroy SCHW from within as HUAC destroyed it from without. The downfall of SCHW, beginning in the wake of the Birmingham conference, is well described in John Egerton, *Speak Now Against the Day* (New York: Knopf, 1994), pp. 292–301 and 439–46.

22. For this section on the Durham and Atlanta statements I am greatly indebted to Raymond Gavins's biography of Hancock, *The Perils and Prospects of Southern Black Leadership: Gordon Blaine Hancock, 1884–1970* (Durham: Duke University Press, 1977). See also Morton Sosna, *In Search of the Silent South: Southern Liberals and the Race Issue* (New York: Columbia University Press, 1977). Both of these are perceptive studies, but Gavins understands better than Sosna the economic and social context of the South within which Johnson, Odum, Hancock, and others had to function. See also Egerton, *Speak Now Against the Day,* pp. 302–12, and 432–39.

23. Gavins, *Perils and Prospects,* p. 148.

24. Will Alexander, "Our Conflicting Racial Policies," *Harper's,* January 1945. In contrast, see William T. Couch, "Publisher's Introduction," in Rayford W. Logan, ed., *What the Negro Wants* (Chapel Hill: University of North Carolina Press, 1944).

25. Quoted in Sosna, *In Search of the Silent South,* p. 155. The letter, written January 9, 1945, is in the Odum Papers, Southern Historical Collection University of North Carolina, Chapel Hill.

26. On the value of the Johnson research program, see Edgar T. Thompson, "Sociology and Sociological Research in the South," *Social Forces* 33 (March 1945): 356–65.

27. Charles S. Johnson, *Education and the Cultural Crisis* (New York: Macmillan, 1951).

28. I wrote about both Stoddard and Bowles in the *New Republic*. In 1953, at the height of the McCarthy hysteria, the trustees of the University of Illinois used Stoddard's leadership in UNESCO to fire him as president of the university. There was a state committee hounding "left-wingers" at the university in the same style as HUAC was hounding SCHW; the trustees were pleased to please it. See Richard Robbins, "Lower Politics in Higher Education," *New Republic*, August 10, 1953. Bowles had a distinguished public career as governor of Connecticut and ambassador to India. But he disturbed the tough "pragmatic liberals" in the Kennedy administration with his concern, which he shared with Johnson, for the peoples of Africa and Asia. I took a satirical view of the controversy in "The Bowles Affair," *New Republic*, October 9, 1961.

29. Unprocessed Boxes, Johnson Papers.

30. Wesley's liberal democratic creed was the same as Johnson's. See his "The Negro Has Always Wanted the Four Freedoms," in Logan, ed., *What the Negro Wants*, pp. 90–112. Ironically, Wesley and Johnson were the two candidates for the position of American commissioner on the League of Nations commission on forced labor in Liberia sixteen years before. That time, too, Johnson won out.

31. See A. Philip Randolph, letter to "Dear Charles," October 26, 1949, Unprocessed Boxes, Section 5, Johnson Papers. On the bitter trustee battle see Reel 58, microfilm, in the W. E. B. Du Bois Papers, University of Massachusetts-Amherst Library. Du Bois's appreciation for Johnson's support is in *The Autobiography of W. E. B. Du Bois* (New York: International Publishers, 1968), p. 391. The label of "reactionary" is found in Herbert Aptheker, ed., *The Correspondence of W. E. B. Du Bois*, Vol. 3 (Amherst: University of Massachusetts Press, 1978), p. 281. In his article "The Crisis at Fisk," *Nation*, September 7, 1946, pp. 269–70, Du Bois argued that if the white businessmen dominating the board *had* to put in a Negro as president instead of a "complacent" white man, they would prefer an equally complacent black man, "not an advocate of the FEPC, the abolition of the poll tax, or any New Deal policies" (p. 270). But Johnson, like Wesley, had spent a lifetime advocating just such legislation. Du Bois was right to denounce the Nashville white board members as far-right bigots and wrong to view Johnson as their complacent Negro.

Chapter VII

1. Quoted in Cedric Belfrage, *The American Inquisition, 1945–1960* (New York: Thunder's Mouth Press, 1989), p. 101. Belfrage, an English journalist deported during the hysteria who later lived in exile in Mexico, is rightly indignant about McCarthyism. But, like the work of Du Bois, his book is

marred by a total astigmatism concerning Soviet totalitarianism. His daughter Sally Belfrage, looking back in anger but also with dispassion, provides a better picture in *Un-American Activities: A Memoir of the Fifties* (New York: Harper-Collins, 1994). On McCarthyism see Richard H. Rovere, *Senator Joe McCarthy* (New York: Harcourt, Brace, 1959). As one observer put it, McCarthy did not know Karl Marx from Harpo, but he knew how to exploit fear.

2. Dan Wakefield, *New York in the Fifties* (Boston: Houghton Mifflin, 1992), p. 2. David Halberstam, *The Fifties* (New York: Villard Books, Random House, 1993). The 1950s, of course, should be fitted to the whole sweep of American history, colonial times until the present. On the great transitions regarding race and ethnicity, see the compelling study by Lawrence Fuchs, *The American Kaleidoscope: Race, Ethnicity, and the Civic Culture* (Hanover, NH: Wesleyan University Press of New England, 1990).

3. Riveting were the pictures of black children in Little Rock in 1957 seeking to enter school. "Television now showed mobs of whites threatening the children as they tried again to reenter the school, this time going through a side door. Millions of Americans could see Alex Wilson, a black ex-Marine, hit on the head by a screaming white man wielding a brick" (Fuchs, *American Kaleidoscope*, p. 160).

4. James MacGregor Burns, *The Crosswinds of Freedom* (New York: Knopf, 1989), pp. 320–21.

5. This section is drawn from my paper, slightly modified, "Eisenhower and Little Rock: The Desegregation Crisis in the South After *Brown*," Ike's America, a Conference on the Centennial of President Eisenhower, University of Kansas, Lawrence, Kansas, October 4–6, 1990. See also Stephen E. Ambrose, *Eisenhower, the President* (New York: Simon & Schuster, 1984), chap. 18.

6. Halberstam, *The Fifties,* p. 423.

7. Box 102 and Unprocessed Boxes, Section 9, Charles S. Johnson Papers, Fisk University Library, Special Collection, Nashville.

8. On Johnson's HUAC testimony see Martin B. Duberman, *Paul Robeson* (New York: Knopf, 1988), pp. 359–62. The Lomanitz case is described in Ellen Schreker, *No Ivory Tower: McCarthyism and the Universities* (New York: Oxford University Press), pp. 135–38, 146–47.

9. Unprocessed Presidential Papers, Section 9, Johnson Papers.

10. Quoted in Patrick Gilpin, "Charles S. Johnson: An Intellectual Biography" (Ph.D. dissertation, Vanderbilt University, 1973), p. 593.

11. Some claimed that HUAC and SISS went somewhat easier on celebrated Negro writers and performers so as not to make them martyrs in the mold of Paul Robeson. Langston Hughes testified freely; he had never been a party member; many of his books, he said, were "affirmations" of America. See Victor Navasky, *Naming Names* (New York: Harcourt, Brace, 1980), p. 191.

12. Aimee Isgrig Horton (Myles Horton's widow) has described the hearing and other forms of harassment in her book *The Highlander Folk School* (New York: Carlson, 1989), pp. 190–214. "Correspondence between Charles Johnson and Myles Horton over the years indicates the deep regard of each for the other's efforts" (p. 195).

13. See John Egerton, *Speak Now Against the Day* (New York: Alfred Knopf, 1994), pp. 99–102.

14. Quoted in Morton Sosna, *In Search of the Silent South: Southern Liberals and the Race Issue* (New York: Columbia University Press, 1977), p. 161.

15. Howard W. Odum Papers, Southern Historical Collection, University of North Carolina Library, Chapel Hill.

16. See Egerton, *Speak Now Against the Day.* Egerton says justly of his liberalism, "Both his head and his heart told him what few other Southern white leaders were ready to acknowledge: that nothing could keep the black minority from rising with the flow of the democratic current" (p. 489). On the contrast between the true white southern liberals like Graham and those who claimed the title but defended segregation, see Harry S. Ashmore, *Hearts and Minds, the Anatomy of Racism from Roosevelt to Reagan* (New York: McGraw Hill, 1982). Stetson Kennedy typified this group: "The best way to rid the South of segregation is to set out to rid the segregation of discrimination" (quoted in Ashmore, p. 109).

17. *Herald Tribune Forum,* New York, October 16–18, 1954.

18. Young's letter of resignation from SERS and the stream of correspondence about SERS discussed here may be found in Box 109, Johnson Papers.

19. Interview with Nelson Fuson, professor of physics, and with Marian Fuson, Fisk University, at Fisk, June 12, 1975.

20. This situation did not change substantially until several years after Johnson's death (interviews with Vanderbilt faculty and with Ernest Campbell, dean of the Graduate School, January 1975).

21. Interview with Leslie Collins, professor of English at Fisk, February 6, 1975.

22. Langston Hughes to Charles Johnson, September 13, 1945, Unprocessed Boxes, Johnson Papers.

23. Lillian Smith to Charles Johnson, Unprocessed Boxes, Johnson Papers.

24. "Edwin Rogers Embree, 1883–1950," typescript, not boxed, Johnson Papers.

25. Edwin R. Embree, *Thirteen Against the Odds* (New York: Viking, 1944), p. 48.

26. Robert Johnson to Charles Johnson, June 14, 1954, Box 69, Johnson Papers.

27. I am grateful to Professor Robin Williams of Cornell University, Robert Johnson's mentor and teacher in sociology, and to Melvin L. Kohn,

Robert Johnson's colleague and close friend in the Cornell Graduate School and now professor of sociology at Johns Hopkins University, for background material on Johnson's life. In particular, Professor Kohn, who knew him well, has permitted me to quote from correspondence concerning the relationship of son and father. In a letter to Kohn (August 2, 1955) Robert Johnson writes that, finally, he and his father have reached a real understanding: "My recent relationship with my father has really been wonderful. He is no longer critical, scornful, or ridiculing; he is helpful, encouraging and supportive. . . . My mother has immense hopes that I will make her proud . . . it is she rather than Dad who keeps me upset, but with her own loneliness and health problems, I'm willing to go along." There is no doubt of Robert Johnson's talent and ability as a sociologist in his own right. In his letter to Robin Williams, Melvin Kohn writes: "I can certainly attest to his being a fine sociologist and a fine human being. He was wonderfully insightful and had a splendid gift of language, inventing such marvelous terms as 'the exemption mechanism' and 'whitewardly mobile.' I learned more sociology from him than from anyone else with whom I've ever worked, with the single exception of you" (Melvin Kohn to Robin Williams, October 22, 1993).

28. Embree, *Thirteen Against the Odds*, p. 69.

29. Charles Johnson to Marie Johnson, December 5, 1946. Quotations from all the letters cited are from Johnson's side only. They are in Box 144, Johnson Papers. In two long interviews at Fisk in April 1975, Patricia Johnson Clifford was gracious and forthcoming, but she did not wish to talk about the Johnsons' personal crisis. After much thought, she decided against giving me access to their private correspondence, which she kept at home.

30. There were Negro associations as well as white that were not interested in closer cooperation on an interracial basis. Conservative and parochial, they had what E. Franklin Frazier called "a vested interest in segregation." A classic case in the 1950s was the National Baptist Convention, USA, then and now the country's largest black religious body. It proclaimed the need to concentrate on the spiritual, not the social gospel and the protest movement of Rev. Martin Luther King. That position has now changed toward more involvement in black community social issues. See E. Franklin Frazier, *Black Bourgeoisie* (New York: Free Press, 1957).

31. *New York Amsterdam News*, November 9, 1956.

Chapter VIII

1. Marie A. Johnson to "Betsy" (Mrs. John Hay Whitney), February 27, 1957, Box 146, Johnson Papers.

2. Lewis W. Jones, Johnson's student, then close friend and confidant, was another logical person to write the biography. He knew the man and

his work well. See Lewis W. Jones, "The Sociology of Charles S. Johnson," draft notes for a paper, Fisk University Library Special Collections, p. 8. But serious personal problems kept him from sociological work for long periods of time.

3. Robert B. Johnson to Marie A. Johnson, February 2, 1957, Box 154, Johnson Papers. Robert's letters to his father date from 1951 to 1956. The one to his father, June 14, 1954, on his career plans also discusses perceptively the Supreme Court decision in *Brown* (Box 69, Johnson Papers).

4. Fred Brownlee to Marie Johnson, September 27, 1957. Box 148, Johnson Papers.

5. Interviews with Theodore Currier, professor of history, emeritus, January 15–16, 1975, Fisk University campus.

6. These difficulties are insightfully analyzed in Butler A. Jones, "The Tradition of Sociology Teaching in Black Colleges: The Unheralded Professionals," in James E. Blackwell and Morris Janowitz, eds. *Black Sociologists: Historical and Contemporary Perspectives* (Chicago: University of Chicago Press, 1974). This section on the assessment of Johnson's sociology and the significance of his research-advocacy bridging role is drawn, with considerable modification, from Richard Robbins, "Charles S. Johnson," ibid., pp. 75–77.

7. Henry Lee Moon, *New Republic,* March 8, 1943.

8. Interview with G. Franklin Edwards, professor of sociology, February 17, 1978, Howard University campus, Washington, D.C.

9. August Meier, *A White Scholar in the Black Community, 1945–1965* (Amherst: University of Massachusetts Press, 1993), pp. 14–18, 73–87.

10. Jones, "The Tradition of Sociology Teaching," p. 137.

11. Ibid., p. 136.

12. William H. Chafe, *Civilities and Civil Rights: Greensboro, North Carolina and the Black Struggle for Freedom* (New York: Oxford University Press, 1980).

13. David J. Garrow, *Protest at Selma: Martin Luther King, Jr., and the Voting Rights Act of 1965* (New Haven: Yale University Press, 1978).

14. Quoted in Pat Waters and Reese Claghorn, *Climbing Jacob's Ladder* (New York: Harcourt, Brace & World, 1967), p. 161. On the mood of hope and the faith in change in the freedom movement in the South, see Richard Robbins, "Negro Politics in the South," *Dissent,* March–April 1968, pp. 181–83.

A NOTE ON SOURCES, PAPERS, AND COLLECTIONS

For Charles S. Johnson, his life and work, the indispensable source is Special Collections, Fisk University Library, Nashville. Special Collections also holds the papers of the Julius Rosenwald Fund. Correspondence to and from Johnson may be found in some of the other collections listed below.

The W. E. B. Du Bois Papers are at the University of Massachusetts-Amherst Library; I have made extensive use especially of the thick file of correspondence on the protracted and bitter battle inside the Fisk Board of Trustees in 1946 over whether to choose Charles Johnson or Charles Wesley as Fisk's new president, with Du Bois weighing in emphatically against Johnson. See also Herbert Aptheker, ed., *The Correspondence of W. E. B. Du Bois*, 3 vols. (Amherst: University of Massachusetts Press, 1978).

The papers of Will Alexander are at the Dillard University Library, New Orleans. Edwin Embree's papers are at the Bienecke Library, Yale University. (Langston Hughes's Papers are at the same library, in the James Weldon Johnson Memorial Collection.)

The Southern Historical Collection, University of North Carolina Library, Chapel Hill, has the papers of many of the southern white liberal group. Included are those of Howard Odum, Will Alexander (partial), Guy B. Johnson, Jessie Daniel Ames, Frank Graham, Arthur Raper, and Rupert Vance. The collection also has the papers of the Southern Tenant Farmers Union (STFU). The papers of Aubrey Williams and Eleanor Roosevelt are at the Franklin D. Roosevelt Library, Hyde Park. The Woodruff Library, Atlanta University, holds the papers of the Southern Conference for Human Welfare (SCHW) and those of Carl Foreman. The Schomburg Center for Research in Black Culture, New York Public Library, has Robert Weaver's papers. It also holds the files of the National Negro Congress.

The Harlem Renaissance writers are represented in several places. Hughes's and James Weldon Johnson's papers are at the Bienecke, those of Frank Horne and Countee Cullen at the Amistad Research Center, Tulane University. (Chester Himes's papers are now there, too.) The Zora Neale Hurston Collection is at the University of Florida Library, the Claude McKay Papers at the Schomburg Center, the Jean Toomer

Papers at Special Collections, Fisk University. The Arthur Schomburg papers are, of course, at the center named for him. The Carl Van Vechten Collection is at the Manuscript Division, New York Public Library. Alain Locke's papers, naturally, are at Howard University, as are the Spingarn Papers, at the Moorland-Spingarn Research Center. The E. Franklin Frazier Papers are also at Howard University.

Robert E. Park's papers are in the Joseph Regenstein Library, University of Chicago. Louis Wirth's papers are also there. The activities of Johnson and other noted southern sociologists of his time, such as T. Lynn Smith, Wilson Gee, and Katherine Jocher, are described in an excellent study by Ida Harper Simpson, *Fifty Years of the Southern Sociological Society* (Athens: University of Georgia Press, 1988).

The papers of the NAACP and the Urban League are in the Manuscript Division, Library of Congress, Washington, D.C. The Manuscript Division also has the files of A. Philip Randolph's Brotherhood of Sleeping Car Porters. Some university and metropolitan libraries carry bound volumes or microfilm of Johnson's *Opportunity*, and Du Bois's *Crisis*.

Material on Mary McLeod Bethune's work in government on Negro affairs can be consulted in the National Youth Administration (NYA) Archives, National Archives, Washington, D.C. On earlier black leadership a valuable source is Louis R. Harlan and Raymond W. Smock, eds., *The Booker T. Washington Papers*, 14 vols. (Urbana: University of Illinois Press, 1972–   ). The Marcus Garvey Papers are still being edited; see Robert A. Hill, ed., *Marcus Garvey and the Universal Negro Improvement Association (UNIA)*, vols. 1 and 2 (Berkeley: University of California Press, 1984), and my essay addressing these volumes and Garveyism in general, Richard Robbins, "Marcus Garvey's Place in History," *Boston Sunday Globe*, March 18, 1984.

For all scholars of black sociocultural life in the African American community before, during, and after Charles Johnson's time, the indispensable source is the Schomburg Center for Research in Black Culture, New York Public Library. For this biography I should also like to express my thanks, again, as I have in the Preface, to Anne Shockley, director of Special Collections, Fisk University, for her valuable assistance. That she happened also to be a very gifted writer made our association even more stimulating.

Index